SYSTEMS, STATES, DIPLOMACY AND RULES

SYSTEMS, STATES, DIPLOMACY AND RULES

J. W. BURTON

Director, Centre for the Analysis of Conflict,
and Reader in International Relations,
University College London

CAMBRIDGE
AT THE UNIVERSITY PRESS
1968

Published by the Syndics of the Cambridge University Press
Bentley House, 200 Euston Road, London N.W. 1
American Branch: 32 East 57th Street, New York, N.Y. 10022

© Cambridge University Press 1968

Library of Congress Catalogue Card Number: 68–29653
Standard Book Number: 521 07316 2

Printed in Great Britain
at the University Printing House, Cambridge
(Brooke Crutchley, University Printer)

CONTENTS

[*v*]

PART II: THE BEHAVIOUR OF STATES

FOREWORD

In 1966, University College London established a Centre for the Analysis of Conflict for the purpose of studying communal and international conflict. A major research activity of the Centre consists of private discussions between parties to contemporary international disputes or to disputes between communities within States. Present are political and social scientists who control and take an active part in discussions. These meetings help in the formulation of hypotheses and lead to theoretical and empirical studies.

University College has received support from the Joseph Rowntree Charitable Trust, the Social Science Research Council of the United Kingdom and the Carnegie Endowment for International Peace. At an earlier stage, and before support could be sought, a pilot study was made possible by the generous hospitality of the CIBA Foundation, London.

The views expressed in this and other publications of the Centre are those of the authors.

G. W. KEETON
Chairman of the Board of Management of the
Centre for the Analysis of Conflict

PREFACE

The research programme of the University College Centre for the Analysis of Conflict is based on theoretical studies of conflict, and on empirical studies of on-going communal and inter-State disputes, employing whenever possible face-to-face discussions between nominees of the parties concerned.

This research programme was stimulated in 1965 by a discussion that was then current in the United Kingdom, and which had commenced in the United States of America a decade or more earlier, regarding the theories and viewpoints of the many scholars, mostly American, who had taken part in what will for a long time be regarded as the most important decade of thought in international studies. (See bibliography.) Arguing the relevance of their theories by reference to case studies of past situations did not do justice to these scientists. One needed to be in a position to ask, in relation to whatever case was being examined, the answerable questions posed by their hypotheses. Official, historical, journalistic, and even analytically descriptive accounts, written up after a crisis, do not provide answers to the kind of questions that are prompted by contemporary behavioural approaches. Many of these can be answered only by analysing perceptions and misperceptions, interactions and features of State decision-making, and these are best observed when the parties in conflict are in an inter-acting situation.

The obviously desirable procedure was to select a current conflict, preferably one in which there was actual violence, and to create a situation in which the parties involved would expose their perceptions of each other, their motivations and goals, their internal political problems, their interpretations of events that led to the conflict and then to its escalation, and anything else to which contemporary theories of relations between States and of conflict might point. Accordingly, in 1965 a request was made to the governments directly involved in a particularly interesting violent conflict to co-operate in this academic inquiry. They were asked to nominate representatives who could reliably reflect the views of their governments and be in a position to maintain communication with them, to take part in discussions with each other in the presence of a panel of political and social scientists. It was made clear that the purpose was not conciliation or mediation, and not to settle the conflict—though it was hoped that the communication established between the parties would be helpful to them. The conference took place in London within a few weeks of invitations being sent. It continued for one week, and other meetings were held from time to time, some at the request of one or other of the parties. Some purposeful communication was established.

This was an academic exercise that had a particular and limited research purpose. However, it was clear that it was most rewarding academically, and if repeated in relation to other types of conflict could lead to insights and hypotheses, and perhaps to means of testing propositions. Furthermore, the experience suggested that an important technique might have been evolved, as it were by accident, for the avoidance of conflict, and for the resolution of conflict even during violence, because the parties themselves seemed to gain from the exercise in ways not possible from more traditional conciliation, arbitration and negotiating procedures. Consequently visits were made to other governments that were involved in conflict situations to see whether they would co-operate in the same manner. The response was positive, and a programme of conferences was arranged, and more careful consideration was given to the preparation of propositions prior to discussions, to techniques, and to means of recording and processing data generated. The Centre for the Analysis of Conflict was established to carry out this programme.

Those of us who took part in the pilot study, when for the first time representatives of governments in conflict were brought together within a controlled academic framework, were not at the time fully aware of the nature of the exercise. Some of us thought it was analogous to psycho-analytical procedures—despite the fact that the participants were highly educated and aware persons with no apparent personal adjustment problems. Others, according to their interests and experience, regarded it as an adaptation of industrial psychology, or of systems analysis, or of the type of meeting Quakers arrange. The technique seemed to have much in common with the social casework method which is now widespread in the handling of persons in conflict with their environment. It was clear that it had features in common with many techniques used in quite different conditions; but it was equally clear that it was different from all others.

During other experiences of these face-to-face discussions the technique underwent change and development. It is now possible to describe it, and to examine its potential as a means for the analytical examination of world society, and conflict avoidance and resolution. This is done in a study, shortly to be available, *The Use of Controlled Communication in International Relations.*[1]

The Centre does not confine itself to this face-to-face analysis; on the contrary, most of the time of its members is taken up with keeping in touch with developments in theory, examining similar techniques employed in other social sciences, making comparative studies and typologies of conflict, and advancing hypotheses in theoretical writings. The conduct of the actual case studies, and the processing of data generated, rest upon this theoretical work. However, the time spent on analysis in a controlled face-to-face situation is an important source of hypotheses, the period in which theoretical studies are stimulated, and the occasion for re-examining hypotheses and propositions. *Systems, States, Diplomacy and Rules* is one direct outcome of these experiences. The two studies are complementary and 'see companion study' is used as a convenient form of cross reference.

The study of International Relations is now moving out of the philosophical phase of the fifties into a period of consolidation. Terminology and clarity of concepts, tested against actual conditions, are the preoccupation of the sixties. The one calls for a high degree of imagination, and the other for questioning. The former is usually the product of individuals, but detailed discussion with colleagues is essential for the latter. I have had the benefit of a great deal of co-operation from my colleagues. Professor Georg Schwarzenberger read through two early drafts. His comments were especially valuable because his approach to international politics and international law is a different one as his own works show. I also had the opportunity of a round-table discussion of a draft led by John Groom, who made many observations of which I have taken full advantage, and without specific acknowledgement in the text. Other participants were Michael H. Banks, Robin Gollan, Rosalyn

---

[1] Macmillan, London, 1969.

Higgins, Christopher R. Mitchell, and Michael B. Nicholson. Leone Burton, who took part in these discussions, had already been working over drafts for some years. These discussions were enjoyable in themselves, and invaluable to me.

Any study such as this depends tremendously upon the published work and thinking of others. Mostly, due acknowledgements are made in the text, but one tends to acquire concepts, and if some acknowledgements are not made that should have been made, this merely serves to show that at last the literature of International Relations is becoming a common property.

The exacting work of preparing the manuscript and compiling the index has been done by Anna McClelland.

To all these, and to those who have given support to the Centre for the Analysis of Conflict, I am grateful.

J. W. B.

January 1968

PART I

Systems and States

1

SYSTEMS

The study of international relations has employed many models: maps, useful to determine geographical relationships, the thread of history drawing attention to continuity, the wheel of fortune which helped to explain cyclical movements, balances drawing attention to some aspects of power strategies, organization which by analogy with organisms demonstrated the interdependent and functional nature of relationships, medical concepts of structure and function which better enabled studies of comparative politics, and cybernetic models with their displays of feed-back. Each of these models or concepts was drawn from the environment, and became available as technology developed: thought in this area, as in others, drew upon developments in thought generally. Cartography, weaving, carrying, weighing, anatomy, medical science, electronics, have provided models that seemed at the time to be improved means of describing social organization. Each was more complex than the previous one. Society itself was becoming more complex, especially world society, and more complicated models were required for this reason. Social relationships are such that even in their most primitive form the most complex of models is needed for their description. Consequently, most recently developed models are as useful to anthropologists as to students of world society, and with their help the study of history can better be undertaken.

Models are useful as analogy. The presence or absence of features in a model does not necessarily indicate their presence or absence in world society: the only features of a model that are relevant are those that are useful in describing or explaining features of world society. Misconceptions about the nature of international relations have been promoted by a tendency to identify the actual with the model, by using models as evidence, and not just as analogy. Concepts of power balances, power vacuums and escalation ladders influence thinking and policy more than is justified by the features of the model to which reference is made. The model we all seek is the one that most closely approximates to the conditions being explained; but even this model could be employed only as analogy. World society cannot be expected to be so accommodating as to conform to the structure and behaviour of an analytical model designed to elucidate hypotheses advanced about it. In any event, models become more and more complex as they are improved and approximate to reality. Their purpose of providing a means of analysis is thus destroyed.

Some students, faced with these problems of analysis, are attracted to regional and institutional studies, others to the study of economic, psychological or strategic aspects of world society. Such studies have an important part to play in the study of the whole subject; but often they are misleading in their conclusions because of the isolation of the chosen area from the totality of world society.

I. A SYSTEMS APPROACH

What we require is some means of taking apart world society, or a particular situation or problem being investigated, in a way which enables analysis without eliminating interactions and complexities, and without drawing arbitrary boundaries within which to make an investigation.

World society is comprised of sets of relationships. Some are universal, as, for example, communication networks; some are scattered throughout the world but nevertheless do not cover the whole, such as wheat, rubber, tin trading networks, and English-speaking relationships; and some are regionalized, as is most frequently the case with ethnic and cultural connexions, or even localized, as are family and village associations. Relationships differ in character as well as in spread: there are trading, cultural, criminal, ideological, tourist, entertainment, educational, and an infinite number of other sets of relationships. The feature that most distinguishes contemporary world society from previous forms is the increased number and spread of relationships that have occurred under pressure of technological changes, especially in communications. Expectations and values of individuals and communities have altered in consequence: increasing interdependence, comparisons of ways of life, and the growth of sympathies and envies, create further and altered relationships. Invention, innovation, discovery, philosophic thought, calamity or fear at any point in a social relationship quickly affect other members of it. As different sets of relationship have members in common, others are affected in due course. This is the infectious process of social change in world society.

In each separate set of relationships there are exchanges and transactions confined to members. Analytically, each of these sets can be abstracted from the whole, even though some of the persons involved in one are, in another capacity, involved in others. Trading relationships can be separated from educational ones. But some of the operations of one set affect others. Educational levels affect trading. International society is, in this sense, an intricate network of systems acting upon each other and therefore affecting the units that comprise each.

One means of analysing world society, or a problem or a region within it, is to examine separately some of these networks of different, but overlapping and interacting relationships. This approach does not of itself supply a model—except in the sense that by working progressively from simple to more complex sets of relationships, each preceding one is a model of a subsequent one. At the same time it is not a departure from the trend in this area, which is the use of more and more complex models: it is suggested and made possible by the existence of complicated cybernetic models that by their nature have drawn attention to interactions and responses of sets of relationships. It is a procedure or an approach that independently supplements models, and also helps in examining them, once they approximate to reality, and arrive at such a level of complexity that they might otherwise become self-destructive as useful models just because of this complexity. The breaking down of society into sets of relationships serves to simplify its examination by making possible an orderly step-by-step advance toward the details of complex relationships without losing a perspective of the whole.

This procedure is based upon General Systems Theory which postulates that there are features of relationships that are common to all systems, whether physical, biological or behavioural, and that it is helpful in studying a particular one to study first features of relationships generally. Systems increase in complexity, that is they have a greater number of units and distinctive features, as they progress through an evolutionary scale from the inanimate, to the animate, to the human, to the social, to the political. Each system contains either features of the preceding systems, or the preceding systems as sub-systems. The systems approach to the study of international politics is, therefore, one that involves a progression from the relatively simple—features common to all systems—to the very complex—features common to particular types of highly developed systems. Apart from analytical usefulness there are, in practice, some unexpected benefits to be derived from a systems approach especially in exposition and in giving precision to widely used but ill-defined terms.[1]

II. SYSTEM TYPES

The concept of 'system' is well understood: it connotes relationships between units. The units of a system are of the same 'set', by which is meant that they have features in common that enable a particular relationship. A telephone system is a relationship between telephones—the units have some special features that make them relevant to the system.

Relationships imply communication between units, or transactions and exchanges. It is possible to regard the parts of a static construction as forming a system: an art composition is a set relationship, a chair or a table can be regarded as parts in a relationship, a mobile has some additional features because stress at one point affects others. There is in these cases communication by physical contact. These systems could be termed *basic systems*, and it is by first examining these, and then other systems of greater and greater complexity, that an analyst is assured that important features of the complex system with which he is concerned are not overlooked.

A system more complex than a basic system is one in which relationships and transactions between units enable repetitive movement. The movement is one that is relevant to predeter-

---

[1] General Systems Theory: see R. Handy and P. Kurtz, *A Current Appraisal of Behavioral Sciences* (The Behavioural Research Council), 1964; articles by J. G. Miller in *Behavioral Science*, vol. x, no. 3, July 1965, and vol. x, no. 4, October 1966. For applications to political science see in particular D. Easton, *A Framework for Political Analysis*, 1965, p. 43; C. A. McClelland, *Theory and the International System*, 1966; P. Nettl, 'The Concept of System in Political Science', *Political Studies*, vol. xiv, no. 3, October 1966; M. B. Nicholson and P. A. Reynolds, 'General Systems, the International System, and the Eastonian Analysis', *Political Studies*, vol. xv, no. 1, February 1967.

mined purposes; examples are a printing press, or a stationary pump. This is an *operational system*. Functional institutions are of this type. They are constructed for specific purposes, and their use for other purposes is usually limited. For example, the international communications institutions have special operational purposes, as do health, agricultural and others. A great deal of public administration is based upon operational systems of this kind. Their activities are routine, no matter how important they might be, and continue with little external control. They might cease to operate and be dismantled once the purposes for which they were constructed are fulfilled or are no longer being pursued. Though designed for a purpose they can operate without purpose; they can remain in operation after their relevant purpose has been fulfilled, or when the purpose has been eliminated, as is the case with much ceremonial custom.

Behavioural systems have a range of capabilities in addition to those of basic and operational systems. The characteristic feature of behavioural systems is that they have abilities to respond to their environment. They may be inanimate: an automated aircraft in flight is a behavioural system capable of self-response to the requirements of the environment in relation to a predetermined goal. Animal and vegetable systems respond to their environment. A flower bed is a behavioural system when each bloom has a pollination relationship with others, and all together respond to the environment. In each case, abilities to respond to the environment determine functional capability in relation to the attainment of fixed functions in changing condition.

Purposeful systems have in addition a capability to determine goals, to change goals, and to alter means of attaining them. These are the cultural and economic systems of a society. The making and remaking of value judgements, and the use of strategy in the pursuit of values, are the unique features of these highly developed social systems. *Controlling systems* have also a limited ability to alter the environment as an alternative to response to it, or as a means of avoiding adjustments to environmental demands that are beyond the response capability of the system. The capability of systems to alter their environments rests mainly upon their relative abilities to influence the behaviour of each other. This depends upon a great many factors such as the extent to which the role of the system is important to others, the extent to which its values and needs are shared by others, the number of members within it that are also members of other systems, and its ability to create an image of itself as a system that has these features. The influence of a church to control the social environment of Britain is greater than the influence of rationalists, and in some societies sporting institutions can exercise greater influence on legislatures than social welfare organizations. These capabilities of purposeful and controlling systems make them more intricate and therefore subject to functional disorder; but they are, at the same time, the means of survival, persistence and growth.

We could construct a model of a world based upon these static, functionally operative, behavioural, purposeful and controlling systems embracing economic, political, social and cultural activities. The map of this society would appear like millions of cobwebs superimposed one upon another, covering the whole globe, some with stronger strands than others representing more numerous transactions, some concentrated in small areas, and some thinly stretched over extensive areas. Each separate cobweb would represent a separate system— trade flows, letters exchanged, tourist movements, aircraft flights, population movements and transactions in ideas, cultures, languages and religions, traffic flows within towns and social interactions within village communities.

This would be a world society without geographical boundaries, for systems have no such boundaries. There are points between which there are interactions or transactions. The transaction points of a system are within the area that encloses them: this may be a small or a world one. But boundary, meaning a continuing line, has no relevance to systems: mobiles, machines and social systems do not have boundaries. However, systems have relationships with other systems. They are linked functionally; a pump has a function in relation to complex pumping systems. They are linked also by reason of shared units, and sometimes have shared values. This is particularly so of social systems: the same people belong in different roles to many systems. *Linked systems* create clusters that tend to be concentrated geographically: communication, trading and other systems tend to be linked and to form societies. The areas covered by these societies are determined by the frequencies of social interactions amongst units within the systems comprising them. Deutsch has defined boundaries negatively as 'marked discontinuities in the frequency of transactions and marked discontinuities in the frequency of responses'.[1]

This model of a world society would not only have no administrative boundaries, but no restraints on the operation of systems except those imposed by their own interactions. It would be a society of uncontrolled change, for each environmental change, or alteration of units within systems, would require alterations in others. It would be a *laissez-faire* society *par excellence*, in which when one system became functionally irrelevant it would cease to operate, allowing others to evolve.

Linked systems tend to consolidate into administrative units, and this is the case in industry no less than in social life. There are *administrative systems* including parliaments, cabinets and civil services, and others in industry and finance, that restrain the free interaction of systems. These administrative systems, unlike others, do tend to be confined to conventionalized geographical boundaries that include major clusters of systems. As will shortly be seen, they have power to control the interaction of systems within given areas, thus limiting the consequences of change.

Once consolidated and accepted by other clusters, linked systems and their administrative controls acquire an identity and a legitimized status within their environment. City States, local governments, nations and States are examples of clusters of linked systems. They acquire their own cultural and ideological symbols and values, and act as though they were systems existing in, responding to, and changing their environment.

It would be misleading, however, to regard these concentrations as systems. This may have been the case in a past age when each was relatively self-contained and isolated: the transaction points of systems tended to be within the boundaries of the linked systems. But this is no longer the case. Over the years the cultural unity of communities has been altered by conquest and migration, relationships have been altered and extended, and communications and specializations in the

---

[1] See K. W. Deutsch, 'External Influences on the Internal Behaviour of States', in R. B. Farrell (ed.) *Approaches to Comparative and International Politics*, 1966.

modern world have extended systems beyond conventionalized boundaries. The boundaries of systems are coinciding less and less with the boundaries of local government authorities and States. Apart from the many cases in Africa and other former colonial areas where boundaries were drawn by the arbitrary decisions of rival Powers, there is in contemporary world society an increasing number of systems—some basically economic, scientific, cultural, ideological, or religious—that have little relationship to State boundaries. There are in addition international institutions that have systemic values that may not wholly coincide with those of each of their State members: the British Commonwealth, the United Nations, and alliances are examples. Functional organizations have their own systemic values and needs. Whatever significance geographically drawn boundaries had, has been and is being greatly reduced by these developments.

States are better regarded as the resultant of the interacting behaviour of systems.[1] Regarding them as systems does not draw attention to the way in which boundaries disturb transaction flows[2] and prejudices in advance an analysis of the role of States in world society. This approach to systems is a departure from that which has been customary when applied to politics. Systems in the Eastonian analysis, for example, are uniformly of the type described here as 'administrative': that is they are structured, with defined inputs and supports. In reality, systems are not frequently of this kind, and the assumption that they are so would seem to be a carry-over from traditional thinking that regarded States as entities, and moreover, the only actors in world society. It is not intended to imply that States are no longer significant; on the contrary, their role and range of activities has increased, but it is a role in relation to systems. World society is perhaps best analysed by considering systems first, and then the role of States, which is the reverse of a traditional approach. These matters are taken up in the next chapter.

III. THE POLITICS OF SYSTEMS

In the creation of systems there is an allocation of positions amongst unit members. The procedure for filling positions is

---

[1] McClelland, *Theory*, p. 91.
[2] Deutsch, 'External Influences', p. 5.

relevant to the system: it might be the arbitrary selection of one piece of steel rather than another by an engineer, the less arbitrary selection of one football player instead of another by a manager, or by an intensely competitive electoral struggle. These procedures relate to the creation of the system. There is a system need for positions to be filled, for it is otherwise incomplete, but the process of filling positions is not an operation of the system. Furthermore, the selection of occupants of positions, by whatever procedures, is of interest outside the system, whenever the operations of the system affect others. Some systems are of more widespread interest than others. The selection of a president of the local parents' and citizens' association is of less widespread interest than the choice of a president of the local farmers' protection league, which is of less interest than the election of president of the local committee which selects a representative for election to the legislature. The distinctive feature of a system in which the filling of positions is important outside it is that it has a function or role which affects other systems, and even the environment. The leader of a trade union is important, not only in his role of unionist, but also because of his influence in society generally by reason of this role. A relatively inefficient union organizer might be preferred to an efficient one because his political beliefs are more acceptable. Members of a union are, in another role, members of a wider set of relationships.

For these two reasons, because the allocation of positions is part of the process of constituting or reconstituting a system and not of its operation, and because others outside it are concerned with the allocation of positions, the political process within any system cannot be regarded as part of it. There are, furthermore, *political systems* that are concerned with the political processes of systems, and in particular the filling of scarce positions in any systems that are important in the allocation and distribution of resources and values within a community. Political systems are mostly loosely organized. They include mass media and public opinions; but in institutional forms they are the vehicles of ideologies and philosophies that determine value judgements. As such they are not confined within State and national boundaries.

It is the function of political systems to control the creation and filling of positions in administrative systems which, as has been noted, are formally responsible for decisions regarding values and resource distribution. Those in control of administrative systems within a given area have opportunities to control the foreign influences that affect the area through systems that cross administrative boundaries. Typically these functions of internal and external control are confined to government: local authorities and nation States. But this is not always the case: private business organizations frequently exercise similar functions. There are no clear-cut differences between the functions of governmental and non-governmental administrative systems. Systems, whether government or business, that have these functions are obviously important to the whole society. The political processes consequently tend to involve many people, and the competition for scarce positions becomes an intense struggle. In an integrated functional or operational system, who happens to control is unimportant: the goals and means are not in dispute. Indeed, persons have to be persuaded by income inducement to accept responsibilities. But those filling scarce positions in administrative systems have authority carrying with it power over the interests of members of all systems within defined boundaries. The contests leading to the filling of the positions become power struggles between political systems with competing interests.

These meanings of political and administrative systems are more precise ones than those in general usage. There is a clear distinction between the process of filling scarce positions within systems, and the operation of systems once positions are filled. Cabinets, no less than civil services and financial institutions, are the institutional means by which the political processes are translated into decisions, and by which these decisions are executed.

It might be argued that once administrative systems are created, it is they that determine the allocation of resources and values within the community. Over short periods this is so: every administrator, even the most junior, has some political function, some opportunity to give effect to value judgements. But in due course the political processes, operating through political systems in association with other systems that have special and relevant interests to pursue, continue to influence the allocation of resources, interests and values that are formally made at an administrative level. The political decision-maker is an administrator, allocating values according to his appreciation of the political processes influencing him.

A distinction between political and administrative systems helps to explain the alteration in attitudes of politicians once they occupy their decision-making roles and become subject to the influence of the total political process, and not merely to some portions of it. A party leader in opposition usually alters substantially his values when occupying the position of government leader. Such a distinction also helps to place in better perspective the overlapping and interrelated policy-making and executive functions of both cabinets and administrations: the traditional separation of political and administrative functions within a government is not realistic and is misleading analytically. In addition, it helps to show how the political process is finally restrained at the administrative level by the structural framework created by governmental and non-governmental systems of law and order, commerce, finance, alliances, and other environmental conditions in which administrative decisions are made.

It is sometimes a matter of surprise that organizations created within the administrative system—which are in themselves systems—endeavour to, and occasionally succeed in controlling it. For example, the influence of the permanent civil servants over the temporary political occupants of positions within the administrative system is widely regarded as improper or undemocratic. Army take-overs are generally regarded as representing anarchical behaviour. But it is clear that any system, whether it is one that has evolved in society because of social and economic needs, or whether it is one that has been created deliberately as an administrative tool, has its own values and interests, and will interact with other systems in society. An administrative organization is linked functionally with other systems. It has overlapping membership and shares the values of other systems. This is an additional reason why it is inappropriate to make the traditional distinction between political and administrative systems: members of administrative systems, be they professional politicians or professional soldiers or administrators, are all subject to political processes by reason of their linked relationship with society. In a real sense all members of a society—be it private enterprise or centrally planned—are civil servants. All have some role in relation to the whole because society is a cluster of linked systems. It would be unreasonable to expect members of systems to confine their interests and values to those directly relevant to the operations of those systems. Defence and civil services are systems interacting as do all others within a society, with their own values, and their own influence in society.

This observation raises some questions about legitimization of administrative systems, reactions to political decisions that do not reflect political processes, and the use of coercion to compensate for an absence of legitimized status. These are better taken up later.

The concept of linked systems, which have no boundaries, and are controlled in their activities within a defined area, draws attention to two phenomena of growing interest in contemporary world society. The first is the spread of disputes from internal strife to international conflict, which is discussed in a later chapter. It is easily understandable that whenever transactions cross boundaries, disputes within them are likely to extend beyond them. The second is the way in which repressive attempts to control behaviour in any system give rise to reactions not only within it but elsewhere, by reason of overlapping membership and shared values. In Nazi Germany, and at centres of repression such as South Africa, coercion of members of some systems within the society affects members of others with shared values. Because systems are operationally linked by overlapping memberships, it is necessary to spread coercion wider and wider within the society, and ultimately beyond it.

IV. FEATURES OF SYSTEMS

Within a system there are parts than can be isolated as separate systems, as, for example, the switchboard or the exchange: these are *sub-systems*. In addition, there are different *systems levels*. The international network of telephonic communication is a high system level; national, regional, local and office are lower levels. Whereas the sub-system is a system in itself that can be isolated (though in isolation its functional relevance will not always be apparent) a system level refers to a complex of relationships comprising all units at that level. Systems have different features at different levels.

As we shall see later in this study (and as is demonstrated in the companion study) it is particularly important in international analysis to determine precisely whether systems or sub-systems are being examined, and what levels are being analysed, and to be aware of differences in features between systems and sub-systems, and between systems at different levels. The typical international 'problem' comprises disputes involving many States, and these can usually be separated out at different systems levels into a series of different disputes between different parties with different issues at stake. A problem or event can be described by tracing developments chronologically, regardless of systems levels. The Vietnam war can be described by recounting an event in South Vietnam, an event the next day in the United States or China, and so on. Such an account features those events which seem at the time to be the most important to the observer. In writing his account the observer is influenced by his philosophy, ideology and culture. His explanation of events fits into his theoretical framework. But analysis of a problem is not description and is not directed by a theoretical supposition. It is an attempt to distinguish the sets of relationships and their interactions. Any problem needs to be broken down into issues in dispute between different sets of parties, and the interactions of these sets. Similarly, in the resolution of a conflict an international problem as such is usually insoluble; but some of the different disputes over specific issues that exist at different levels might not be.

Each unit within a system is relevant to the system because of its *role* in relation to the system. Each may be capable of performing several roles, and therefore can be relevant to several systems. A telephone can be an antique and belong to that 'set'. In analysing units within a system it is their system features that are relevant: the antique telephone need not function as a telephone, but it must have the properties of an antique. The private personality and views of a leader are not evidence of his likely behaviour in an official role: role and system must be matched. The behaviour of a State in an alliance or defensive role should not be assumed to indicate its behaviour in an aid-giving role where it is involved in a different relationship.

Systems emphasize *wholeness*. A relationship involves units influencing or being influenced by each other. The related units have, therefore, features in addition to or even different from those of their separate parts. *Gestalt* psychologists have pointed this out. The accurate perception of the features of a system depends upon the simultaneous perception of the system as a whole: features may be perceived that are not those of the system unless it is perceived as a whole. Movements seeking social reform, independence struggles and repression of political oppositions, need to be examined in the context of the whole of the relationships involved, and these usually extend beyond national boundaries. This is one of the weaknesses of some regional and specialized studies that are undertaken out of the context of the wider relationships that exist.

All systems, even mechanical ones, are subject to *systems change*. Alteration in unit-members, caused by environmental influences, use or growth, can change their relevance. This is the nature of mechanical wear and failure: for any system to retain its original function, altered units must be replaced, or additional units added to compensate for their altered structure. By improvisation it is possible to include units within a physical system that are more relevant to other physical systems, as all mechanics know, to include physical units within a human organism, as all surgeons know, and to include different ethnic groups in one social community, as all sociologists know. Such units may alter toward greater systemic relevance, as do parts of a new machine, or may disintegrate as does a faulty or non-set part, and cause a disorder in the system. Over a period of time unchanged function is obtained by repaired or changed structure. Change can also occur as a result of increased or decreased unit-members: an additional line to a drawing can alter all relationships, and the character of a social group changes with numbers present.

When a system undergoes change, some units within it become redundant or irrelevant—alienated—others not previously part of it may become relevant. Machines are remodelled, and social organizations shed members and gain others. Despite changes in membership and in values of some members, systems can retain their functions and values provided some form of coercion is introduced to control unit behaviour. This again directs us toward consideration of legitimization of authority, which we have postponed.

System change and adaptation are well understood in biology; survival of species depends upon adjustment to environmental alterations. The possibilities are elimination, or survival in an altered form. The two processes, maintenance and adjustment, interact, and the outcome depends upon the level of adjustment required by environmental change, and the system ability to alter.

This type of change and adaptation is concerned with adjustment of structure, and over long periods of time. Adjustment of behaviour to meet current environmental conditions is a more complex process, and requires perception of the environment, feed-back into the system and response. Vegetable and animal systems have some of these capabilities, as when they respond to changes in light and temperature.

The capability of social systems to adjust to the environment rests upon many factors: abilities of units to perform different tasks, to do without inputs from the environment when they are no longer available, to find other sources of supply, and to deal with additional inputs.[1] Factors such as these are relevant to an examination of the consequences of sanctions and of war, when sudden changes occur, or to any unexpected changes that some systems might impose on others by reason of invention, innovation or deliberate policy.

It was stated above that systems do not have geographical boundaries: there are transactions between set units. However, systems operate within an environment comprising other systems, and 'boundary' is a useful concept to describe the operative limits of systems. In some cases operative limits correspond with geographical or sociological boundaries, in others the connexion is less clear. The concept is an important one because it helps in an understanding of systems change. It is the boundaries of systems that respond to the environment, and it is out of this response that change occurs. The boundaries of a green–red–amber traffic system are reached when it is found that drivers do not have sufficient warning to stop and are faced with a moment of indecision as the lights change. An alteration in the system is required, and a circular disk, half green and half red with a clock hand moving around may be substituted so drivers can see when the change will occur. The 'boundary' of the new system is wider. The transactions of Somalis in Kenya were more with Somalia than with Kenya, and cut across the territorial boundaries of Kenya. Some change was required in

---

[1] See P. M. Blau, *Exchange and Power in Social Life*, 1964.

formal arrangements between the two States—not necessarily a change in territorial boundaries.[1]

Any alteration in the boundaries of a system alters its relationships with other systems: the new traffic system influences traffic flows, and altered local arrangements on the borders of Somalia and Kenya alter all their relationships. There is, therefore, an ability within some systems to alter their environment.

Systems failure can occur as the result of an internal breakdown in communications, as when there is a mechanical fault in a communications system, or an administrative weakness in a social system. It is more likely to be due to the existence of demands made by the environment of greater magnitude than the system can absorb: communication flows and inputs from the environment vary in quantity and quality, and from time to time can be beyond the capacity of systems to handle. This is one explanation of breakdowns, deviations and adaptive changes in individual behaviour, and it applies to systems generally, mechanical, animate and social.

It is a systems need that rates and types of change should not require adjustment beyond the capability of the system. It seems to be a general rule that the higher systems are in an evolutionary scale, the less are their abilities to adjust: mechanical systems can survive most conditions, and it is the lower forms of life that can best survive nuclear fall-out. Social systems, on the other hand, are greatly affected by altered environmental conditions. It also seems to be a general rule that the higher systems are in an evolutionary scale, the greater is a compensating ability to control environments, and thus to limit the needs for adjustment. Lower forms of life must adapt or perish, but some social systems have a capacity to influence both their physical and social environments.

These two capabilities, the ability to be indifferent to the values of others and to adjust to altered conditions, and the ability to influence the environment so as to avoid the need to adjust to it, together constitute *systemic power*. The term 'power' usually refers only to this second ability, the ability to impose patterns of behaviour and values on others; but the ability not to be affected by this power is no less an expression of power.

[1] For a discussion of systems boundaries, see C. A. McClelland, 'Systems Theory and Human Conflict', in E. B. McNeil (ed.), *The Nature of Human Conflict*, 1965.

The two processes, adjusting to and changing the environment, interact. It is probably not accidental that abilities to adjust diminish with the acquisition of abilities to change the environment. The latter is likely to be preferred as causing less hardship to members of the system concerned. If monopoly conditions can be created it is easier to take advantage of them than to alter productive structures. In this sense the ability to adapt is limited in practice by whatever ability there is to alter the environment.

This form of exposition helps to clarify what are the *power needs of systems*. Power is a need of a system to the extent that environmental adjustment-demands are greater than its adjustment capabilities: power is the means of bringing these demands within system capability. Every system endeavours to increase its power because its use can be an alternative to system change; but as a system it can do this only to the extent that its role is important to others, and its values are shared by others. Its power is derived from its social relevance. It is relative systemic power that controls systemic change and gives stability to social systems; but as it is derived from role relevance and shared values, it is limited. Consequently a flow of system change and adjustment takes place.

It will be apparent that though a social system will tend to try to alter the environment rather than adjust to it, this is not necessarily so. The use of power to control the behaviour of other systems can impose upon them adjustments beyond their capacity, leading them to respond with whatever power they have. A power contest would follow. Consequently, every system has to balance costs of adjustment against costs of conflict. This is the problem faced in employer–employee relations, in church relations with educational systems, and in competitive commercial relations.

The processes by which decisions are taken within purposeful and controlling systems are cybernetic ones: goals are set, perhaps altered after a reassessment of the response of the competing system, and the balance between costs of adjustment and costs of attempting to alter the environment is reassessed. Compromises may be the outcome; but if information and assessment are faulty, both systems can lose by trying to avoid making adjustments. The efficiency in operation of a system depends upon its accurate assessment of the adjustments which it must make, and its ability to make them.

The notion of systemic power, which relates to system inter-action, is different from the notion of *State power*, or that threat or coercion that an administrative system can employ to control the behaviour of other States, and of systems that are within and which extend beyond its boundaries. This is a power that is exercised, not as a result only of system interaction and decisions taken at a systems level, but by administrations that endeavour to assess the interests and values, current and future, of systems and the society as a whole. They are in a position to mobilize the resources of systems, including defence systems created by them, to achieve these interests and values. Systemic power can oppose or support State power, and in the analysis of any situation these two forms of power need to be distinguished.

It has already been observed that States are not systems, but they comprise systems, linked and administratively directed to achieve common goals. State administrative systems have abilities to adapt to the environment, to alter it, to change direction and circumvent obstacles, and if necessary to change goals and values. It is to explain these complicated processes that electronic and cybernetic models have been used, such as flight of an aircraft that allows for drift, flies around storms, corrects its position, and may finally be required to alter its goal. A systems analysis is a method, and provides a set of concepts or tools with which to analyse change in structure, function and values; resistance to change; the use of power to control the environment; and conflicts amongst systems, between States and systems, and amongst States. This is the important area of the contemporary study of international relations, and the one with which this study is concerned.

V. SYSTEMS ANALYSIS AS A METHOD

Some incidental advantages of a systems approach in the study of international relations appear with its use; the following are some of those of which one becomes aware in empirical studies, and in exposition.

The generality of systems provides a means of clarifying some of the inter-disciplinary problems and issues causing disagree-ments amongst scholars. By reference to systems it is possible to determine, on the one hand, what is common amongst systems and, on the other, where there is but analogy. For example, the individual, as a system, has features in common with States: beyond this his aggressive and other behaviour can be employed only as analogy. Psychology and the study of politics are thus given a precise relationship. As Boulding once observed: 'General Systems Theory is the skeleton of science in the sense that it aims to provide a framework or structure of systems on which to hang the flesh and blood of particular disciplines and particular subject matters in an orderly and coherent corpus of knowledge.'[1]

The personality of a leader is sometimes a characteristic feature of a situation or a dispute; systems analysis helps to place personal characteristics in perspective. The individual in society plays a role in many overlapping systems—his occupation, his church, his sports club and his political system. He may act in some roles in ways which an outsider might consider inconsistent with his behaviour in other roles. Only that part of his behaviour that is enacted within the system being examined is relevant: it would be misleading to predict the behaviour of a system on the basis of the whole personality of the actors. The peace-loving Christian cannot be counted on to act as such when head of a State. Conversely, it could be misleading to build up a character, as is done in some biographies, on the basis of behaviour in a particular role. President X may give observers of his presidential behaviour the impression that he is irresponsible, emotional, unpredictable. In fact, in other roles this same president might be cautious and capable of responsible reaction to reasoned approaches. The appearance of irresponsibility may be due to a variety of political pressures entering into political decision-making. A hard-line policy of other States, designed to counter the irresponsibility of the president, may do no other than force the president to respond with even more determination along the same, apparently irresponsible lines. The behaviour of Hitler in relation to a particular role appeared to have an element of madness. In the same circumstances others, with wholly different personalities, may have behaved in a similar way. Hitler was a formal decision-maker, the product of many systems of relationships, and of responses of these systems to an environment; he was the instrument of systems responding to the environment. Deducing a total

---

[1] K. E. Boulding, 'General Systems Theory: The Skeleton of Science' in *General Systems*, vol. I, 1956, p. 17.

personality from behaviour in one known role, or deducing from a known person his behaviour in a particular role, can both lead to errors of policy. Simple explanations of events in terms of personalities, racial characteristics, lack of respect for freedom, the possession of 'double standards', can satisfy politically and emotionally, but not intellectually; they are not an appropriate basis for analysis or policy.

From the point of view of psychologists, systems are systems of persons, even though it is acknowledged that the individual is sometimes playing a political role. Hence the fears, responses and decision-making processes of the individual are a starting point. From the point of view of the sociologist, systems are dominated by group behaviour, and public opinion surveys should help to indicate what States' responses are likely to be. Certainly we need to know far more about the role of the individual and of groups in States; but State values can dominate individual and group responses. One finds Arab and Israeli students, and Chinese from Formosa and China, Greeks and Turks in Cyprus, Indians and Pakistanis, all adopting stereotypes and mirror images, and using apparently uncritically the arguments of their side; in discussion it becomes clear that these are not altered by reference to fact or reason. Is it an individual or group response, and if so, why should it be confined to the issues in conflict and not spread to other values which are held in common? Or is it a systems response that is transmitted to the individual through his identification with the system and its needs? Easton has drawn attention to systemic needs, and the life processes of systems.[1] He points out that they respond to disturbances, stress and change of all kinds in ways which enable survival and growth: the preservation of values and acceptance of them within systems is part of this process. Systems persistence is a feature that requires explanation. Part of the explanation lies in the influence of the system upon its members, their identification with it, their conformity, and therefore their defence of its values and interests. Clearly the system does not always impose values: demands are also made upon the system. However, to the extent that the system satisfies demands, it receives support; individual behaviour in part reflects the values of the system, and its goals and strategies. It is this systemic influence that accounts for commonly held

[1] D. Easton, *A Systems Analysis of Political Life*, 1965, p. 17.

stereotypes and uncritical acceptance of policies; psychologists and sociologists can, within a systems framework, avoid approaching the subject from their psychological and sociological standpoints, and can interpret the role of the individual and the group within the context in which they are behaving.

Systems analysis requires the investigator to perceive the system from a point within it. Descriptions and interpretations of State behaviour from a point within another culture, or another point of time, produce most bizarre results. Take the common view held in the West of political procedures in new States. It is only in recent decades that many non-western peoples have been decision-makers in their own right; previously decisions were made for them. Anthropologists, sociologists and political scientists are now examining non-western decision-making, and in due course we may have more insight into processes that are widespread in Asia and Africa. The slow and apparently inefficient process of finding a consensus at one level after another before a final decision is taken is not even yet understood by western decision-makers. The debating and simple majority system of party politics is not a democratic ideal to which many cultures aspire: from many viewpoints it could be regarded as an inefficient, wasteful and undemocratic form of decision-making. The non-western political pattern of decision-making is an intensive and time-taking consultative process in which different views are argued until consensus emerges, and this is confirmed in a final vote. It is very like the 'free' or non-party vote in western parliaments when an issue of great public interest like hanging or divorce is being debated. It is to be noted that in western social organizations there are usually no formal oppositions, and different views are debated before a final vote is taken. From within the western system the western observer perceives the adoption of non-party procedures in some important circumstances, as consistent, rational and desirable; the same procedures in new States are regarded as undesirable or in some way inferior because they do not conform with another pattern of western behaviour. Their relevance to decision-making at a State level is not understood because they are not perceived in the context of the political systems concerned. Foreign office officials, while aware of these problems, have built-in resistances to identification with the societies being analysed. The foreign office official—who is, in any event, moved after a few years to another post—cannot afford to identify: there are on record many cases in which an official has been reprimanded and transferred for interpreting too sympathetically the attitudes and policies of the government to which he is accredited. In any event, every national, especially a national employed to press the interests of his own culture, has to overcome great personal as well as official resistances to perception from within a foreign society. A systems, rather than a descriptive, approach, helps the investigator to avoid the error of making valuations about 'rational' and 'irrational' behaviour, and helps to expose the reasoning of decision-makers within the system and environment in which they act.

A general theory is a guide to perception universally; a systems approach provides a method by which any particular society or State may be analysed. Because it deals with a particular set of relationships—those that are being investigated —and not the behaviour of the whole of international society, it could prove inadequate in some degree when tested, even in relation to the particular system under examination. Knowledge of the interaction of systems, that is analysis of systems wider than those of immediate interest to the investigator, is essential to an understanding of any particular social system. The most detailed analysis of the political relations within a trade union that is contemplating strike action would give no reliable clue to effective policy in the absence of an analysis of political relations with employers, the government and the public. A systems approach helps to draw attention to the reality that a particular situation comprises many systems and sub-systems. The Indonesian–Malaysian confrontation, for example, was originally a function of a number of systems at various strategic levels. Soviet arms were supplied to Indonesia, and the United States and Britain were strategically involved, making relevant the bi-polarized East–West relations. Chinese minorities, and China's interests generally in the area, brought in Chinese–United States relations. The wider Asian–African relationship, and the narrower Philippine–Malaysian–Indonesian inter-action had their influence. There were others which affected the main system of relations between Indonesia and Malaysia, and the sub-systems of race and religion. From a descriptive and ana-lytical point of view all related systems are important, and it is these that are to be taken into account in any longer-term 'if — then—' prediction to be made.

Precise analysis of each relevant system and sub-system is required. Generalizations about a conflict being a function of personalities, an ideological influence, maladministration and a wish to divert public attention, or some other popular belief, do not lead to an understanding of the complex relationships that exist. The obvious factor of geographic proximity will usually be an important one to take into account in examining relations between States. But far more important may be kinship ties, the religious systems that cut across political boundaries, occupational relations that involve population movements across borders, trading relations, the ideological and racial systems that are internal causes of external tension, the physical presence of other Powers, and such features that all together explain the total relationship. Systems analysis guards against significance being attached to the obvious and the conspicuous merely because they are obvious and conspicuous, and against the absence of attention to features of a situation that are less conspicuous but nevertheless relevant and essential.

Systems analysis draws attention to the ability of States to alter responses, because it is particularly concerned with the operation of systems within an environment, and with communication and feed-back processes. Power balances and capabilities are perceived as reserve resources to underwrite inefficiencies in decision-making. Behaviour, whether it be of men, groups, animals, machines or States, is characterized by a normal or typical range of responses to stimuli, and also by an abnormal range. Socially, normality is determined by reference to predictability, and in some respects to acceptability. The range of agreed normality tends to increase with increased knowledge of structure and function: with knowledge, predictability and acceptability tend to be less important as criteria. Aggressive responses in the individual are more likely to be perceived as normal if the observer is aware of all the circumstances of the stimuli, and the exact nature of the response. It is not appropriate to regard the behaviour of States as being normal or abnormal in the sense that the individual might be: States are inefficient in decision-making, they have structural and functional breakdowns, but they remain sovereign and fully responsible for their actions. Nevertheless, the analogy with the individual helps to describe State behaviour: the more that is known of the structure and environment of a State, the more its behaviour will be perceived as normal and predictable. Normality and abnormality in the behaviour of States are better considered in terms of capability of varied response: an irrelevant or self-defeating response may be taken deliberately and rationally, but on false or inadequate information. Persistence with this same response in the face of hostile feed-back from the environment to satisfy ideological, political or some other such considerations, leading finally to conflict, could reasonably be regarded as an abnormal response. International politics have not been characterized by varied response: hostile feed-back from the environment within a system of power politics has led to alterations in response only in so far as power has been lacking. In the behaviour of States, unlike the behaviour of individuals, the use of power to counter hostile responses in the environment, and thereby to make unnecessary adaptive behaviour, has been regarded as normal behaviour. In the contemporary world environment in which there is increasing resistance to the use of power as normal behaviour, capability of varied response is important to States. The persistent policies of western States to support unpopular governments in Asia is an example of failure in learning, failure to alter responses, and of the employment of power to offset the effects of this failure. Systems analysis helps to demonstrate the processes and possibilities of varied response.

A special merit of the systems approach is that it provides a means of removing subjectivity in respect of the concept of 'national interest'. When the interests of States existing with a world society of States are determined by reference to system and State needs there can be some precision in the definition of legitimate intervention, aggression, self-defence, and other terms that have led to academic and political argument, as will be seen in a subsequent chapter.

2

THE NEEDS OF STATES

A distinction has been made between systems and States. The former are transactions between set units. The latter are clusters of systems and parts of systems within geographical areas, controlled and integrated in some degree by politically created administrative systems. Systems have their own properties, powers and interactions; they are the product of the needs of the societies in which they operate; they are subject to change and even elimination. New ones emerge, and their persistence finally depends upon their social relevance. States, by contrast, are the on-going structures created by these clusters of interacting and altering sets of relationships. State authorities have power to control the operations of systems, and a limited power to control the environment in which they operate. Some of this power is derived independently from resources and systems under their direct control, some is derived from the systems they create.

System survival is not vital to the life of a society. On the contrary, system change, elimination and creation are vital because it is through these processes that a society adjusts to its environment and develops. But supra-system authority exercised at a local or State level, to maintain control of systems, and to influence the wider environment in which they operate, is a vital and distinguishing feature of social life. For these reasons it is appropriate to refer to the needs of States, that is the conditions necessary for survival and continuing operation in relation to these two functions, whereas the needs of systems relate only to their impermanent social relevance.

The needs of States, for example, needs of survival and independence of action, are important determinants of the structure and operations of world society. Other determinants are the activities of States when they attempt to influence the wider environment in favour of the systems they control. State needs and activities in defence of systems are interdependent. But analytically it is important to make the distinction, for some State activities within world society can be explained only in the context of State needs, while others can be explained in the context of the needs of the systems whose interests the State is pursuing.

I. STATES AS ENTITIES

In International Relations and Diplomatic History it has been customary to treat world society as though it consists of relations between the States within it. Two assumptions have been implied. The first is that States and relations between them alone comprise world society: International Relations is still the commonly used title of the appropriate discipline. The contemporary flow of ideas, universal changes in values, the influence of technological advances, and the widespread activities of commercial enterprises, have been treated as separate phenomena, to be noted in passing, because they could not readily be examined within this traditional framework. Yet they have been amongst the most influential aspects of world society: States have been powerless to control them. Even international governmental functional institutions have not found a convenient place within this framework. Any framework or description of world society which does not embrace all of these relationships is inadequate, not only for a study of world society, but also for a study of inter-State relations within world society.

The second implied assumption in traditional studies is that States are entities, and that relations between them are relations between integrated units. Traditional international law and the concept of the legal authority reflect this. This is a carry-over from a period when rule was by feudal power, and States were entities as far as other States were concerned. In short, the framework of analysis to which we are accustomed is one suited to a period of history when relatively isolated States co-existed. The relations between them appeared to be State-power relations, and a State-power framework seemed adequate as a means of analysis.

In important respects this approach has been misleading even to those concerned primarily with relations between States: as has been observed, States are boundary areas that do not coincide with transactions, and some of the most significant and persistent aspects of relations between States are missed when they are treated in this way. However, States as entities do have their unique properties and needs, and it would be as misleading to ignore these as to miss the significance of systems. Nationalism, national attitudes and stereotypes, experience of threat and national defence are State phenomena that affect greatly relations between States, and the systems within and crossing States.

Furthermore, one of the roles of authorities is to ensure that the State responds as a whole to environmental circumstances: responses to threats and to war are obvious examples of total State response, and all systems and parts of systems are mobilized accordingly. Less obvious, but even more general, is State response to commercial, cultural and other changes experienced initially by some particular system or systems: a tariff that protects a particular industry is a State response, and units within all systems may be involved in their role as consumers.

It is not implied that these State responses are necessarily in the general interest of all systems. The protection of particular interests might be damaging to the community as a whole. Many protective devices are clearly damaging in the long term when they lead to inefficient productive structures. The pursuit of particular interests may be costly to the community. Hobson has argued that British imperialism was in the interests of groups, but not in the longer-term interests of the community.[1] But it is particular interests that are most affected by innovation, invention, discovery and changes in the environment; it is these that are required to make adjustments and to take risks. Regardless of the interests of all other sections of the community, State authorities accept an obligation to respond to their demands for protection and support, and to spread the costs widely.

If systems within a State and their environments were static these problems would not arise: there would be little need for a State to act as an entity. But change anywhere requires adjustment somewhere, and not necessarily at the point of change. Production of cotton goods in India and Japan required changes in England on a scale that could not be sustained by capital and labour concerned. Nationalism in Asia made possible by Japanese occupation led to changes in European States which affected some special interests very directly. A condition of peace would follow automatically if every change were followed by a passive adjustment to it: if English workers could have been transferred out of the cotton industry into others

[1] J. A. Hobson, *Imperialism*, 1948.

relations with Japan might have been different. If new ideas of Communism could have been passively absorbed in other States where they satisfied felt needs, the Cold War would have been less of a problem. In practice, some change is absorbed passively, some is resisted. A role of authorities is to protect its citizens against the adverse effects of internal and external change, and sometimes it is expedient to do this by preventing change taking place (for example, by legislating for a limited production of margarine to protect butter producers) or by isolating the system (for example, by imposing tariff protection or quotas, by banning political parties and controlling mass media). The passive acceptance of all change, while it might result in a condition of peace, would no less result in the elimination of some systems, and certainly of some of their values. It is the responsibility of State authorities to determine what changes are acceptable, and to ensure that adjustment burdens are shared.

II. THE ROLE OF STATE POWER

It is in this perspective that the State need for power, including force, becomes clear, at least in the absence of international functional institutions that provide rules for the management of change. State power—in all its aspects—has a functional use in providing some deterrence against the forcing on a State of the whole burden of adjustment to change, leading to final destruction of its systems values. To take some extreme cases, a drought in one State could readily be offset by migration to neighbouring countries or by forcible acquisition of the produce of neighbouring States. Adjustment to industrial development that made oil essential could be made by forcible acquisition of oil resources from others. In the contemporary world national defences may still be relevant to this systemic need: obvious cases of aggression attract reactions from other States, and perhaps from the United Nations, but only after some national resistance has been made. The growth of national forces in new States is in part a response to the need to deter the influence of greater States on their own freedom of decision-making. However, this problem of change and adjustment is not solved by national power. The greater States can always export unemployment, control terms of trade, export ideologies and use aid and capital loans as bargaining weapons and, if necessary, intervene directly in the affairs of other States. If the power of States were only military power, then a logical solution would be to give all States equality by giving them nuclear weapons. But even if all States were nuclear Powers, this would still not prevent the imposition of policies by greater States upon others by various threatening means.

This problem of change and adjustment was not faced in traditional approaches. Power balances and collective security arrangements merely preserve the rights of greater Powers to impose their policies upon others. GATT and UNCTAD represent some first signs of attempts to substitute functional rules for power dominance, but as yet the powerful have managed to avoid many obligations not to discriminate. The struggle by new States to industrialize and to diversify reflects an awareness that the problem is not basically a military one. Alliances, such as that attempted by the Arab League and the Organization of African Unity, seek to offset the systemic weakness of developing States by attacking regimes within the region that respond to foreign pressures.

Thus, looking at the interaction of States and at world society as a whole, it is possible to discern a functional and a dysfunctional use of power. Because each State within international society is in a constant condition of change, each State faces the option of absorbing or forcing upon others the adjustments required. Powerful States, in which most technological change takes place, seek to maintain existing structures and practices by which they can use others to cushion the effects of change, and by which they can prevent change taking place elsewhere. While this was more conspicuously so when powerful States had colonies or satellites, it remains so despite political and institutional restraints that exist in the contemporary world, and the behaviour is now dubbed 'neo-colonialism'. Power or force, in all forms, has a functional value when employed to prevent systemic changes that are dysfunctional to the State, and required merely to suit the convenience of other States.

III. ISOLATION AND NONALIGNMENT

One of the roles of the State is to protect a geographical area, bounded by fixed borders, from the uncontrolled influence of transactions that tend to cross those borders. It can do this by internal assistance, protection at the border, and activity beyond the border. The extent to which authorities do this determines the degree to which they isolate the community systems from international ones. A condition in which systems boundaries are identical with authority boundaries is one of perfect *isolation*. This was a general condition before the development of the international system; but in the contemporary world, isolation is a virtual impossibility. It is proving impossible to isolate communities even from the influence of ideas. But a degree of isolation over a short term is possible, and it is the short term with which authorities are concerned. Ultimately internal tensions and conflicts between community members that do and do not wish to be protected from the influence of foreign systems, and inter-State tensions and conflicts that arise out of interrupted transactions, tend to reduce the power of authorities, and to defeat isolationist policies.

The question arises as to whether it is possible to isolate a State from world politics, that is to eliminate intervention in the political processes of other States, when the systems clustered within the State extend beyond its boundaries and have significant sub-systems centered in other States. This is the position of the United States of America: would it be possible for the United States to avoid its political and strategic involvements in other countries while its commercial, cultural and ideological systems extend into them?

Isolation is not *neutrality*. Neutral States in war try to eliminate the influences of war by refraining from acting in the interests of any belligerent. This may or may not involve reduced transactions. *Nonalignment* is a system designed to widen and not to confine transactions. It is a condition in which there are interactions and interdependence at a systems level: each State asserts the right to determine its own values, but not to impose its values on others. Foreign commercial firms would, in these conditions, be obliged to negotiate with authorities within the States in which they were operating without any support from their own governments. As a foreign policy, nonalignment seeks to allow the community to be open to the influence of all foreign systems. Provided the indigenous values and interests of the authorities and the community are secure, and provided there is a widespread adjustment capability, nonalignment policies could lead to the integration of the domestic community with world systems.

IV. THE WELFARE STATE

The role of the State is essentially to serve the interests of systems and parts of systems within it, and therefore, in foreign policy, to act, not as a barrier to transactions, but as a filter of them, in order to ensure that change is within the capacity of systems to absorb without destruction of social values. In addition, the role of the State is to act positively to promote flexibility and adjustment, and to promote values. A systems analysis does not lead to the conclusion that States are becoming irrelevant to world society; on the contrary, while the role may be changing, it is becoming more, and not less important, as increased initiatives are taken within boundaries to promote welfare by redistributing resources, and to balance the interests of wider systems with internal values thus created.

Authorities vary in the degree to which they are prepared to control systems within their boundaries. Whether they are more or less active depends upon the demands made upon them by internal systems, especially those that influence political processes. Demands upon authorities vary according to internal conditions, for example, levels of economic and social development, and the presence or absence of differences that create ethnical and religious systems, or agricultural and industrial ones, that have competing values, and which, in the absence of authority, would interact according to the *laissez-faire* manner of our earlier model. Authorities are required to control systems behaviour and to determine competing system values. In conditions in which social values are changing, authorities find that they are required to be more and not less active in influencing systems.

Authorities also vary in the degree to which they seek to isolate or protect their area from external influences, and the reasons for this are also internal demands. In conditions in which the role of authorities is to act as a buffer between external and internal influences in such a way as to facilitate responses within their boundaries to wider system changes, and thus to eliminate the significance of boundaries, they are more active in internal than in foreign affairs. For such conditions to exist, a high degree of internal unity and satisfaction with the operation of wider systems must be present. In conditions of internal dissatisfaction, authorities endeavour to isolate the economic, social, ideological and other systems within their boundaries from the influence of wider ones. In these cases welfare is a value of less importance than internal security. A State seeking to protect an enterprise or an ideology within its boundaries from the changes taking place in wider trading or ideological systems, is in conflict with other States within these systems. Insecurity thus spreads, and welfare tends to become a secondary value. The Welfare State is thus dependent upon its environment: it can thrive only when in other States there are conditions of stability, and no demands made upon it to defend itself against severed transactions and actual intervention in its affairs.

The view of Kant and Bentham seemed to be that the less authorities intervened, apart from the needs of law and order, the better. In the inter-war period the State became intensely active in protecting internal industrial systems from external competition. This was restrictive intervention designed to hold workers and capital where they were at a time of high unemployment. The State apparatus, evolved largely for this purpose, was later able to respond to increasing demands for social services, some of which arose out of the oppressive conditions of the inter-war and post-war period. Gradually, and especially after 1945, the role of the State became more constructive; rehabilitation and retraining schemes, rehousing, re-equipment of industry, and education generally were post-war functions demanded of States. This set States upon a course which led them to respond to community demands, rather than to group interests: goals of welfare led to policies quite different from those traditionally promoted to protect group interests. Consumer interests began to offset group interests in demands for protection. The modern welfare State is more and more acting as a buffer against systems change, and less and less as a barrier to it. A trend in economic relations is toward bringing State boundaries into line with systems boundaries: GATT and the Kennedy Round are examples. Communications are beginning to force the same trends in ideological relations. But this is not a return to a Bentham ideal so much as an extensive use of State power to eliminate the significance of boundaries—which Bentham would probably have supported in contemporary conditions. The Welfare State is not, as popularly conceived, one in which benefits are given at random, but one in which authorities intervene to assist those affected by change to adjust to it, thus spreading the burden of change suffered by some systems across the whole society. The intention is not to prevent change; on the contrary, it is necessary at times to promote it as part of the adjustment process.

V. RATES AND TYPES OF CHANGE

Assuming that the final role of authorities is to allocate values and resources in such a way as to satisfy needs, to prevent conflict between systems operating within their jurisdiction and to distribute burdens of change, probably the main need of States is that rates of environmental change, and abilities of systems to respond to change, should be so balanced as never to have States faced with rates of change beyond their capacity to respond. This is also a condition necessary for peaceful relations between States, because if a State is faced by environmental conditions that are likely to destroy it as an organized cluster of systems—if, that is, it is likely to fail operationally and disintegrate into separate States—its powers will be used, not to protect systems interests, but to secure survival and independence. The phenomenon of a State risking destruction to itself, in the sense of damage to the system clusters that comprise it, in order to survive as an entity, is one with which we are familiar.

States have a greater ability to accept and to adjust to natural disaster than to the same damage inflicted by identified agents: floods and droughts induce responses different from protective duties against the exports of the country concerned. Responses to damage caused by discriminating treatment by another country differ from responses to the same damage caused by a non-discriminatory policy. Change that is sudden promotes responses that the same change over a period of time would not involve. Change that is inflicted by a foreign agent, that is discriminatory against one State, that occurs in conditions of inflexibility, and is sudden, will certainly be unacceptable and lead to desperate responses. Whether change is economic or political the same considerations apply.[1] While it is possible to have rules governing rates of change in mechanical systems, such as manufacturers lay down for the running-in of new machines, and to have laws

---

[1] For a discussion of responses to different types of change, see J. W. Burton, *Peace Theory: Preconditions of Disarmament*, 1962, chapter 3.

governing flexibility, as registering authorities have for moving vehicles, it is not possible to have laws and conventions governing rates of change in systems, States and their environments. However, an acknowledgement of the relevance of rates of change draws attention to two aspects of decision-making. It suggests that States in their own interests need to avoid actions that place unacceptable burdens of adjustment upon others. The conditions of the inter-war period in which States were making adjustment demands on each other beyond the systemic capacity of those without colonies and strong economies finally led to desperate attempts by these States to alter the environment by force. It also suggests that flexibility of response, that is, efficiency in decision-making, and flexibility of internal systems, are of the greatest importance to the security of States.

A second need of States arises out of the fact of change: systems require freedom to adapt to and take advantage of changes that they perceive as favourable to them. The discovery of new resources brings no benefits until they are exploited, the acquisition of new ideas and values gives no satisfaction if they are suppressed. Attempts to prevent States taking advantage of favourable change lead to the same desperate moves to alter the environment as do unacceptable levels of change. The frustration of expectations was the reason for the failure of balance of power policies which tended to prevent change and adjustment to it, and is the fallacy of collective security. It is the reason for social revolt. In due course, frustrated demands assert themselves. After wars, after revolutions, the conditions previously demanded by those demanding change tend to be accorded even when those resisting it are the victors: Japan now has its co-prosperity sphere, and independence movements have been accorded self-government. Some changes are important in the progressive development of States. They include day-to-day alterations in values and attitudes, and day-to-day introductions of new technologies that day-to-day are imperceptible. They become perceptible, and of political consequence, when resistances inhibit them to the point at which they accumulate and give rise to discontinuous or step-level change. The ideal type of world society is one which is fully permissive of change and never requires adjustment by a State or its systems other than that which is slow-moving and continuous.

VI. INTERNALIZED NEEDS

In addition to the needs of systems that States reflect, and the needs of States as entities, there are also felt needs that do not relate to systems, and cannot reasonably be regarded as State needs: the preservation and promotion of cultural and ideological values, observance of traditions, roles in world affairs and such extensions of national identification. These would appear to be less fundamental than the needs to which reference has been made, and some might seem to be even transitory; yet they are no less important politically. They may have origins just in propaganda, but once values are internalized they become State needs, which authorities are prepared to promote and defend at great cost. The precautions taken over many years by the United Arab Republic to prevent contact with Israel, and even travel to Israel by other nationals, reflected a felt need which was not necessarily a State security one. Attitudes become widespread: Arab and Israeli citizens when in contact have displayed regular stereotypes. The same could be said of the widespread fear of Communism within the United States of America, which lent support to anti-communist activities even outside the United States. It is difficult to ascertain whether the fears and aspirations that individuals have lead to policies, or whether policies reflect the needs of the society that have been internalized by its members.

VII. THE SPECIAL CASE OF DIVIDED STATES

There is one special case in contemporary world society which a consideration of State needs might help to clarify. This is the case, such as exists in Germany and Korea, and to some extent in Vietnam, in which, as a result of intervention by other States, two separate States have been created where only one existed before. Each has very little systems relationship with the other. There were strategic reasons for the separations, and these had ideological implications that required the creation of two different types of States and systems within them. Questions arise as to whether the two States, comprising the same ethnic and language communities, and existing in the same wider environment of world society, can retain their distinctive systems, and whether the administrations can both attain and maintain a legitimized status. If not, what are the processes by which the divisions will progressively decrease? These are important questions in policy formation, for it is tempting in many situations of internal conflict to adopt the solution of partition, despite the fact that each time there are potential conflicts arising out of pressures for re-unification and others for the maintenance of the separate States. Indeed, the hypothesis that new States, comprising systems that are at first alien and foreign-backed, can be created and made stable after one or two generations of control, seems to be fundamental to policy thinking within the great Powers. The Soviet would argue that it has created administrations in East European States that will remain communist, and the West would maintain that it has created States in its own image in the Philippines, Korea, Vietnam, Greece and elsewhere in the developing areas, where without its intervention different forms of administrative systems might have emerged. How permanent is this intervention, what systems changes will occur, whether States now divided will be re-unified, are questions as yet unanswered.

What has happened in each of these cases is the creation of relatively isolated and firmly controlled States with many of the features of traditional societies. The new generations know no other: alternatives are not clear and values do not change. There is in each a potentially low level of stability which will be in evidence once the States are exposed to the world environment, and once internal control through the power of the State and of foreign States is relaxed. What we need to know, for policy reasons, are the conditions that must prevail before authorities feel they can expose the systems under their jurisdiction to the influence of world transactions, and the likely consequences of this exposure.

The Soviet Union and Yugoslavia appear to be two examples of States that were relatively isolated from world systems, and that are now less isolated. The level of support for authority would appear to have increased and not decreased, but no conclusion can be drawn as to whether it was increased support that made possible the opening of the State to external influences or whether the relaxation of restrictions increased support. In other States, such as China, Spain, and many of the States of Asia, Africa and Latin America, there appears to be a fear that exposure or internal relaxation of control would lead to reduced support, if not actual revolt. In some cases, such as in Greece in 1967, political processes were bringing change too quickly for them to be acceptable to some interests, in this case the army, and they were prevented from operating. It would seem from these different cases that the level of political support for authorities is not a function of leadership, ideology and the values and interests of authorities, but a function of two variables, first the rate of change, and second the capacity of authorities and systems to adjust to change. This latter seems to depend upon levels of internal security, and the degree of shared values within the society generally. If this is so, then the future of separated States might depend most upon the behaviour of other States. If they are allowed to develop through the stages of a traditional society and render secure their institutions and internal processes of change, as the Soviet Union and Yugoslavia finally did, then they will be in a strong position to tolerate foreign sources of change. If, on the other hand, they are constantly on their guard against foreign threats to their security, as the Soviet Union was before industrialization, then they will be less flexible and more traditional in their internal controls. The threats that China has perceived as a result of containment and non-recognition by the West seem to have resulted in recurrent attempts to prevent alterations of values internally that made even the Soviet Union appear to be a threat. In this sense the policies of the West may have been self-defeating. A controlled extension of trading and cultural transactions at a pace consistent with the abilities of administrative systems to organize adjustment, and to maintain their political support, may be the means by which isolated societies can adjust to exposure to world society.

The same analysis can be applied to communities of different ethnic origins within States: the security of communities seems to be a first requirement, and in many cases this might require their own separate administrative controls. Once this is attained, systems transactions across boundaries or between different ethnic groups can more readily take place.

In summary, the needs of systems, communities and States seem to relate most to rates and types of change, to abilities to adjust to and spread the burden of change, and to the preservation of State values, including internalized social values.

3

LEGITIMIZED BEHAVIOUR

In addition to system and State needs of the types that have been described, there are State goals which if attained would deprive other States of these needs: acquisition of territory, control of resources, and influence on the ideologies and policies of other States. Many system and State needs can be satisfied by inter-State co-operation and co-ordination of activities, and this is the basis of functional institutions and treaty arrangements. But these other goals involve competition, rivalry, and power struggles: there can be no co-operation and co-ordination of activities when two States seek the same indivisible object, or when one State seeks to control another. The study of international politics, and the practice of diplomacy, have been directed primarily to finding ways and means of controlling these conflicts of interests. To prevent violence, laws defining aggression, and a threat of force greater than that available to any one State or alliance of States, would seem to be required. Disarmament and collective security arrangements suggest themselves as means of solving this problem of 'aggression'.

It is not within the scope of this study to argue that these measures cannot succeed: this has been done elsewhere.[1] What is being inquired into here is why or in what circumstances States pursue goals that deprive other States of their system and State needs: is it inevitable that States will have such goals, is this form of aggression inherent in a world society that comprises independent States of unequal power?

There are aspects of or approaches to such an inquiry which can be passed over. It is self-evident that one of the conditions required for States to pursue these apparently aggressive goals is an unequal power relationship. Whether States always tend to take advantage of power superiority, whether States are by nature aggressive and expansionist, has been argued on many occasions,[2] and debating the issue further would not advance

---

[1] See J. W. Burton, *International Relations: A General Theory*, 1965; and I. Claude, *Power and International Relations*, 1962.

[2] See, for example, J. D. Carthy and F. J. Ebling, *Natural History of Aggression*, 1964.

our inquiry. Nor need we concern ourselves with the question whether aggressive goals are ends in themselves, or means of attaining other State interests; there is no way of assessing motives and justifications, and in any event the consequences are the same. It could be that the widespread assumption that States do have these goals gives rise to policies and practices that help to promote aggressive behaviour. This self-fulfilling aspect of policy has been observed many times,[1] but by itself it does not explain aggressive behaviour in many particular instances. There is an opinion that conflicts of interest of this nature are inevitable, and inevitably lead to a condition in which more and more States come under the effective control of fewer and fewer great ones.[2] Historical evidence can be produced to support this view: today there are but two thermonuclear Powers. Historical evidence also seems to refute it: changes in values have led to demands for independence, and the most powerful States are experiencing higher and higher costs in denying needs to smaller States. One effect has been to lead them to reassess and to reperceive their needs and interests, and to be less inclined to force the burden of technological change on to weaker States, as was the practice of colonial Powers. Furthermore, systems that originated within the boundaries of the greater States have now extended beyond them and are linked to systems within other State boundaries. The needs of these systems, and the values of their members, are not always compatible with State needs. Greater Powers are, consequently, restrained both by the smaller States whose interests they threaten, and also by systems and values within their own jurisdictions. In practice, the conflicts which occur in contemporary world society take place amongst less powerful States, and the greater Powers cannot, for fear of being involved with each other, do anything effective in preventing them.

These and other aspects of the problem of aggression are better dealt with in the systems framework in which system and State needs have already been discussed. There appear to be two main issues involved in considering behaviour that seeks to deprive other States of their values and needs. The first is whether State authorities, when they are acting aggressively in this sense, are pursuing system and State goals, or whether

---

[1] See Burton, *Peace Theory*, chapter 4.
[2] See G. Schwarzenberger, *Power Politics*, 3rd ed. 1964.

they are acting in response to pressures upon them that are not inherent system and State needs. This involves, in any particular instance, an empirical inquiry into whether the aggressive behaviour is merely an easier alternative to some difficult internal adjustment: we have already noted that control over the environment can be used as an alternative to internal adjustment. It also involves clarification of the concept of 'national interests'. These two are related because authorities are required to make value judgements in which they balance costs of adjustment against costs of altering the environment. In each case the question raised is the extent to which authorities reflect system and State interests. It is this inquiry into legitimacy which is the subject of this chapter; an endeavour is made to distinguish between legitimate intervention and aggression.

The second issue which is relevant to an inquiry about conditions in which States act aggressively is whether authorities, when acting aggressively, are aware of alternative means and goals, of possible responses of other States, and of costs of conflict. These are issues of decision-making which are taken up in following chapters. These two inquiries, the interests which authorities reflect, and the efficiency of authorities in decision-making, should provide a basis for an assessment of whether aggressive policies are inevitably pursued because of the inherent power structure of international society, and if not, of the extent to which they are pursued because of a failure to perceive consequences in terms of State interests, and because of the pursuit of special interests and non-systemic needs.

I. LEGITIMIZATION

By looking at States as clusters of systems it is possible to examine the behaviour of State authorities in relation to their systemic and State roles. Their obligations are to allocate system values, to protect systems from external influences, to spread burdens of adjustment, and to do this with a view to promoting transactions outside their boundaries where these are required by the general interest of the systems that comprise the State. This provides a normative concept of behaviour. Any action that has neither a systemic nor a State value, and is promoted in the interests of authorities or pressure groups at the expense of the State, is outside the range of this behaviour. Means that are adopted to pursue systemic or State interests that provoke hostile responses from other States when alternative means or goals are available, and to this extent are self-defeating, may also be treated as outside this range of behaviour. In short, systemic and State interests provide a basis on which a standard of behaviour can be constructed.

Whether authorities are acting in accordance with their role, and pursuing systemic or State interests, cannot be determined by subjective estimations of what these interests are. It can be determined by reference to their legitimized status in the enactment of their role: this can be determined by operational tests such as electoral support, evidence of opposition, stability of government, the presence or absence of coercion in the maintenance of authority, and the nature of external responses.

There is an important distinction to be made between that which is described as 'legal' or in accordance with law, and that which is 'legitimized' or which is valued for itself.[1] That which is lawful, be it procedures or authorities, is not always valued, as a government of a State is aware when it suffers the consequences of widespread rebellion. Legal status is not necessarily legitimized status; legal status is sometimes obtained by force, and even when it has been derived from processes which are respected, it is sometimes maintained by force. Perhaps it is here that some approaches to international law and political science are most in disagreement, and also where political scientists are still most unclear. Subject to interpretations of law and obligations imposed upon citizens and States, lawful behaviour is a clear concept: constitutions and agreements are observed, and the legal authorities respected. The employment of power in order to require this observation and respect is legal. On the international stage, a State that defies the decisions of the United Nations acts unlawfully, and is sometimes coerced into submission by sanctions or more direct actions. However, once consideration is given to legitimization, that is, the value attached to legal forms and authorities, then this formerly clear concept becomes muddied: there is no longer any expected behaviour. Applying the tests of legitimization, those that uphold constitutions and agreements, and the legal authorities themselves, may, if they are no longer valued, be regarded as the reason for social disorder.

---

[1] See Max Weber, *An Intellectual Portrait*, 1960, and S. M. Lipset, *Political Man*, 1960.

The illegitimacy of lawful behaviour, the legitimacy of unlawful behaviour, and social obligations on the individual in society in some circumstances to behave unlawfully to promote legitimized institutions, have not yet found a place in serious political analysis. Yet it is this factor of legitimacy, whether or not it happens to conform with law, that is fundamental in social and inter-State relationships. Once we have a clear understanding of what constitutes legitimacy, we will have an understanding of what constitutes intervention, aggression, conflict and other phenomena of which we are only vaguely aware.

Legitimacy is closely linked with levels of participation in the political processes by which values and interests are allocated; if values are to be attached to structures and processes, participation in them would clearly help. But it is possible to have very low levels of participation, and yet an acceptance of the value of institutions, as was frequently the case in some new States immediately after attaining independence. Legitimization would appear to depend more upon performance in the satisfaction of needs than upon the particular forms and processes involved. It was only when independence leaders like President Sukarno of Indonesia failed to meet demands for stability and welfare that their legitimized status declined. On the other hand, democratic institutions, whatever their form, are not necessarily legitimized.

Probably the most important single influence affecting levels of legitimization is change in the demands made upon institutions and processes by reason of changed values and circumstances. Traditional or primitive societies were mostly under authoritarian rule by one or a few leaders, and sometimes even under hereditary rule. Yet authority remained legitimized. There were no alterations in values because there were few environmental changes that required alterations. The roles of leaders and led were accepted and stable. Even feudal societies, in which reciprocal roles favoured the few, were accepted and stable, there being no awareness of other institutions, and no expectations. Most contemporary societies had a powerful traditional influence until the technological revolutions of this century, which both altered environments and provided means of communicating these alterations. The demands made during the first half of this century upon institutions by the peasants of feudal China and the Philippines, and demands for independence and internal change in the rest of the world, were demands that reflected new values (which originated largely in the West), and which existing institutions could not satisfy. These demands, based upon changed circumstances and knowledge of alternatives, reduced the value of many authorities, structures and processes that had been acceptable over centuries.

Systems analysis helps to some degree in clarifying the concept of legitimacy. Each unit within a system has a role and a pattern of behaviour in relation to it: this is the meaning of unit relevance or 'set'. In basic systems the roles are equal. In closed social systems, however, some units carry with them a degree of control over other units. The chairman of a meeting, by reason of the role he enacts, has a higher degree of control over members that he would have if he were one of them on the floor. But the influence he exercises is derived from the meeting. Within a closed system there are no influences or powers that are not derived from the system: it has all the characteristics of a traditional society in which roles and values do not alter. Legitimization of authority is complete. However, in practice social systems are open: they have overlapping membership, and they are linked to other systems that do not necessarily have all the same interests. Members of different systems cannot keep their different roles entirely separate. There are, therefore, many sources of external influence on a system. Whenever there are external influences being exerted upon a system, and its authorities have altered values, or units have altered values without being accompanied by any alteration in those of the authorities, there is a condition of non-legitimization. An example is when members of a political party alter their values because of religious, financial or other influences; alterations then occur within the system, and this leads to conflicts between members, and breakaway groups are likely to be formed.

In some cases the external influences are more directly applied, as when the administrative systems of government intervene, perhaps on the side of minorities, forcing the majority to accept voting procedures that ensure continued control by non-legitimized minorities. This has happened in some countries where election of officers in trade unions is controlled. There is in these cases an authority within the system—the legal one—whose non-legitimized status is supported by external influences.

In practice this is a more usual condition in any social system than one of complete legitimization. There are few, if any, systems that are subject to changing environmental conditions, and whose authorities remain wholly legitimized: for this to occur they would need to be systems of little value to and isolated from the rest of society, like a society for the watching of steam trains. Generally speaking, social systems have values and interests that are mixed with the values and interests of other social systems. Directors, club presidents, secretaries of organizations are selected under the influence of political processes that are wider than those existing within the system as such, and frequently under the influence of political systems designed for the purpose. A high degree of non-legitimization is therefore general.

When the concept of legitimization is applied to the structure and processes of administrative systems an additional factor is introduced. Whereas systems derive their influence over each other through their social function, and whereas authorities within them have a power limited to the support they have within the system and whatever support they can obtain by reason of the values they share with other systems, administrative authorities have powers over systems that are not related to values shared by the rest of the community: police and military forces are established outside systems, and deliberately to give administrative authorities non-systemic power. The practical reason for this universal procedure is that administrative authorities have the formal function of allocating resources and values within their area of jurisdiction, and of protecting interests within this area from external influences. Every decision they make affects some systems favourably, and others unfavourably, and it is therefore necessary to have an enforcement capability at least in reserve. The more unified are the interests and values of all systems, that is, the more integrated is the society as a whole, the less intervention by administrative authorities is required.

There is a tendency to identify authorities with government, and for practical purposes this is convenient; but decision-making is better understood if it is noticed that in most societies, authorities—persons filling roles concerned with the allocation of values and resources—are not confined to those in government. The political process is such that public and private authorities tend to act to promote the interests they most represent: their first loyalty is to those institutions that placed them in their positions. But in no society is there just one set of interests and goals: elements of nationalism, group interests and a diversity of values always exist. Authorities have the function of distributing resources and determining values in ways that reflect the interests of all systems in society. Consequently, in their own personal interests, and because it is often conventionalized political behaviour, they have the task of marrying their own political interests with those of the total political system. In practice, authorities are sometimes more inclined to cater for the values of opposing political institutions than those of their own, because they believe they can count upon the electoral support of their own. A party supported by workers feels itself more able to restrict trade union activity than a party supported by capital.

The degree to which authorities can pursue special interests within the area of their jurisdiction, and deviate from important system demands, is high, at least in the short term. The degree to which they can promote the special interests of some systems that also operate outside their boundaries, to the detriment of other internal systems—that is, the degree to which they can expend resources in intervening in the affairs of external systems and other States—is also sometimes high. But wherever there is a difference between systemic interests, on the one hand, and the goals and values of authorities, on the other, there is at least some loss of political support for authorities: there is a reduced level of social legitimization. Propaganda and controls can affect this; a critically low level is reached when threat, coercion and the use of force are required to maintain authorities in their administrative roles.

The nature of legitimization is best demonstrated by taking the two extreme cases of political stability and communal conflict. Political stability is a condition in which authorities are both socially and legally legitimate. For this to occur the felt needs and interests of the population must be met by the administrative system within the State, and an ideological, ethnical and cultural identity must develop, so that both law and the State are supported as ends in themselves. Kelman has represented this condition in the following way:[1]

---

[1] H. C. Kelman: a diagram produced at a private seminar.

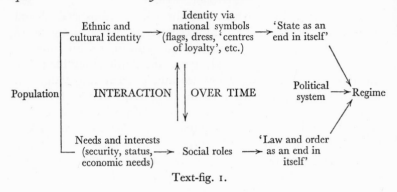

Text-fig. 1.

He has restated this condition by reference to requirements of the system:

	Consolidation	Mobilization	Conformity
Sentimental appeals	Cultural integrity	Symbolic involvement	Commitment to State as an end in itself
Instrumental appeals	Functional integration	Social role involvement	Commitment to law and order as an end in itself
Examples:	New States	States facing a threat	Stable, well-established States

This framework suggests that in any State with two antipathetic ethnic or cultural communities, common needs and interests might overcome other differences and create a stable society, provided the organization of different ethnic or cultural values were kept separate from, and not allowed to disrupt the organization of needs and interests. Common needs and interests might in due course modify other values, and promote a wholly integrated society.

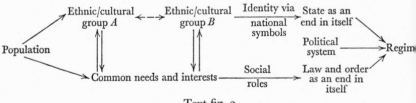

Text-fig. 2.

The usual condition, where there are two major communities, is the one in which the authorities give priority to the needs and interests of the cultural group they most represent, thus causing discontent within the other. This was, in the view of the Turkish Cypriots, the position in Cyprus; in the view of the indigenous Chinese, the position in Malaysia; in the view of the local Indians, the position in Fiji; in the view of the Africans, the position in Rhodesia. The motivation of the authorities in each case might have been racial, fear, protection of economic interests, or some other: in all cases the policy was self-defeating in that tension was created between the communities concerned.

The position is no different, analytically, when the communal factions are divided, not by race, religion or ethnic origins, but by ideology or class. Radical and conservative opinion both require needs and interests to be satisfied, and in the absence of this there is a level of legitimization so low as to threaten political stability. In most societies there are more than two different ethnic, religious, economic and other communities of interests, but the same processes are involved. To the extent that authorities fail to satisfy felt needs and the values of groups, they lack a highly legitimized status.

The usual procedures for political change and legitimization are not always effective, especially in conditions in which societies include different communities each with their own sets of interests and values. Even the mature party-political parliamentary systems enable governments to remain in office despite lack of political support as measured by non-electoral processes—strikes, riots, opinion surveys and local government elections. In many States in Europe, and in most elsewhere, there are no regular procedures for political change. Authorities maintain themselves by preventive detention, coercion and military rule. Once this occurs resistance tends to develop within civil services, and within armed services in particular. If the latter consider that authorities are inefficient, corrupt or not reflecting the interests and values of society, they are in a strong position to react because they have the means of taking administrative control. They must then endeavour to interpret and give effect to the interests and values of the clusters of linked systems. The test of their legitimacy is the extent to which their authority does not require the support of threat or coercion. Ultimately participation demands require some formal test of legitimization, such as elections.

II. INTERVENTION

A concept of legitimacy also provides the tests by which it can be determined whether authorities are acting within their State role when engaged in foreign relations. The argument to be developed is that intervention is aggressive in conditions in which either the authorities inviting intervention, the authorities intervening, or both, lack a legitimized status as measured by empirical tests of political support.

We have already made a distinction between systemic and State power. The same distinction is required in relation to systemic and State intervention. Let us return to the model of a world in which there are no governments, and imagine the discovery for the first time of oil, and means of using it in road transport. There would develop amongst the interests that owned the oil, and those that were exploiting, distributing and using it, a set of transactions, and the system would finally take shape under pressure of commercial dealings. There would be foreign influences operating in the societies in which parts of this system operated. The countries where the oil was discovered would be affected, and the life of the consumers of the oil would be affected. But this is not what is meant by intervention, even though government agencies were involved in the commercial relations. This would be the usual process of change and development through discovery and invention which creates new systems and alters others. The influences are systemic influences.

Now let us superimpose State boundaries upon this oil system. Another type of influence immediately occurs, this time the control by each State of the operations of the part of the oil system that happens to fall within its boundaries: taxation, control of trade practices and safety measures are enforced. Each State is free to exercise this control in whatever way it chooses: it could nationalize the resource, take over distribution, or alter in any other manner that part of the oil system that operated within its boundaries. The system as a whole would be required to adjust and to meet the demands made upon it by each State. This is the ordinary control of systems by State authorities with which we have dealt. This is not intervention, even though other States are affected. In other words, systemic influence on system, and State influence on a system or part of one that is within State jurisdiction, are not examples of intervention. But if one State were to act in any way either within or outside its boundaries in a manner designed to influence the behaviour of the system or any part of it in another State, this would be intervention. For example, withholding resources from usual markets could be regarded as intervention in the affairs of another State, and could be a serious form of intervention if there were no other source of supply. This is the intervention of sanctions. The use of State influence, exercised by diplomatic or other means, in order to prevent nationalization would also be intervention. Intervention is, in this view, a concept relevant only to the behaviour of States, acting either upon other States or parts of systems within them. It is the use of State power and not systemic power. Intervention and imperialism are therefore closely linked concepts: imperialism is any form of State activity that seeks to promote systemic interests outside its boundaries in such a way as to protect these interests from control by other systems and authorities in other States.

Earlier it was observed that system authorities and State authorities both affect the distribution of resources and values. It may seem inconsistent to argue that systemic influence, in our case influence of the oil interests, is not intervention, but State influence is. The reason is that within a State, while systems have an influence, they remain under the control of State administrative authorities. They must accept the values of these authorities. So, too, that part of a system that happens to operate within one State but has its main interests elsewhere is under the control of that State. The State can nationalize it, eliminate it or impose controls. The effect of foreign State intervention, on the other hand, is to remove systemic influence from the control of the State in which it operates. System influence extending from one State to another is legitimate provided, first, that the system influence that originates in another State is not derived from the power of that State; and second, that the system influence within the State affected remains subject to the control of that State as are all internal system influences. Unless these two conditions are fulfilled there is a condition of intervention.

The underdeveloped States of Africa, Asia and Latin America perceive interference in their political life by commercial and other non-governmental interests. They tend to refer to this as intervention in their affairs. It is clear that the bargaining position of the small or underdeveloped States is weak, and that they are subject to the influence even of interests that have no governmental backing. But this is not intervention. Frequently the activities of private interests are backed by their governments in many subtle ways; unfavourable trading agreements that provide the framework of systems operations are negotiated between governments. What, in fact, these small countries are demanding is a withdrawal of this form of intervention by foreign governments, and greater intervention in other ways so that they will obtain more favourable terms of trade, more capital, and favourable loans: they seek foreign intervention to increase their bargaining power against systems over which they have difficulty in exercising control. They seek foreign State power to support their own State power against foreign systemic influence. Lumping all foreign influence under a heading like 'neo-colonialism' misleads analysis, and is thus misleading in policy formation. It results in attitudes to and images in other States and systems within States that are probably false.

III. AGGRESSION

These forms of intervention could reasonably be termed aggression, but this latter term usually connotes a direct physical intervention. This is a form of intervention that only larger and more powerful States can adopt. A great deal of contemporary political thought was developed in powerful States, or States that were powerful at the time, and this form of intervention has been justified by imaginative extensions of rights of self-defence and protection of foreign properties. Whether justified or not, it is to be noted that intervention means intervention by States into the affairs of other States, by exercising control over them or systems within them, and that this form of intervention is a practice within the capability only of authorities that are more powerful than those they are endeavouring to control. Just as it is possible with sufficient authority or force to alter internal systems, so it is possible to alter systems outside State boundaries, and to create new ones with different values and interests. This has happened in Korea, Germany and Vietnam, and the creation of Israel was due to this process. It is the fact of this relative power that States exercise on one another which is the basis of power theories of international relations. International law as traditionally conceived tends to sanctify these relationships: intervention has been held to be a legal right of powerful States in some circumstances.

Intervention by a State into the affairs of another, whether it be indirect or direct, takes one of two forms: either it is without, or it is with, the knowledge and consent of the authorities concerned. Suez was an example of the first when in 1956 the United Kingdom, France, and Israel endeavoured to impose their wills upon Egyptian authorities. There is little difficulty in designating such actions as aggressive. Vietnam, Hungary and many other instances are examples of the second in which foreign governments have given support to existing authorities, and perhaps at their request. The latter may be separated into two different classes. First, cases in which the inviting authorities are legitimized and can be regarded as acting in the interests of the community: this was usually the case where countries facing invasion by Germany in the late thirties sought foreign help. Second, cases in which the authorities are not legitimate ones except in the narrow legal sense, and do not apparently represent the values and interests of the systems within their boundaries. In this case the authorities are seeking support to compensate for their lack of legitimization and authority, and they are likely to receive it to the extent that foreign Powers assess some advantage in using the opportunity to support values and interests important to them. British support to Malaya, Soviet Union support to Indonesia, and United States support to South Vietnam were examples. In every respect this type of case is identical with that in which intervention occurs without the knowledge and consent of authorities, because the legal authorities represent only some interests. In this way a distinction is possible between legitimate intervention and aggression in these more complex cases in which intervention is invited. It hinges more upon the degree of legitimization of the authorities in the State in which the action takes place than upon the motivations of the intervening Power. There may be as strong a case for intervention at the request of some rebel group that can give evidence of support, as for intervention in the interests of the legal authorities that lack support. In practice neither side can give convincing evidence, and intervention is difficult to justify. Friedmann has arrived at this same conclusion by arguing that in cases of civil warfare no foreign State has a right to accept an invitation from the legal or recognized authorities as this would prejudge the issues involved, and it is for the members of the communities affected to determine these.[1]

When authorities in States act outside their boundaries, with all the risks and costs involved, it can be assumed that they have some important interests to promote: these may be systemic and State interests; or alternatively the authorities may be aware of domestic trends or challenges that threaten values and institutions they seek to preserve, and which they cannot control by internal or border control. In either case their intervention at the invitation of other State authorities is an intervention for their own purposes, and not related to their systemic or State needs. The legitimized status of the intervening authorities is, therefore, a second test to be applied in determining when intervention is legitimate, and when it is aggression. Each of the two types of intervention referred to above, those in which the authorities within the inviting State were and were not legitimized authorities, should, therefore, be sub-divided into two in order to take into account the legitimized status of the authorities within the State that is intervening. Taking into account the various combinations of legitimized and non-legitimized States, and invitations to intervene taking and not taking place, it will be found that aggression occurs in all cases except that in which a legitimized authority invites a legitimized authority, and in some circumstances (depending upon the legitimized status of opposing factions) that in which a legitimized authority intervenes without an invitation from a non-legitimized authority.

Foreign intervention is likely to decrease and not increase the support non-legitimized authorities have, and in due course their legitimized status will decline further. There is then a condition of conflict between systems and authorities which is likely to spread to other States through interacting and linked systems. This raises an interesting empirical question, whether fully integrated communities controlled by fully legitimized authorities ever engage in aggression.[2]

---

[1] W. Friedmann, *The Changing Structure of International Law*, 1964.

[2] This is a study at present being conducted by the Centre for the Analysis of Conflict by C. R. Mitchell.

The concept of legitimate intervention rests upon the legitimization of authorities within their own boundaries; it does not rest upon the acceptance of the intervention by another authority, or upon international undertakings to intervene. If this were not the position, State authorities would be required to act legitimately in two different, and possibly incompatible senses: legitimately in the sense of representing the values and interests of their State, and legitimately in the sense of acting in accordance with demands made on their State by some contractual obligations. The former in practice takes precedence over the latter, particularly when demands made upon States arise out of agreements entered into by previous governments, and in different conditions.

That this must be the position is even clearer in cases in which authorities do not have a legitimized status. It is possible for State *A* and State *B* to enter into an agreement under which systems and authorities in *A* acquire special rights within State *B*. If the authorities in *B* have merely a legal status, and not a legitimized one, the agreement is, in effect, between State *A* and some individuals in State *B* who fill positions of authority, but who are acting as individuals outside their State role. If the agreement were held to be the basis of relationships between *A* and *B*, *A* would have certain rights despite opposition in *B*: if the legitimized status of *B* were taken into consideration, the agreement would have no validity.

The legitimized status of the authorities in *A* is no less relevant: an intervention by a non-legitimized authority in State *A*, even at the invitation of a legitimized authority in State *B*, cannot be held to be valid: it would, in effect, not be State intervention, but the intervention of persons acting outside their State role. It would be opposed by systems within *A*, and therefore by others in other States. Stated more generally, the exercise of rights under an agreement entered into by State authorities, one or more of whom has not a legitimized status, is not legitimized, and leads to internal conflicts that spread to other States through shared systems and values.

This reasoning can be extended to multilateral agreements such as those that establish international institutions with powers to coerce members. When a State has signed an agreement, such as the United Nations Charter, a right of intervention to control its behaviour domestically, or its behaviour in relation to other States, depends upon the legitimized status of the institution, and of the authorities in the State concerned, in respect of the particular matter in dispute. It is clear that legitimized State authorities cannot be placed in the position of accepting the right of other authorities or international institutions—or international lawyers—to determine for them their values, or in any way to deny to them their political function of determining distribution of values and resources within the area of their jurisdiction. On the other hand the absence of a legitimized status exposes an authority to intervention into matters of domestic jurisdiction, as, for example, when human rights and other values of systems that cut across boundaries are affected: unless authorities can demonstrate a legitimized status in relation to their policies, no claim can be made for protection on grounds of domestic jurisdiction. In practice this view is widely adopted, even though it may also have widespread opposition on legal grounds. For example, it is the absence of legitimized status of the governments of Rhodesia and South Africa in respect of their control of Africans within their territories that is used to justify United Nations intervention in matters which might otherwise be claimed to be matters of domestic jurisdiction. Whatever might be customary law, legitimization or the absence of it is the test which is applied, though not explicitly stated, in determining whether intervention is justified.

The interplay of intervention and the aggressive responses that it is likely to stimulate are important in practice. The common pattern of conflict is one in which there is intervention by States in the affairs of others in a non-legitimized framework, as for example when States promote or defend sectional interests in foreign States. In due course there is an aggressive response once these States find adjustment burdens, or reduced expectations, imposed upon them to be greater than the capacity of their systems to absorb. Germany, Italy, and certainly Japan could be regarded as being in this position before the Second World War. In a traditional legal sense these States were the aggressors; they struck the first blow. The Western States were defending themselves. Every State can find some justification for its aggressive policies, usually the claim to self-defence. Responsibility for the background conditions is never accepted. This makes the concept of legitimization all the more relevant and important: it helps to cut through the more subjective arguments of what is and what is not aggression.[1]

These two different bases for normative behaviour, the legal and the legitimized, need not, in practice, be greatly different. The second determinant of legitimate behaviour, decision-making, bridges the two. Decision-making includes the taking into consideration of alternative means and alternative goals in the pursuit of systemic and State interests. The demands of other States or international institutions are part of the environment or input of States. The task of legitimized authorities is to promote adjustment to the environment, and to assess the costs involved in trying to alter the environment or isolate the State from it. Consequently, the demands of States and obligations to institutions, those that arise out of agreements and all others, have to be taken into account. Inefficient decision-making by authorities, that is failure to be aware of choices or to act in systemic and State interests, is no different in character from non-legitimized decision-making: in practice inefficient decision-making leads to reduced legitimization. Consequently decision-making bridges the gap between State needs and environmental demands, and thus bridges the gap between legitimacy in the sense of representing the values and interests of the State, and legitimacy in the sense of acting in accordance with agreements or demands made on the State. It is to decision-making that we now turn.

---

[1] For a discussion on 'aggression' see Burton, *International Relations*, pp. 34 ff., and *Peace Theory*, pp. 48 ff.

4

DECISION-MAKING

Decision-making ranges from the administrative procedures by which messages are distributed and filed, to the quality of perception and interpretation, and the degree to which action is guided by adequate consideration of all possible choices. It includes the execution of the decision, and readjustment to cope with environmental responses to the decision. The decision-making process can be faulty at many specific points: any one weakness in the total process can affect the efficiency of the whole. One's first inclination is to look at the routines, the lower levels of communication processes, the system of receipt of messages, filing, distribution, preparation of submissions for decision, and the routines that follow decision. In the contemporary world these are always under review; foreign offices are fairly efficient in these matters. In practice, failures are not due to the mechanical systems, and are more frequently due to parts of the total process that cannot be reviewed by public service inspectors, and by operational research consultants. These are the parts which are the responsibility of senior and final decision-makers. Failure here is not acknowledged contemporarily, and when historically revealed, it is interpreted as failure that is beyond human control. Eayrs has commented, 'A physician whose patient dies through malpractice or neglect faces an inquest or a suit for damages; an engineer whose bridge collapses through faulty mathematics or through too much sand and too little cement faces a Royal Commission or a penitentiary sentence. But the statesman whose policies bring ruin to a nation does not even ask forgiveness. There is, he says, nothing to forgive.'[1]

I. THE AREA OF CHOICE

In order to examine efficiency in decision-making, how the inter-State system operates, whether States can achieve consciously stated goals more reliably, whether they can avoid conflicts with other States, the area of choice that decision-

[1] J. Eayrs, *Right and Wrong in Foreign Policy*, 1965, p. 38.

makers have must be determined. What authorities should do in particular circumstances, on the basis of some ideology or normative rules, is not immediately relevant: what alternatives exist is the first consideration.

An interaction process within and between systems can be a mechanical one not involving choice. In basic systems this is the case. In social interactions there is at least some part of the interacting process, no matter how small, that does involve alternatives of behaviour. In historical or descriptive studies areas of choice are not apparent: they tend to record choices that were made. In any event, the canvassing of alternatives usually reflects ideological opinion. What is required is an analysis of the area of choice of decision-making generally, in the light of which alternatives in particular situations can be examined.

A usual means of defining areas of choice is to refer to static and dynamic influences on States over which they have little or no control, and the changing environment that might be more subject to influence, and in relation to which States might be in a position to choose alternative policies. This is an arbitrary distinction useful in describing an environment, but less useful in determining areas of choice. The more direct way is to examine areas of the environment or conditions that are alterable and unalterable by the deliberate decisions and policies of States. This draws more attention to the relationship which is of immediate interest: the relationship between decision-makers of States, and the systems and environments in which they operate.

Alterations in environments must be treated as part of the unalterable data to be taken into account within the total decision-making process of States. Authorities may be able to influence the nature of change in some small ways, but not the fact of change. Conditions of extensive and discontinuous change, presenting States with adjustment problems beyond their capacity, might often be held to be a sufficient cause of conflict between States. History draws attention to altering rates of change, and an expectation would be an increase in situations of conflict associated with increased levels of change. Before the First World War, former colonial areas were industrializing rapidly, forcing widespread adjustment upon metropolitan powers, and war accentuated this. In 1830 cotton manufactures accounted for 50 % of British exports, and only 24 % the year before the war. Japanese industrial production rose from 183 (base year 1899 = 100) in 1909 to 827 in 1931. Canadian wheat exports rose from 95 million bushels in 1914 to 286 million by the end of the twenties, and similar changes took place during the war in Australia and Argentina. This was the order of change that was widespread within States and between them. Adjustment to sudden change on this scale was beyond the capacity of States like France and Britain, and certainly beyond the capacity of Germany. The problem was accentuated by the requirements of post-war rehabilitation, the objective of which was to solve pressing human and political problems, and not the longer-term structural ones. Policies were defensive and restrictive because it was easier politically to impose tariffs and to reserve colonial markets for the exports of the colonial Power, than to move capital and labour from some industries to others. The Great Depression of 1929–31 was evidence of structural maladjustments, and of self-defeating restrictive policies, and its intensity led to further defensive responses. In due course the political effects of restrictive economic policies became apparent. The rise of Hitler to power was against this background. Japan's demands for a South-East Asian co-prosperity sphere were directly related to the restrictive policies of the West. This was not a case of a war that was inevitable because of some fundamental psychological drives: it was a war occasioned by interactions of a character that led governments to aggressive acts in the protection of their interests. In the contemporary period, the failure of powerful States to adjust to changing circumstances is more in relation to political values than to living standards, but the processes and consequences are comparable. In the period before the Second World War demands for greater participation in internal decision-making were widespread in feudal economies, and even in the major States where minorities were excluded. The war gave opportunities to independence movements for electoral reform.

The internal conditions of the State must also be treated as unalterable for purposes of decision-making. There are changes over periods of time in the abilities of the State to appraise its environment and to adjust to it, and changes in structure. The Keynesian era was one in which insights into financial policy enabled States to adjust to altered economic conditions by means less likely to promote tariff wars. But increased communications have brought States into closer contact, and the process of adjustment remains difficult despite increased governmental controls. Furthermore, governments are now as much concerned to place barriers against ideas as against goods. The State structure, its pressure groups, its nationalism, and its fears of the environment, are unalterable within any span of time that is relevant to decision-making processes. Even State institutions and practices are unalterable. In the party system of politics statements are made more for domestic than for foreign consumption: this affects inter-State relations but cannot easily be controlled. The influence of pressure groups can help to escalate conflict between States once it occurs, but authorities must respond to it. History, tradition, leadership interests, government control of information services, traditional alliances and sentiments, the size of armed forces, religious views, language differences, dependence and interdependence factors, and many others, have a bearing upon the course of State relations. These are of importance to the philosopher, the historian and the political scientist; they are relevant features to point out to students who are studying the behaviour of States. But they are part of the environment which decision-makers must accept as unalterable in their day-to-day planning and making of policy. Like gravity and friction in the operation of a machine, they are factors to be taken into account and offset: they cannot be eliminated, and their presence is felt most when the machine is operating under stress.

This is an approach of political realism, though different from that of the classical school of realists. They were realistic in facing up to the nature of Man and the State, from which they drew conclusions about the nature of society. This approach takes the objects of their realism as unalterable data. Attention is confined to those decisions and acts that are within the capability of States in their contemporary environment. This realism also requires the exclusion of many areas that may be within the decision-making capability of States over long periods. For example, educational systems—even the kind of history textbooks used—have an important bearing on international society, but in practice changes in culturally based educational policies do not take place within a time span relevant to the avoidance or resolution of a conflict, or the management of inter-State relations.

Alterable factors are probably few and insignificant. To base an analysis of decision-making upon them may seem at first sight to be reducing it to an unreasonable level of detail. It may seem to exclude all manner of variables that have traditionally been regarded as directly relevant. More radical decisions, for example the creation of federations, the elimination of States or some types of States, the creation of supranational organizations, disarmament or arms control, or single-tax, give more scope for imagination, and may seem more relevant to the problems of international relations than an examination of decision-making by States in a very restricted area of choice. But in the real world of politics it is not possible to decree that in the interests of avoiding a Third World War and its consequences, States must be disarmed, or that certain types of systems must be eliminated. Sweeping descriptions and generalizations about the behaviour of men and States in international society, and bold solutions to problems, have been a feature of most studies of international relations. They no longer satisfy the student who wants a clear picture of the movements of history, and who wants to see at the micro-level what the processes are that give rise to these broad movements, and in this way to see at which points, if any, systems can be altered or influenced by deliberate decision.

At the macro-level the relevant questions to ask are: why do States enact unacceptable roles? why do they pursue policies that provoke aggressive responses? why do they endeavour to deny participation to those seeking it? what are systemic influences? what is the result when States resist them? These questions can be answered only in part at the macro-level by postulating systemic and States needs and interests. But the processes that lead systems to change, that give rise to States responses, that finally render States and systems, or States and States in conflict, can be seen only at the micro-level of decision-making. This is to some extent true of any system: a breakdown is obvious, but the reasons for it usually require more exact attention. This level of analysis involves empirical studies, hypotheses and reality testing, and is recent in the study of International Relations. The questions at the micro-level are: how are the decisions taken within political systems? what use is made of information? how accurately is the external world perceived? what capability do States have of responding to their environment, and of altering their response?

That the range of choice in the making of decisions is narrowly limited at any given point of time might be discouraging: no easy and quick solutions to serious political problems can be contemplated. But even the limited range of choices that exists at a particular time is responsible over long periods of time for systemic changes, and for resistances by States to systemic changes that ultimately lead to conflict between them. If States finally become irrelevant to world society, if supranational authorities are created or if disarmament occurs, this will no less be due to decision-making processes—to limited choices made at many points of time. For these reasons the details of decision-making—trivial matters in comparison with the great movements of history—are of particular interest in the study of international politics and conflict.

II. DECISION-MAKING PROCESSES

Within this restricted area of choice, authorities operate with varying degrees of efficiency in attaining their goals, according to levels of awareness of available alternatives. When authorities act in certain ways because they have no alternative, this is not necessarily because there are no alternatives, but because they were not aware of any. The Cuba crisis of 1962 seems to have been an occasion when decision-makers increased their efficiency by making themselves aware of alternatives. Information, experience, training and time for consideration, are amongst factors relevant to efficient decision-making which, along with legitimization, determine the degree to which States can respond to their environment in ways which do not deny needs to others.

Efficiency in decision-making depends upon efficient operation at many points in the total process, and decision-making models show these. One of the first decision-making models was one developed by Modelski to describe decision-making in a power framework. It was essentially a model based on the State, any international aspect being introduced only by reason of alliances and collective security that follow the failure of State power to ensure security. Modelski defined power as 'the community's present means to obtain the future desirable behaviour of other States'.[1] When referring to the community's

[1] G. Modelski, *A Theory of Foreign Policy*, 1961, p. 39.

means, he was concerned with community power available for use by governments. 'Power is the product of co-operation between the policy-makers and their community.' For Modelski, power-inputs and power-outputs are the variable elements of foreign policy. The foreign policy operations of a State are limited by the amount of power at its disposal, and a picture of the foreign policy operations of a State can be inferred from an account of its power-output. His diagrammatic representation is:

Text-fig. 3.

This simple model is an apt one. We have made a distinction between systems and the State, and between systemic influence and State power. The power of a State is derived in the first instance from the enforcement agencies its administrative authorities create; but its potential power is that which it can derive from systems within its boundaries.

However, we require a model that tells us more of the nature of decision-making both at a government and at a community level. Furthermore, the input in which we are most interested is change; power enters into the model only in so far as it is a means of preventing change, of enforcing adjustments internally or externally, and generally in giving effect to some types of decisions. The following change-input model demonstrates some aspects of international society and its processes not otherwise apparent.

This model draws attention to features of decision-making, and points where failure is likely to occur, such as perception of change, different interpretations of change according to the ideology of the country of origin, the manner in which change is reported by the mass media; classification and memory of the community, past experiences of conflict and aggressiveness, traditional thinking; responses as determined by perception and memory, the influence of leadership, of educational levels, and of knowledge of the environment; the interrelations between government and community, the effect of feed-back from dom-

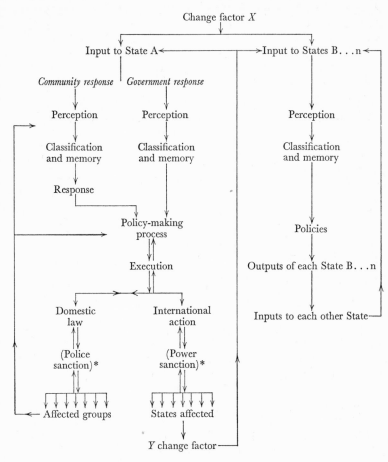

Text-fig. 4. Decision-making model.

* Operative when authority exceeded: indicative of conflict situation: includes foreign assistance and alliances.

↓ Input.   ↑ Feed-back.

estic and foreign sources on policies contemplated or being implemented; the role of both domestic and foreign executives such as police and the armed forces; the nature of organized pressure groups seeking to promote or to prevent change, the nature of national and international pressure groups, and the interplay between the two directly and through governments and international institutions; and the general nature of domestic and international consensus, how it develops and becomes codified. A model such as this shows decision-making to be a process: while the formal or constitutional decision-maker is a head of State or a government, in reality the decision-maker is not a man or a group of men, but a process. Final responses may have no relationship to the responses, in similar situations, of individuals or small groups. The decisions affecting foreign policy are those in which decisions are required as to whether change and adjustment are to be accepted or resisted, and the consequent decisions as to whether they are to be enforced upon domestic or foreign interests. These decisions are affected not only by the availability and willingness to employ power, but also by the level of efficiency of the State and its ability to adjust to change; a State with unemployment and no re-training programmes, greatly dependent on a few exports and a few markets, has a low capability for adjustment. Its power can be employed to compensate for this. Inefficiencies in decision-making, such as faulty perception and information, ideological or other commitments that prevent assimilation of new facts, barriers to feed-back, all threaten the change-adjustment process and invite the employment of power.

This is a decision-making model of one State; but the output of one State is the input of other States. The output of a State—for example, economic aid—may bring favourable or unfavourable responses from the recipient. Whatever the responses, they become the input of many other interested States, and are, therefore, of greater magnitude than a bilateral relationship would suggest. The behaviour of one Power toward another is part of the world environment perceived by all States.

III. THE ROLE OF PERCEPTION

As Text-fig. 4 indicates, it is the perception of the environment that is the operative link between subject and environment. It is at the point of perception that decision-making commences, and any misperception automatically renders responses inappropriate. If power were perceived as the motivation of other States, certain defensive policies would follow logically; if participation were perceived as the drive of international society, policies would take different forms. The United States perceived China as power-oriented, and looked for evidence of Chinese intervention in the affairs of neighbouring States, and interpreted events in Korea and Vietnam accordingly; if it had—rightly or wrongly —perceived the motivations of Chinese as being the drive to control their own affairs without foreign or domestic overlord-ship, United States policy calculations might still have had to take into account the strategic loss of a sphere of influence, but this loss would have been evaluated in a different perspective.

It is probably at the point of perception, already conditioned by theories, that there is the greatest source of irrelevant response. The origins of conflict can be frequently traced to false perception. In the Cyprus conflict the issue most debated was 'Enosis' or union with Greece. Turkish Cypriots, the minority community, feared for their position within a State that would be controlled by Greece. For political reasons Greek Cypriot leaders constantly made statements suggesting that the long-term aim was Enosis. Coldly appraised, it is difficult to believe that most Greek Cypriots, especially the younger generation, wanted Enosis; it would probably have meant lower living standards, apart from giving up indepen-dence and all that this means to ruling élites. This does not mean that there did not exist a strong Greek sentiment. Australians talk of 'going home'—meaning, visiting the United Kingdom; but this does not prevent them being allied with the United States, and being strongly nationalist in many respects. Greek Cypriot sentiments were similar. Perception by Turkish Cypriots of the real position was difficult in the light of past experiences, and of Greek statements; and a resolution of the conflict depended upon an accurate perception by them— and an accurate perception by the Greek Cypriots of Turkish fears.

The study of perception is not new: but its significance in decision-making has been examined only in recent years. In 1960, Abercrombie demonstrated 'the selective and inter-pretative nature of perception', and showed how 'the infor-mation that a person gets from a specified part of the outer world depends on the context, or total situation, and on his past experience, which is usefully thought of as being organized into schemata. Human relationships play an important role in perception both in that they are often a significant part of the context, and in that they have contributed to the formation, testing and modifying, of schemata.'[1] She then went on to show how perception affected the processes involved in the formulation of scientific judgements. This study rested to some degree on work on visual perception done previously, and with which we are more familiar. In the study of international politics we are concerned with non-visual perception; there are non-visual and conceptual images of other States and people that cannot be analysed as can the apparently unequal lengths of equally long lines enclosed between inwardly and outwardly pointed arrows. We know from visual presentations that form can be 'seen' even though it cannot exist. For example, below is a drawing of a triangle that cannot be made.[2]

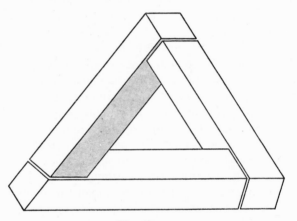

Text-fig. 5.

Even more easily, and with far less opportunity of correction, entirely impossible images of States and people, and their relationships with other States and people, can be 'seen'. 'Aggression', Nationalism', 'Communism' and 'Capitalism' are perceived where they do not exist, and in forms they do not have. The very clear-cut images the United States and China have had of each other seem to be very different from images many other States have of them. Each successive event perceived seems to confirm past perceptions because of the selective and interpretative processes involved. A decision or action that does

---

[1] M. L. Johnson Abercrombie, *The Anatomy of Judgment*, 1965, p. 18.
[2] From L. S. and A. Penrose, *British Journal of Psychology*, 1958, no. 49, p. 31.

not fit into schemata is likely to be treated as a trick. There can be escalation in perception of threats quite apart from that which arises out of successive defence actions and responses. The problems of perception are many and varied, and this is not a study of them. Transference, the influence of fear, the effects of education and tradition, are all relevant studies. Mention is made of them here to draw attention to aspects of decision-making that are alterable. Abercrombie seemed to show that a self-correcting process operates once the subject is aware of the process of perception, and of his own false perceptions. The degree to which perception by States is subject to influence is still to be demonstrated.

IV. EXPECTATIONS

Interaction processes and perceptions are not by themselves necessarily critical sources of aggressive behaviour. A State may react passively to seemingly adverse environmental conditions, despite its inadequate adjustment capabilities and its inefficient decision-making processes; another may react aggressively in circumstances that seem favourable. In the early thirties Japan refrained from retaliation in the face of extreme provocation arising out of western trading policies, and in the sixties the United States acted aggressively to change in the little island of Cuba. There is a third factor which preconditions both interactions and perceptions; for want of a better term this might be called 'expectations'.

Expectations are analytically distinct from interactions and perceptions because they concern future behaviour. Being judgements about the future behaviour of others, expectations are subject to even greater distortion than perceptions. They give free play to prejudice and preconceived notions because there can be no reality-testing as is frequently possible with perception. Moreover, expectations are usually even more strongly self-fulfilling. United States expectations of Chinese expansionism led in the forties to policies of containment that provoked responses that appeared to the United States to be aggressive. The expectations western European governments had of German political trends after each of the World Wars led to demands to restrict German strategic capabilities, and these provoked responses in some political factions that were interpreted as evidence that the expectations were justified. Egypt's foreign policies in the last decade have reflected expectations of British and American behaviour. The roles of each of these States in respect of the Middle East could have been altering significantly in Egypt's favour, but Egyptian expectations of their behaviour, based on past experiences, lead to policies that make alteration of their behaviour more difficult to achieve.

Expectations are legally, historically, behaviourally and theoretically derived. Expectations based upon constitutions and agreements are held to the extent that legal arrangements are enforceable, or are in any event likely to be observed for reasons of mutual self-interest. In the international field where there can be little, if any, enforcement, they derive from behavioural experience. Historically based expectations are derived from accepted interpretations of State behaviour such as the expansionist tendencies of States, and the use of power and force as an instrument of policy. These are strongly and universally held, and modify legally based expectations. Only consistently maintained roles that contradict traditional expectations are credible, and usually even these are confined to States, such as Sweden and Switzerland, that are deemed not to have aggressive motivations because of their size and geographical positions. Historically based expectations seem to be held more firmly than behaviourally based ones, and this means that States have difficulty in creating an image of themselves different from that already created by them, and perceived by others, in a previous and totally different world environment.

Theoretically based expectations, once established, are the most firmly held, especially if the theories appear to reflect current and historical experience. Power theories now dominate popular thinking and condition expectations of governments and people: they are simply grasped. Alternative theories are difficult to establish, even though analytically they might serve better to interpret history and contemporary behaviour. Experiences with students undertaking simulation exercises suggest that under stress there is in decision-making a reversion to simple and popularly held notions. Students excuse themselves, when asked why they did not adopt alternatives that would have had a greater pay-off, by saying they did not have time to think. Unless and until alternative theories become part of conventional wisdom, expectations that seriously restrict choices of policies will continue to dominate decision-making.

It is in relation to expectations that contemporary theories of politics and international politics have most to offer to the practitioner. Theories of power, participation, communication, functionalism and regionalism enable him to examine possible choices, and to broaden his range of choice. Guarantees have little political significance, but expectations of behaviour based upon theory and example can sometimes supply the required assurances. No constitutional devices or official statements could guarantee that Turkish Cypriots would not in due course find themselves under Greek domination. Perhaps if they had examined independence movements, struggles for participation in decision-making, and other features of decision-making such as this, they would have had different expectations, guarantees or no guarantees. Indeed, if they had examined cases, such as Australia, where a religious minority holds the balance of power between political parties that are comprised of the same ethnic and religious groups but differ only in their political beliefs, the Turkish Cypriots could have had expectations of political and physical security within a unified Cypriot community. Fear typically confines choices to familiar responses, and it is the contribution of theory that it points to alternatives.

It could be argued that when students revert to power responses under stress in simulation, and when States reduce their range of choice to familiar responses, they are demonstrating political realism: it is not realistic to think that States can be induced to expect in others, or adopt themselves, behaviour that might be suggested by cybernetics, functionalism, or communications and participation theory. Herein is a misinterpretation of theory. There is nothing so practical and realistic as good theory. Theory represents an attempt to explain behaviour: Political Science is not a normative discipline, it is not dealing with 'oughts' and 'shoulds', or idealistic solutions. Communications theory, cybernetics and decision-making theory attempt to show how policies are arrived at: functionalism attempts to explain why certain types of institution are more efficient than others, and regionalism seeks to explain some features of behaviour. While these theories can be used to point to inefficiencies and, therefore, to changes that could be made to overcome them, they are essentially explanation. If cybernetic theory is an advance on power theory, it is only because it better explains the behaviour of States. Theory explains the behaviour of other States, so that perceptions and expectations can be adjusted to accord with reality. Without theory parties to disputes regard their antagonists as behaving in ways they themselves would not: they believe that they are rational and consider alternatives, while others do not. In the day-to-day world, political theory helps decision-makers to anticipate and to control the behaviour of others. In the critical Cuban crisis, conflict was avoided by the consideration each party gave to the behaviour of the other on the basis of what was rational, and of the choices that were possible. In this particular case, deliberate and obvious attempts were made by the United States to demonstrate alternatives available to the Soviet Union. The two States involved were both overwhelmingly powerful; the outcome could be explained only as a cybernetic solution, and not as a power one. Theory demonstrates possibilities, it enables prediction, and can thus guide behaviour and point to means of reliably achieving goals. Knowledge of it expands possible choices, some of which will be deemed to be politically realistic in particular circumstances.

At the present state of conventional wisdom, and despite any theories which would make reasonable quite different expectations, typically States expect hostile responses from others. There is, as we have seen, a historical preconditioning which accounts for this, but there are specific influences in a world environment that lead to more conflict in one period of history than in another. Contemporary conflicts do not involve the great Powers directly, they have their origin in the smaller States of Asia, Africa, Latin America and the Middle East. Frequently they have their origins in internal unrest in these countries, and the strategic and ideological interests of the great Powers sometimes lead to intervention by them. Potential conflict exists between groups of developing States and the established ones, but so far this has not gone beyond irritations such as nationalization of property and tense relationships. A power model cannot adequately explain contemporary tensions and conflicts, and great Powers have resorted to power in Malaysia, Philippines, Korea, Laos, Vietnam, Guatemala, Cuba, Dominican Republic, Hungary and Poland, because they lacked sufficient knowledge about these situations to arrive at sound expectations: in all cases it seemed expedient to control by force situations the future of which was uncertain. In each case the 'doves' (including a large proportion of scholars with an analytical interest in the behaviour of States and national groups) and the 'hawks' have had different expectations based on different theories. In each case the use of force has brought responses that could be used to justify the theories of the hawks, and looking back on each case the theories of the doves seem no less to be vindicated.

It will be seen that expectations in international politics are typically conservative, being derived from traditional views on the behaviour of States, and typically pessimistic, being based on the most cautious assessment of these views. There is, therefore, despite agreeable interaction experiences and informed decision-making, a propensity toward policies, and interpretation of the policies of others, that favours escalation of tension and conflict. Changed behaviour of States brought about by altered political and strategic conditions and values is not accompanied by altered expectations in respect of that behaviour. Two possible influences that might correct this are those of theoretical analysis, and increased insights into the motivations of political factions and States.

V. OVERLOADING OF DECISION-MAKING

We have been dealing with aspects of decision-making which contribute to aggressive behaviour. To a limited degree misperceptions and false expectations occur because of inadequate information, an inability to digest all available information, and lack of opportunity to make assessments of possible explanations. But misperception, stereotyped images and prejudice usually exist over long periods of time; increased information and opportunities to reassess do not necessarily alter them, and may reinforce them. To some degree misperception occurs because of too much information, and the need to select. Selection accentuates prejudices.

Whenever more information is being received than can be processed, or more decisions are required within a given time span than can be taken, or more action is required than is within the abilities of the system, there is a condition of overloading. Overloading is an important origin of aggressive behaviour, and in the contemporary world of centralization of State organization it is becoming increasingly important. With education, improved communications, and a growing awareness of the problem of perception, overloading as a source of conflict may tend to decrease; but with more and more State control of the Welfare State, with greater interdependence internationally and increasing difficulties of co-ordination, it is likely to increase.

Overloading takes many forms. At a systems level, the flow of information into administrative departments creates problems of co-ordination that cannot be solved by increasing consultations, which in any event reduce time available for decision-making, and finally require other co-ordinating superstructures. Sifting cannot solve the problem of selection. North and Holsti found in their analysis of the 1914 crisis that the bureaucracies were snowed under by information; much could not be assimilated, and decisions were delayed with serious consequences.[1]

Overloading is more dramatically evident at higher levels of decision-making, and the general picture seems to be a pre-occupation with one or two situations, others being pushed aside, or left to the judgement of junior officials. Those which are politically (domestically) important receive a high priority; those that are currently of less immediate interest receive a low priority. In this way the shelved problems of today become the critical issues of tomorrow. The decision taken by the United Kingdom government in 1966 to give Fiji a constitution that placed Indians in an inferior electoral position was one recommended by officials, and the full implications seem not to have been examined at a high political level. We do not know enough about the details of decisions that finally led to partition of India, to conflict in Cyprus, to confusion in the Middle East: there is a strong presumption, supported by case studies of similar situations, that origins of conflict could in these cases be traced to overloading of decision-making that results in priorities being determined by immediate political interests, and not the relative importance of situations current and developing.

[1] See in particular, O. R. Holsti, *Perceptions of Time, Perceptions of Alternatives, and Patterns of Communication as Factors in Crisis Decision-making* (Stanford, mimeograph), 1964, and in *American Political Science Review*, vol. LIX, 1965, pp. 365–78.

VI. POLITICALLY RELEVANT TIME SPANS

Quite apart from problems of perception and overloading, there are origins of conflict associated with political time spans. It is especially true of party systems of government that longer-term planning, anticipation of problems, and steps to avoid decisions that might be self-defeating in the future, are not valued at a political level, yet each case study reveals points of time at which anticipation could have resulted in avoidance of conflict. It could be argued that we are here concerned with a typically unalterable origin of conflict; but this is not necessarily so. Governments, especially within a party system, cannot be persuaded to trade a future value for an immediate political gain; but usually administrations are not even equipped to consider the long-term implication of policies. It is within the decision-making capability of States to create pressure groups, such as research units, both within administrations and the private sector of society, that would lead to greater freedom of choice in selecting alternatives that satisfy longer-term interests.

Furthermore, as with misperception, the time-span problem tends to be overcome once decision-makers are fully aware of it. It was not just political expediency that persuaded governments in the thirties to increase tariffs and to devalue currencies despite the ultimate consequences. Self-defeating or self-prophesying policies, such as many defence and alliance policies, are entered into in the belief that they will achieve their goals. It is only when the consequences of interaction are clearly demonstrated that such policies can be avoided. Thus the time-span factor may be more influenced by theory than by politics: if longer-term interaction can be shown to be destructive of future values, this could affect decisions on contemporary ones.

VII. THE 'EXPERT' AND THE SELECTION PROCESS

Facts have to be translated into data relevant to decision-making: the process is administratively an involved one, including selection and interpretation at a number of levels, committee discussion, and submission for decision of recommendations in a form likely to be acceptable. Specialists on regions, on special topics, and on international institutions are responsible for most of this processing. Their experience in relevant areas, and knowledge of relevant topics, may be wide; but their formal training may not have been relevant. Hence the 'expert' within a decision-making process is likely to be so regarded because of a knowledge of local languages and history; he may be entirely unaware of the way in which systems and States behave. Knowledge of the language, geography and history of an area is inadequate if alternative policies and goals are to be considered. Similarly, knowledge of strategy will tend to blind the 'expert' on strategy to non-strategic solutions to a problem. Take, for example, a decision regarding sanctions. The expert on local resources, financial experts, institutionalists, and political advisers are all involved. But there are behavioural influences that seem to be relevant, for example, the inclusion in a sanctions policy of specific and practical demands to be met: the effects of sanctions will be to weaken the unity of those imposing them, and to strengthen the resolve of those against whom the coercion is directed, unless reasonable and specific options are made known. There are involved here some serious problems associated with threats and deterrence, about which there is an extensive literature.[1] The 'expert' on behavioural responses is usually not within a panel of advisers. The absence of professionalism in decision-making, for so long a conspicuous feature of industry, is still the conspicuous feature of State decision-making.

VIII. CRISIS BEHAVIOUR

Crisis behaviour in international politics cannot usefully be studied by examining individual and small group crisis behaviour. It demonstrates once again the dangers of trying to apply psychological and sociological studies directly to international behaviour. Under stress individuals and groups display known and recognizable features: there is increased rate of error, stereotyped responses, diminished tolerance of ambiguity and many other such traits. Decision-makers of States are not necessarily under stress during crises: on the contrary, it is common experience that in a crisis other problems are pushed aside, and there is more opportunity than usual for considered and analytical examination of the problem on hand. Wilson of

[1] See P. Green, *Deadly Logic: The Theory of Nuclear Deterrence*, 1966; and J. David Singer, *Deterrence, Arms Control, and Disarmament*, 1962.

Britain took time off to meet Smith of Rhodesia on board a warship to discuss the Rhodesian problem; Kennedy gave undivided attention to the Cuban missile crisis. The consequence of crisis is frequently more careful examination of the problem in hand, and the neglect of other problems, which in turn, because of this neglect, lead to crisis. State decision-making has always this strong element of crisis behaviour—some matters are dealt with because they are more 'urgent' than others, and those not of immediate concern in due course become 'urgent'.

There are, however, certain distinctive features of State crisis behaviour: values and administrative processes alter. To a large degree what happens in a crisis is merely an accentuation of the misperception, overloading and other features of decision-making that prevent all options in respect of all decisions being examined. The study of crisis behaviour is valuable in itself; but its main value is that it points dramatically to inefficiencies that go unnoticed in ordinary decision-making. In crisis, and despite increased attention given to the problem, misperceptions are greater, perceptions become more stereotyped, every action of the enemy is interpreted as a threat, the history of the conflict is reinterpreted to substantiate the theory that aggression was always the intent of the enemy, belief systems become closed and alternative policies unrealistic, the administrative processes by which facts are examined are by-passed to secure quick decisions, facts that do not support policies are disregarded and their purveyors treated as hostile agents, advisers are those who give the advice that is wanted, priorities lead to the neglect of matters not related to the crisis, power becomes centralized and intimidation of parties with opposing views increases. In these terms some States are always in a condition of crisis, and most States have a propensity in the direction of crisis behaviour. In so far as day-to-day decision-making is made more efficient in terms of ability to consider all options, crisis behaviour will also be more efficient.

IX. DECISION-MAKING AND LEGITIMIZATION

It has been argued that the test of legitimization of authority is performance rather than means by which power is acquired. Consequently, efficiency in decision-making is a component of legitimization: authorities, no matter how established, may have their legitimized status increased or reduced by their decision-making efficiency.

Foreign policy is not usually as important electorally as domestic policy. The area of foreign affairs is one that people are prepared to leave to governments. It is only when they fail, or when there is a national emergency, that foreign policies are debated and criticized. In less developed States, political leaders have a wide discretion on foreign policy matters, popular demands being confined to independence, racial equality and such broadly stated values. These conditions give authorities a freedom to interpret State interests that they do not have in respect of domestic matters. But they also enable authorities to accede to the demands of pressure groups that may not reflect State interests. In the short term many failures in decision-making are due to political processes which require decision-makers to take into account domestic pressures of many kinds which if ignored would threaten their political existence. Studies of particular conflicts make one acutely aware of the interplay of domestic and international politics in foreign policy decision-making. The Australian Labour government refused to recognize China in 1949 because ministers feared the reactions of a 'Catholic Action' minority within the parliamentary caucus.[1] The British government's handling of the Rhodesian problem seemed to be conditioned by pressures from supporters and opponents, far more than by considerations affecting African Rhodesians. These pressures exert the day-to-day limitations on freedom of decision. They lead States into conflict with systems, and with other States. But these are, in the sense we have used the term, unalterable influences, unless there are institutions such as committees of legislatures that are constantly examining the making of foreign policy. In short, in the making of foreign policy there is a complex interplay between legitimization measured by achievement, and decision-making that is influenced by group pressures. One result can be drift and indecision, based upon compromises and inconsistencies, such as seem to have characterized British policies since the Second World War. Another can be dominance by ideological, industrial and military pressures, as seems to have characterized United States policies for the last two decades. It remains to be seen whether developed socialist States, that are less subject to

[1] See H. S. Albinski, *Australian Policies and Attitudes toward China*, 1965.

the influence of organized interests, succeed in arriving at foreign policies that serve the longer-term interests of the State, and avoid policies that deprive other States of their needs.

We are thus led to a concept of normative behaviour that does not rest upon past practices or upon power, but upon the behaviour of authorities that have a legitimized status and whose decision-making efficiency enables them reliably to achieve their goals, or to alter goals and strategies so as not to be involved in dysfunctional conflict.

5

CONFLICT

Concepts of systems and States, of their needs and values, of legitimization and intervention, and an analysis of the processes of decision-making, provide the means of examining the nature of communal and inter-State conflict, the conditions in which it is functional and dysfunctional, and how it escalates and spreads.

Conflict may take the form of competition or, at the other extreme, an acute form of a struggle between parties to attain goals that are vital, even by injuring or eliminating opponents. For our purposes conflict can be said to exist when the following conditions apply: 1. there are at least two parties or analytically distinct entities; 2. there is a condition of 'position' scarcity in which a location or a role cannot be held or enacted by more than one party, or a 'resource' scarcity that does not enable both parties to satisfy their demands; 3. there is behaviour by one or all parties designed to threaten, injure, destroy and control another party; and 4. there is action by at least one party to seek scarce positions or resources by coercion of another.[1]

I. SYSTEMS AND STATE CONFLICT

A condition in which clusters of functional systems are linked and interacting, and in which their main concentrations are organized by administrative systems with jurisdiction within fixed boundaries, is one of continuing conflict between system and system, system and State, and State and State. These three types of conflict are present in every international situation of conflict; they are analytically distinguishable.

A system that adjusts to its environment is in conflict with it: at any one time in a society many systems are in conflict with others. Values held in a commercial system are in conflict with values held in cultural and religious segments of society. Values

---

[1] In 1956 R. W. Mack and R. C. Snyder set down many conditions of conflict, and these four relate to only some of them. Others seem to be sub-conditions. See the *Journal of Conflict Resolution*, vol. 1, no. 2, 1957, p. 218.

held in relation to defence are in conflict with values associated with welfare. Within each of these areas there is conflict as, for example, amongst business firms and religious organizations. Conflict between system and system is a part of the on-going process of change within any behavioural group. This conflict can result either in the elimination of a system, or merely in changes that make some units redundant or irrelevant. In the latter case, which is the more usual one, conflict occurs between units within a system, at least until adjustment to the environment is complete. This in-fighting is a conspicuous feature of most social systems. In industries that are depressed by reduced market demands, redundancy disputes and conflict between unions are usually widespread. In-fighting takes more dramatic forms in linked systems and communities that face a hostile environment: alterations in tactics and values affect the roles of members. Suppressed conflicts amongst colonial peoples prior to independence—which usually come to the surface after independence—the internal conflicts that took place in Germany and Japan in the thirties before military control, domestic disputes in the Soviet Union and more recently in China, were evidence of difficulty in adjustment to frustrated endeavours and environmental pressures.[1]

A different type of conflict occurs between functional systems and States. Conflict in this case arises, first, out of the fact of territorial boundaries that interrupt transactions, and, second, out of the function that authorities have of allocating values and resources.

Boundaries tend to impede or prevent commercial, financial, linguistic, cultural, ideological and other relationships. If transactions continue, despite restraints, this is likely to lead to conflict between system and State, as when two parts of the one ethnic or commercial system, that are separated or restrained by a State boundary, perceive their interests in more closely linked relationships. If, on the other hand, boundaries provide barriers sufficient to encourage the growth of separate functional systems, then these will tend to be in conflict with each other, as is the case when trade controls lead to the growth of protected industries. The State is then pressed to give increased support to the systemic interests affected, leading to conflict between system and State. To the extent that competing

---

[1] For a case study, see F. Fanon, *The Damned*, 1963.

systems both sides of the boundaries obtain support, conflict between States occurs.

The second source of conflict between system and State arises out of the power of States to determine allocation of resources and values. This involves problems of legitimization to which reference has been made. Even legitimized behaviour within a State affects parts of systems lying outside its boundaries. Control by a State of flows of trade and ideas brings it into conflict with systems that may be widespread and powerful in the sense that they have a functional value in other States, as well as in the State imposing the controls. Whereas systems interact and are in conflict only to the extent of their influence as functional systems, States have their own independent power, and also a power to mobilize systems. Conflict between powerful systems—oil, chemical, ideological and cultural—and a State can therefore escalate to levels that force upon authorities altered values, and perhaps threaten their legitimized status. Financial inducements to authorities, and interference by foreign business interests in domestic political processes, are evidence of this form of conflict.

Conflict between State and State brings into play State power on both sides, and escalation is likely to higher levels of conflict than is possible in conflict between systems and States. Conflict between States can be in promotion and defence of special interests, for example, trading and investment interests, and in promotion and defence of internalized State values that are widely shared, for example, national security, ideology and cultural values. The two tend in practice to overlap: ideological values are used to mobilize communities in the defence of specific interests. In a particular situation it is sometimes difficult to distinguish systemic and internalized values: a great Power pursues its strategic and trading interests simultaneously with its cultural and ideological values. Internalized State values may emerge as a result of frustration in the pursuit of sectional interests, and may become more influential than more structured ones, as happens when States seek to eliminate colonialism from their continents, even at the cost of particular trade and aid opportunities.

II. THE SPREAD OF CONFLICT

It will be clear from the preceding analysis that it is rarely possible to have a condition of conflict within a State which does not affect systems that cross State boundaries, and equally rare to have a conflict within or between systems that cross State boundaries that does not have consequences for the State. It is probably misleading ever to regard internal conflict and inter-State conflict as separate conditions, or for any particular case of internal or international conflict to be treated as though it did not involve both. Similarities between inter-State and communal conflicts can be demonstrated by reference to the Kelman model referred to above.[1] In so far as the felt needs and interests of communities *A* and *B* are met by a wider and common administrative system, which implies adequate participation by *A* and *B* in decisions affecting them, systemic conflict between *A* and *B* does not occur. Whether *A* and *B* are communities within one State, or States within the wider international system of States, the proposition applies. Conversely, in any society in which satisfaction of the demands of systems does not fulfil expectations, or in which discriminatory advantages occur, there is a condition of conflict. There is usually an imbalance between parties in conflict. The weaker party, and perhaps even a stronger one that expects to lose support by reason of population changes or ideological influences, looks

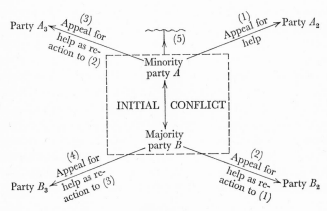

Text-fig. 6.

[1] See Text-fig. 1 on page 48.

for external support. The conflict widens when the minority party seeks outside aid from other parties, and the majority party, seeing its secure position threatened, follows a similar policy. The conflict escalates to an international level.

Additional influences are present in a community after a colonial power withdraws. A local colonial administration tends to rely upon the loyalty of those factions that have most to gain from continued foreign control. In Cyprus the British administration recruited Turkish police during a period of Greek Cypriot resistance to colonial rule. After independence, communal conflict is likely to occur in any event, having been repressed during foreign occupation; but it is aggravated by the identification of one group by the other with the overlordship of the colonial Power. The process appears to be 'divide and rule'. In practice, the intention is not to do this; 'divide' is the inevitable result of 'rule' when the ruler finds an ally in a weaker minority. Once 'independence' is gained and the controlling Power withdraws, the remaining, and by now mutually hostile parties, may call on outside support in the resultant conflict. The process described above then takes place. There is a scapegoat element in this process. When the communities within a foreign-controlled area have no means of gaining their freedom, or eliminating frustration and racial or other discrimination, they tend to turn on each other, or upon a small minority in their midst. This accentuates the 'divide and rule' effect, and extends conflict into the independence period in which all factions are freer to enlist foreign support.

Despite international boundaries, communal conflict, whether ethnic or ideological, tends to involve foreign parties. A question suggests itself as to whether international strife results directly from communal conflict—that is, whether there can be international, in the absence of internal, conflict. Looking at States with a long history of peace, their internal integration is a conspicuous feature—Scandinavian States are examples. Looking at States that have been involved in war, internal strife is a conspicuous feature—African, Latin American and Middle Eastern States are examples.

III. DYSFUNCTIONAL CONFLICT

Conflict amongst systems, between systems and States, and amongst States, is therefore an on-going and inevitable condition. It has a functional value in so far as it is the means by which clusters of systems are adapted to social needs, and by which State needs are modified to meet the needs of a world society. What is of more direct interest in the study of inter-State relations are the conditions in which this form of inevitable conflict leads, in the absence of supranational coercion and nuclear-power deterrence, to the involvement of people, systems and States in damage and destruction that serves no functional purpose. What are the conditions in which conflict becomes dysfunctional?

A conflict may be violent and yet functional, at least from the point of view of some parties. The test of dysfunctional conflict is not violence, or destruction. Conflict is dysfunctional when it has no objective of value to the State, or is more costly to the State than the worth of the values to be acquired, or is unnecessarily costly in the sense that alternative and less costly means can be found for securing the goals sought.

This cost approach to dysfunctional conflict is analogous to dysfunctional commercial dealings. Competing bidders for scarce resources (including positions) are faced with a series of decisions involving their value systems: at each rise in costs a reassessment of values is required. Decisions may be taken to continue bidding, even though this means selling other assets possessed—an alteration in values. If bidding by a party advances to the point at which the cost to it is greater than the value to it of the resources being bid for, the bidding is dysfunctional. At an auction a bidder usually pulls out at this stage. In an international situation pulling out is difficult for prestige and domestic political reasons. Continuing commitment to attain the goal requires the introduction of new values to justify the increased costs. No matter what the cost, the objective can be justified by invented values. Small-scale conflicts over trivial matters can in this way escalate to major ones, and the goals are restated and revalued accordingly.

This cost concept of conflict begs some important philosophical questions about the concept of value, about State value as opposed to group-interest value, and about how to relate costs to values. In the field of practical affairs, however, these questions are less important. Decision-makers deal with particular situations of conflict in which they have stated goals. The costs of conflict are known in terms of lives, resources and disruption, and judgements are made of the relative value of goals and the costs being incurred. Though these judgements may be subject to alteration and are subjectively made, they are nevertheless made. In practical terms values and costs are related.

It will be apparent that this cost conception of 'functional' and 'dysfunctional' is quite different from the conception of Simmel and Coser, and many others who have been interested in the sociology of conflict: to them what is functional and dysfunctional relates, not to values, but to integration and disintegration. 'Far from being only a "negative" factor which "tears apart", social conflict may fulfil a number of determinate functions in group and other interpersonal relations; it may, for example, contribute to the maintenance of group boundaries and prevent the withdrawal of members from a group.'[1] They have examined conflict from the point of view of the political processes of a society, in which individual and small-group interactions take place in conditions in which cost is not conspicuous, and goals are achieved by one faction. It has been wrongly assumed that the analysis can be extended to conflict between States, where the conspicuous features are escalating cost and the mutual destruction of the goals of the parties. This natural law that postulates functional values of conflict reflects a traditional dialectic approach to social evolution, and as such does not take us any further than the trite observation that the outcome of conflict is another situation, and that conflict is in this sense integrative. In this view conflict avoidance and the resolution of conflict could be regarded as dysfunctional because they prevent the integrative processes of conflict.

That a conflict leads to another situation, and in this sense is integrative, is not to be denied; but the avoidance and resolution of conflict no less lead to a new situation, and are therefore integrative in the same sense. There is no reason to believe that conflict has integrative functions that could not be carried out by any other means. Alternative means imply reassessing values

[1] L. Coser, *The Functions of Social Conflict*, 1965, p. 8.

and costs, and for this reason the cost concept of conflict is a more fundamental one than the integrative one. In international conflict the integrative element is not apparent—peace treaties usually restore the sovereign independence of the defeated party; it is the cost element that is the important one. The judgement by the sociologist that a conflict was positive because it maintained boundaries or prevented withdrawals, is a subjective one of no consequence. It is no more than a rationalization or justification of a phenomenon that appears to be unavoidable; there is no intrinsic virtue in maintaining boundaries or groups. The important question is whether conflict is avoidable, and in what circumstances. The difference between the generalized sociological approach and this analytical one arises, therefore, out of the different way of looking at conflict; we either accept the evolutionary dog-eats-dog approach, or an analytical systems approach designed to show why it has done so in the past, and whether man must eat man in the future, even in cases in which conflict is dysfunctional for all parties. One suspects that when conflict avoidance and crisis management are better understood, the evolutionary significance of conflict will be less credible. When we come to consider propositions concerning conflict it will be found that some widely accepted ones, such as the integrative effects of outside threat, have been deduced within this evolutionary approach, and empirically cannot be justified.

IV. SOURCES OF DYSFUNCTIONAL CONFLICT

A question to be resolved is whether dysfunctional conflict between States is, like a volcano, an inevitable eruption that occurs from time to time when an accumulation of systemic demands is perceived to threaten the existence of a State and its values; or whether it is less mechanical and inevitable than this, and is due to behavioural interactions. If the latter be the case, it would then be of practical use to determine which, if any, of the interactions that are responsible for dysfunctional conflict might be subject to deliberate State or inter-State control. An analogy with trade cycles helps to pose these questions. Trade cycles, like dysfunctional conflicts, were observed over long periods of time. The question economists faced in the thirties was, were these inevitable fluctuations arising out of the operation of economic systems, or were they subject to control by deliberate actions, and deliberate avoidance of actions, and if so what were these actions? Are there State policies to be pursued or to be avoided that would prevent conflict becoming dysfunctional?

The reason for dysfunctional conflict must, by definition, relate to miscalculation of costs. The goals that States cost relate to effective participation in decision-making, control of scarce resources, and the filling of scarce positions of influence. Costing also relates to strategies, including strategies that change goals and sacrifice goals. Strategies are influenced by the existing circumstances of State relations, such as relative power positions, by the nature of the values involved, by expectations of the behaviour of others, and by many such variables. There are two major sources of error in costing goals and strategies. First, initial estimates are likely to be false. Inadequate information about the nature of the environment and possible responses of others, misjudgements made on the basis of ideological commitment or fear, domestic political demands and the influence of pressure groups, all tend to exaggerate the value of goals sought and to minimize the costs involved. In the early fifties the United States exaggerated out of all reasonable proportions their interests in Vietnam, and underestimated the final costs involved. Second, there are political responses and environmental changes that occur once one goal is pursued which destroy the prospect of attaining other goals, and which also create other problems that require solution. Part of the cost of conflict is both the loss of other desired goals, and the creation of other problems costly to solve. For example, Britain's alliance policies and identification with conflicts in which other members are engaged destroy secondary goals such as closer relations with Asian and African States that are non-aligned, thus prejudicing its opportunities to influence their decision-making. Australia may have a choice between maintaining strictly its white population composition, and non-discriminatory immigration policies; it has, in addition, choices in the ways of pursuing these choices. When it selects its restricted immigration goal, and when it selects means which are discriminatory and which ultimately rely upon defences and alliances which involve it in conflicts in Korea and Vietnam, it immediately destroys opportunities of attaining other goals, such as improved commercial relationships and regional security arrangements. In addition, it creates problems in its own relationship with Asian States and amongst Asian States. Choices that are made can always be justified on political and strategic grounds; but justification is not the same as a costing in terms of sacrifice of other goals and of creation of additional problems.

Increased costs do not necessarily lead to termination of conflict. Once conflict is engaged, even at a non-violent level, new values are introduced to offset against the increased and unexpected costs. These new values are not systemic or State values; by propaganda they can be made to appear to be important at the time and they are internalized. United States costs in Vietnam were offset against a duty to the rest of the world to prevent aggression. In retrospect a realistic costing can be made; but at the time governments cannot admit to mistakes, and they are caught up in their own spiral of increasing costs and the creation of values to justify them. Ultimately it is difficult even for authorities to determine which were the values originally at stake, and which were those subsequently introduced. War aims are always difficult to define.

Conflict becomes dysfunctional when costs are miscalculated. Miscalculation of costs is evidence of faulty information and inadequate theories of international behaviour, evidence, that is, of faulty decision-making. Conflict persists even after it has become dysfunctional because it is made to appear functional by rationalization of values by those who originally miscalculated. Conflict becomes dysfunctional, therefore, by reason of decision-making processes and not because of irreconcilable differences of interest.

This can be demonstrated by reference to the zero-sum and non-zero-sum concepts of conflict. A conflict is zero-sum when the gain of one party is the loss of another. If A and B both seek the same territory, and if this common aim is absolute and does not change despite rising costs of conflict, there is no solution other than a zero-sum one. At any one point of time all conflict is zero-sum: at any one moment of conflict A and B are competing or fighting to gain fixed goals. Parties state their disputes in fixed terms: each requires the other to act in certain ways, and nothing short of meeting the demand is acceptable. But in reality values are changing continuously, and frequently those that are stated as being the critical ones, are merely evidence of the existence of other ill-defined and negotiable differences. In 1967 the United Arab Republic stated that it would not allow shipping into a port controlled by Israel. Israel took the position that trade through the port was a vital interest. The conflict, as declared, was zero-sum. In reality alternative means of obtaining oil supplies and exporting products were being explored by Israel and other Powers involved, and calculations were being made of the increased costs involved and whether these were sufficient to justify war. Then the question needed to be asked, was the port the critical matter in dispute, or was this merely the evidence of others, such as the fate of Arab refugees and Israel's ties with the West. An even more far-reaching question in the mind of many observers was whether the officially advertised threats, the emphasis on militarism and finally the confrontation were not means of creating unity both in Israel and in Arab States. In every condition of conflict values are constantly changing: costs of conflict, alternative means of securing the benefits of the object being contested, capacity to do without, altered values because of altered appreciations of the total position, and a great many other influences affect relationships. Because values change, no conflict is zero-sum: even a total gain to one side need not necessarily deprive the other of a value if alternative goals are discovered.

Furthermore, most conflicts relate to values that are perceived to be threatened. When two parties are in a situation of conflict they typically perceive each other as threatening, and the origin of the perception may be defensive action taken by one of them. A perceives a threat from B and takes defensive measures, and when B is aware of these he responds by increased defences, which A regards as proof that his original perception was accurate. The process continues, and conflict escalates. This points again to faulty decision-making, and a failure to test perception, as the source of conflict.

There is, therefore, no such thing as an objective conflict of interests: conflicts of interest are relative to values that are subject to change, and conflicts of interest are perceived conflicts. In other words, it is a reasonable hypothesis, at least one that deserves more exploration than has traditionally been made, that dysfunctional conflict is not due to static or unchangeable features of international society, such as the nature of Man, the State or the inter-State system, but to complex interaction behaviour that, if even partly understood, might be controlled unilaterally by States pursuing their own interests. Partial understanding is as much as can reasonably be expected, but it could lead to policies sufficient for many purposes, as is the case with our understanding of economics that has led to financial policies that help to control levels of employment.

V. THE IMPLICATIONS OF SUBJECTIVE CONFLICT

This is an important observation in relation to means of resolving conflict. If two States were in an objective conflict of interests, resolution could be only by conflict until one side were victorious, or by an enforced settlement. The first solution is one which international society seeks to avoid, and the second is one that proves impracticable because it is not acceptable to the parties, and it is not possible to devise an effective collective security system. A different prospect offers once it is determined that conflicts are subjective. Their avoidance or resolution is by altered values and by reperception of threats. These are both processes that take place within the parties: they are not changes that can be forced upon parties. Any attempt to force a new set of values upon parties is likely to increase the area of conflict: it is the parties and they alone that can determine their values.

The procedures of judicial settlement, and even conciliation and arbitration within a power framework, are inappropriate if conflict is subjective. Alternative procedures, that assist parties to assess values and perceive the environment accurately, are the appropriate ones. The companion study, *The Use of Controlled Communication in International Relations*, is based upon experience with States engaged in conflict, and is a study devoted to an examination of techniques of conflict avoidance and resolution on the assumption that conflicts of interest are subjective, and due to an inadequate assessment of values and costs, and to perceptions of threats and intentions that have not been reality-tested.

VI. ASSESSMENT

An important difference between traditional historical and philosophical approaches, and the contemporary analytical and sociological ones, is the concentration by the former on what are perceived to be basic and unalterable drives, and by the latter on interaction processes subject to control at a State level. There are historical reasons for this. Traditional approaches were originally concerned, for obvious reasons, with the behaviour of great Powers, and European Powers in particular. Small States in Europe had the restricted choice of joining alliances, or of contracting out of power politics by the pursuit of neutral policies. Great Powers had little interest in interactions with smaller States; if they could accomplish their aims with the power at their disposal, and without offending other great Powers, they did so. Their interactions with other great Powers, of which there were few in any case, were at a straightforward power or bargaining level. Decision-making was a relatively simple process, uncomplicated by complex pressure-group activities, public responses, international institutions, and politics outside Europe. There was no need to consider the nationalist and independence responses of smaller States which, in the political and strategic circumstances of the contemporary world, require even the greatest of Powers to think twice before endeavouring to impose their will by force. Historians recording events, and philosophers observing them over long periods of time, had no reason to give attention to motivations other than those that appeared to be the basic and continuing ones: the nature of Man, the State and international systems of States. Nor were they concerned with response and feed-back, and altered response. The study of interaction processes even in social life is a recent development. Historians and philosophers were aware that escalation was an important process, and that deterrence was the purpose of defence arrangements; but these, like power, were seen to be straightforward and continuing features, the raw data of theory, of which no detailed analysis was required. To the contemporary scholar, the process of interaction is no less important, and perhaps more important in an explanation of State behaviour, than any basic drives. Indeed, many scholars would now argue that the debate about basic drives was a digression from the main interest; whether or not the prime motivation of men and States is aggressiveness, fear, power, the struggle for rights of participation, the need for living areas, or merely a desire to exchange products for welfare purposes, or all or none of these, interactions occur, and out of interactions develop both structures and motivations. Even though States were neutral in motivation terms, the fact of change by discovery, invention, innovation, altered values or altered philosophies, would lead to interactions, and these would themselves generate seemingly relevant motivations. Different circumstances would produce different responses, and the behaviour of any one State might be power-dominated to-day, participation-dominated tomorrow in relation to one State, and idealistically dominated in respect of another at the same time.

A systems approach enables a micro-analysis of world society: it attracts attention to details of relationships, such as perception and decision-making, that in a traditional framework of State entities in a power relationship seemed less important. It is also one that requires more precision and clarity in the use of terms and concepts: State, authorities, political systems, power, deterrence and most others that have been employed for centuries are found to need re-examination. Perhaps the greatest contribution a systems analysis will make in the future will be to clarify normative behaviour, and especially the conditions in which a State acts aggressively, and by this means, to clarify for the benefit of authorities the processes by which they are led into dysfunctional conflict.

State authorities act in ways that threaten or deprive other States of their needs, depending upon the following influences:

the pressures imposed on the State and its systems by the external environment, particularly rates of change;

the adjustment capabilities of the State and its systems, arising out of its stage of development, levels of dependence and internal organization;

the levels of State and systems power as compared with the power of other States and systems, especially economic and military powers that can be employed to change the environment and avoid the need for internal adjustment;

the legitimized status of authorities, and the degree to which they act outside their State roles to preserve their values;

and the efficiency of State decision-making, including abilities to respond to the environment, to alter goals, and to adopt alternative means of achieving goals.

Many different cases can be constructed with these five influences. Authorities might be wholly legitimized and efficient in decision-making, but experience external pressures beyond capacity to adjust, and by subversion or guerrilla warfare endeavour to acquire territory or resources. Others that control a State with sufficient adjustment capability, and with a high power capability, might find it more convenient to force policies upon others. Others, that are legitimized and control a State that has adjustment capability, might be led into aggressive behaviour by failures in decision-making. It should be possible to explain all conflict in terms of these variables.

Each of these variables can be defined by reference to operational tests, and consequently a degree of prediction of State behaviour should be possible after comparative or quantitative measurements of legitimization, adjustment capability, exposure to environmental change, and decision-making efficiency. The relevance of these variables, moreover, can be tested in the contemporary period against experience of States that have not and have been involved in conflict that in retrospect proved dysfunctional.

It is interesting to note that we have identified as origins of dysfunctional conflict three sources closely related to the three that Deutsch identified as sources of integration or stability. We, from the point of view of conflict, have been concerned with the existence of adjustment demands, inefficiencies in decision-making, expectations of a hostile environment, and value changes. He, from his point of view of integration, was concerned with the presence of the positive features of these factors. 'In order to achieve integration, therefore, we need a high level of interdependence, adequate cybernetic or self-steering capabilities of each partner to permit mutual co-ordination, and interest patterns which permit coincidence of positive co-variance of expectations and of rewards for both partners.'[1]

[1] K. W. Deutsch, contribution in a CIBA Foundation Symposium, *Conflict in Society*, 1966, p. 304.

PART II

The Behaviour of States

6

THE SYSTEMIC BEHAVIOUR OF STATES

Systems concepts, the attention they direct to the details of decision-making, and the light they throw upon the meaning of terms, make possible a micro-analysis of world society. A complementary analysis at the macro-level brings to attention features of State behaviour that are not satisfactorily explained in systems terms. Internalized values such as nationalist sentiment, prestige, rights to participate in decision-making anywhere that affects the State, ideological commitment, may not be as fundamental and influential over long periods of time as are patterns of transactions. Nevertheless, they are important influences that help to explain, not only State behaviour, but the nature of world society generally. Moreover, it is the macro-level of analysis that appeals to decision-makers, and provided it is made in the light of behavioural interactions established at the more detailed level, it can serve a useful purpose in throwing additional light upon some aspects of the behaviour of States in world society.

In every group interaction there are three basic processes. There is co-operation amongst members on a basis of equality, characterized by reciprocal transactions and a co-ordination of activities. There is also leadership which provides means of co-ordination of activities without necessarily eliminating group participation in decisions. Whenever the exercise of the power of leadership extends beyond the limits of authority there is resistance, and a drive by members to regain participation in decision-making, and a position of greater equality in relationships. These three processes are related in time: the one tends to lead to the next. But at all stages all three continue to exist to a greater or a lesser degree: one is more dominant than others at different times.

Relations between States can be expected to display evidence of these three continuing processes, each more dominant at one time than another, and all present at all times. It is convenient to regard each as an abstraction from the whole, and subject it to analysis as such. The first is the condition of reciprocity and exchange in which there is no important differentiation of power, in which each unit plays an equal part in determining the conditions of total society. In practice, this is a condition likely to be found only in relations between primitive societies. The second stage is the one with which we are most familiar, and which has been the main concern of political studies, and that is the stage after power has been differentiated, and when it is used by some States to coerce and to force conditions of behaviour upon others. The third is the stage of reaction to the employment of power, when tactics designed to eliminate the effects of coercion by the powerful are being employed by the relatively non-powerful. This is a condition apparent in the contemporary world society that has reacted against colonialism, and is reacting against economic pressures.

I. THE CONCEPT OF A NORM OF BEHAVIOUR

A separate treatment of these three processes of interaction is not merely a convenience. It serves to draw attention to the existence of different behaviour patterns that otherwise tend to be lumped together and therefore overlooked. There has not developed in the discipline International Relations any concept of the behaviour of States equivalent to that behaviour of an individual in society which is regarded as within the range of lawful, socially conforming or acceptable behaviour. A wide range of foreign activity by States and their citizens is inevitable in an interdependent world. Some are exercised by all, such as diplomatic rights, and others are exercised only by those States with commercial and strategic interests that are widespread, such as intervention in the affairs of others. Such a range of activity is associated with the individual in society, from behaviour that is common to all to behaviour that is possible only for the few. There are also the extremes of individual aggression. While we have clear concepts of social norms, there is no concept of State behaviour that is universally acceptable in international society—behaviour that is directed toward the development and advancement of the State but which is at the same time acceptable and conforming within world society.

It is important to be able to define the norm of behaviour. To explain monopoly a concept of competition is required, to understand oppression it is necessary to have a concept of freedom, and to analyse differences in human behaviour it is necessary to have a notion of what is standard. The study of inter-State relations is directed toward, amongst other things, ascertaining what is acceptable and what is not acceptable behaviour. Whether the regulation of conduct is to be self-imposed by States themselves or imposed by a supranational body, the problem remains the same: first acceptable or unacceptable behaviour has to be defined.

It is understandable that international law has not provided a concept of a norm. In municipal society behaviour can be acceptable even though outside the law, and behaviour within the law can be unacceptable. This is part of the process of change in law. Likewise, international law provides little guide to acceptable behaviour. It is mainly based upon past patterns of behaviour of States, particularly of powerful States. Some are not generally acceptable to the international society, such as some property rights that new States have challenged, and the right of intervention in the political affairs of other States at the request of a government that does not have popular support. It is from the social sciences that one would expect to derive a concept of a norm of State behaviour. It is psychology and sociology that determine norms of behaviour in municipal society; it is a sociological and not a legal concept.

When previously we discussed legitimization, reference was made to 'normative' behaviour: if authorities wish to attain certain given goals, then policies are required that take into account systemic needs, otherwise there will be self-defeating results or high costs in terms of other values. The concept of 'norm' is a different one: this refers to a standard pattern of behaviour by which to measure other patterns. Both may be described by reference to systemic behaviour. Neither concept has any moral or ideological connotation. The norm in this context is used very much as economists employ perfect competition as a norm for analytical purposes.

Schwarzenberger has come close to a concept of a norm by distinguishing between community and society behaviour. Community behaviour is characterized by a high degree of reciprocity and co-ordination of activities, whereas society behaviour is characterized by relationships based upon power.[1] The individual and the State are capable of both community

---

[1] See Schwarzenberger, *Power Politics*, 3rd ed., 1964, pp. 12–13.

and society behaviour, according to whether they are acting in the one environment or the other. This provides the concept; but when applied to an analysis of behaviour it has a tautological element: behaviour is conforming when in a situation that promotes conformation. The norm of behaviour of the individual in society must be based upon his response, and not the social conditions to which he is responding. What we need to find is the nature of behaviour, and the reasons for it, in a community environment, and to determine to what extent this behaviour can be induced in other environments. Cohn used the term 'neo-neutrality' to describe his concept of the norm.[1] This has the advantage of pointing to types of policy, and thus makes more specific the concept of acceptable behaviour. However, this is a norm of policy, a prescriptive norm, rather than of behaviour.

II. EXCHANGE RELATIONSHIPS

A norm of State behaviour is, in systems terms, behaviour when authorities are fully legitimized, acting in the interests of systems, and capable of perceiving the environment accurately and responding to it appropriately. Such behaviour can be expected in the least complex of conditions, for which reason it is associated with behaviour within a community relationship. The reason for the behaviour is not because of a community situation, but because of the relatively easy responses required in it. Norm behaviour is possible outside community relationships provided the subject is capable of relevant responses.

Simple exchange relationships are those most conducive to norm behaviour; they feature full legitimization because the actors are responsible to themselves, and full knowledge in respect of the transaction. This relationship is the convenient one in which to examine norm behaviour, especially since it accounts for many transactions even in the most complex of social relationships. The simple exchange relationship, involving goods and services, is familiar to anthropologists. It arises out of specialization of function, which in turn relates to resources and skills. It is characterized by reciprocity, which may take ceremonial and institutionalized forms. Organization of exchange at

[1] G. Cohn, *Neo-Neutrality*, Translated from Danish by A. S. Keller and E. Jensen, 1939.

a primitive level includes processes that structure divisions of labour, and enable an interplay between wants and skills. Pure reciprocity occurs only at an early stage of social relationships, for once specialization advances on the basis of diversity of resources and skills, wants cannot always be satisfied by reciprocity: either supplier or consumer has an advantage due to different values attached to what can be supplied and consumed. *A* wants what *B* can supply, but *A* can find other suppliers and can, if necessary, do without *B*'s services; if *B* is not in such an independent position in relation to *A*'s services, then *B* is in a weaker bargaining position: reciprocity does not operate. Exchange by reciprocity thus gives place to transactions in which there is credit or debit, and, as this procedure continues, bargaining power accumulates, and supplier or consumer can ultimately employ power to his advantage.[1]

Even a simple exchange system may involve a great number of actors, and ultimately a differentiation of power may occur between groups. But to dwell upon a purely power politics model is to ignore some of the most characteristic aspects of social organization. In any relationship in which one party has 'power' over others—such as the landlord-tenant relationship, employer-employee relationship, the parent-child relationship —the employment of power in any form, including coercive power, is subject both to expediency and to conventionalized usages. If it is employed beyond these, or if the conventions alter, opposition occurs. The landlord-tenant relationship gives the landlord wide powers, but if these are exceeded the relationship might be challenged; equally there is resistance from the landlord if the tenant alters his values and demands a higher share of the products of his labour. Restraints on power need to be examined, not in relation just to the exercise of power, but also in relation to reciprocal and exchange systems.

The contemporary international system of States commenced as a series of relationships between units already characterized by marked specialization in function, and therefore differentiations of power. There were large and small national groups, each with its own skills, resources and other assets and needs. Mistakenly, this already differentiated system has traditionally been taken as the starting point of inter-State analysis; by commencing at this point, the significance of a mass of day-to-

[1] See Blau, *Exchange and Power in Social Life.*

day transactions that still remain largely reciprocal, despite differentiated power, has been missed. In transactions in the private sectors of relations between States, and even in many of the public sectors, exchange on a near-reciprocal basis is the rule rather than the exception. Yet the student of International Relations is sometimes left with the impression that almost all commercial, cultural, diplomatic and political exchanges are made within a power framework. It is not realistic to postulate that international relations are primarily zero-sum: not all relations are like those involving acquisition of territory when *A* takes 100 square miles of territory, and *B* is deprived of the same amount. There are reciprocal agreements, bilateral or multi-lateral, that are non-zero-sum: *A* and *B* can both gain from an exchange. Less advanced communities are based upon more simple exchange systems whereby a balancing is always the objective, and in Asian cultures today the gift ceremonies are evidence of the non-zero-sum basis of social organization; but the great bulk relationships in contemporary society are also of this order, though less conspicuously so. They are in evidence in the functional arrangements between States that range from health agreements, to tacit and formal agreements not to test certain weapons.

The reality is that international society has an inherent and fundamental non-coercive aspect. While coercion may be a conspicuous feature of world society, it is not essential to it, and therefore cannot provide a basis for analysis. It is possible to have stable relationships amongst units within social groups and between groups, that do not rest upon coercive power; it is rarely possible to have such relationships resting only upon coercive power. Coercive power is the support, the organizing factor introduced when attempts are being made to alter relations or to preserve them. It does extend beyond this: in some conditions policies are based upon bargaining or coercion, to the exclusion of other processes; strategy then becomes concentrated upon the organization of the emergency power mechanism, to the exclusion of the everyday reciprocal one. The more the emergency mechanism is built up and organized, the more it disrupts the rest of the system, and self-defeating processes gather momentum. Relationships then continue within a threat system. But this conspicuous power-dominance of some relationships that exist from time to time and in some circumstances, is superimposed on transactions that create social systems and are on a reciprocal or non-power basis. In world society, the institutionalized forms of reciprocity and co-ordination are of increasing significance. Indeed, in the view of some theorists, 'functionalism' is an institutional form of co-operation which could eat into the area of inter-State relations, commencing with the routine matters of communications, and eventually dealing with difficult political arrangements, thus creating an effective system of international government based on the *ad hoc* consent of sovereign States.[1] Most political scientists approach the theory of functionalism with caution. Nevertheless, it serves to call attention to processes within international society which are widespread, though inconspicuous because of their non-political character.

III. THE ROLES OF STATES

The reciprocal specializations of States endow each with roles in world society. The roles of a State are determined in the main by the static elements of the environment in which it exists: location, resources, population, culture and traditional relationships. These static elements ensure a high degree of continuity in role enactment. In a specialized international system, each of the independent units enacts its own characteristic role, depending largely upon these static influences, and the infinite number of continuing features that characterize a State. Many of these features are unique to each State; a combination of features is certainly unique. As a result, Malaysia has a special role in relation to the export of tin and rubber, Britain has traditionally played a role as a financial centre, the United States has currently an aid role. Each of these States has a great many other roles, which are finally determined by an interplay of all the static and dynamic, domestic and foreign influences that determine the foreign policies of any State. Thus it is that a distinctive image of each State evolves, and associated with this image are the specific roles enacted by the State. Role is, therefore, the behaviour expected of a State, the predictable behaviour to which others adjust and respond, the acts and functions of each State that together create the structure of international society.

[1] See E. B. Haas, *Beyond the Nation-State*, 1964, and I. Claude, *Swords into Plowshares* 1956.

The fulfilment by States of the roles, with which others are familiar, and to which they have already adjusted, is a precondition of stability. Equally, instability is associated with changes in role enactment by States. International roles may alter as a result of altered environmental conditions, including alterations in values and philosophic beliefs. Sometimes the alteration has its source within a State, especially after a significant social or political change; and sometimes it has its source outside the State, as has been the case in the role of Britain consequent upon demands for independence within the British Commonwealth. Even so, it is a mistake always to regard these alterations as being unpredictable. Role-changing may on occasions be unexpected, but it does not follow that it is unpredictable. If false perception, false images, wishful thinking, 'transference' and such difficulties in decision-making could be overcome, expectations would most usually seem to be fulfilled. Scholars of Chinese affairs have not found the altered role of China, consequent upon its social revolution, wholly unpredictable or even wholly unexpected. In the forties, many political scientists were predicting developments in Asia which were at the time so unexpected as not to be credible to State authorities. Western failure to adjust to Asian developments has not been due to altered roles by nations in Asia, but to a refusal to accommodate to longstanding nationalism, and to roles which have been enacted over several decades.

There are special features of role enactment, knowledge of which assists in interpreting world politics. No State can for long enact a role which does not reflect domestic interests and traditions. One of the serious failings of contemporary diplomacy is interpretation of events by undue reference to current and transitory circumstances. Stalin, de Gaulle, Mao, each can be regarded as having determined the course of national policy, and therefore of world relationships; but the lasting changes associated with them can also be explained in terms of system and State needs and trends. This is an occupational hazard of practitioners who follow day-to-day events. Perception of an event or change, and exaggerated response to it because of undue significance attached to it, are frequently the beginnings of conflict.

Roles enacted within an alliance cannot be stable. One of the most important sources of tensions within alliances is an expectation by the dominant partner of uncritical acceptance of leadership roles, an expectation that nationalism and felt needs for independence will continue to be subordinated to allied strategic planning. The expectation is based on experience in the early years of an alliance; but the expectation that the subservient role will continue to be tolerable is incompatible with prediction based on a behavioural study of States. The purpose of an alliance is to create stability, including a sense of stability; once achieved the costs of alliances in terms of independence are reassessed. Far less tension, and increased stability, would be achieved if these alterations were expected, and adjustments made in decision-making processes in anticipation of them. The persistence and strength of the British Commonwealth probably owes much to a traditional willingness of the United Kingdom to acknowledge and to adjust to national aspirations.

Roles will not be stable unless they are widely acceptable. Legitimization rests ultimately upon reciprocity. The roles that States enact emerge over periods of time; the progressive exploitation of resources, the spread of education and the development of industries enable States to acquire roles that are acceptable as part of the structure of international society. Even discontinuities and sudden changes, such as occur through the acceleration of trends during wars, may be acceptable and even welcome at the time; Britain's role of world leadership was being taken over by the United States before the Second World War, and it continued afterwards. The role of the non-aligned States is little understood; but it is acceptable provided it conforms with expectations. The Soviet role of giving political support to revolutionary movements in economically backward communities is expected in certain circumstances where social change is being demanded, and provided it is exercised within certain limits, which are themselves part of the expectation, it is acceptable.

Whatever roles finally emerge out of structural and static factors, and from interplay between domestic and foreign influences, are universally acceptable or unacceptable according to the ways in which they are enacted. If the government of Sweden took advantage of its peacekeeping function to promote trade interests, its role would be unacceptable. The aid role of the United States is subject to the same considerations. Formerly acceptable roles become unacceptable either because the environment makes them so, or because they are enacted differently. Britain's role as a colonial power was acceptable even to colonial peoples, until altered values led to demands for independence—just as landlord-tenant relationships are acceptable until changed demands are made upon the landlord. Britain did not alter its role; if there were any changes they were intended to be adjustments to demands for self-determination. In other cases roles become unacceptable because of changes in their enactment; a State supplying capital can later use its position to political advantage. If changes in the enactment of roles are made in order to meet the demands of an altered environment, then stability can persist. Changing role enactment can equally be a reaction against an altering environment; the aid of major donors has tended to be enacted in order to offset an altering environment. The more a recipient State has moved from acceptable policies, the more has been the aid, and the more rigid have been the conditions; at some point the aid role becomes unacceptable—and even before it is wholly unacceptable it is resented.

All roles, even acceptable ones, have an element of power. Roles are accepted because they contribute to the international structure, and other States gain by their enactment; the recipient is in the power of the donor. This power is not authority, nor is it coercion; it is that power which emerges even in a reciprocal arrangement when each party equally desires the output of the other. It is exchange power, which is integrative of social relationships, and therefore not a cause of conflict. Aid given on a non-discriminatory and unconditional basis to raise living standards is acceptable, and the donor believes he is rewarded by the satisfaction he obtains from giving, and by the expectation of improved political relationships. Each party is to this extent in the power of the other. If either party enacts its role in ways that are unacceptable to the other, and if it is determined to force upon the other acceptance of an unacceptable role, it must be in a position to coerce. It can do this by bargaining if the reciprocal relationship is unbalanced; the donor of aid is usually in a stronger position than the recipient. If the bargaining position is not sufficiently strong, as when a recipient has another donor to whom to turn, coercion may escalate to more direct means of enforcement. Thus the policy of the donor becomes self-defeating: aid designed to improve relationships is instrumental in destroying them. This will be found to be the case generally; once a role or its particular enactment is unacceptable, coercion cannot give it stability. Coercion can be regarded from this standpoint as a limited means of supporting an unacceptable role.

It is not difficult to determine when a role is unacceptable; diplomatic and press reports quickly indicate hostile responses. It is more difficult to determine what constitutes unacceptability. Western aid has, in the opinion of many directly concerned, caused as much ill will as good will. From the point of view of the donor, it would seem better not to give aid on unacceptable conditions, and perhaps not to give it at all, if the response is hostile. However, States tend to continue practices, despite evident hostile responses, at least until these responses can satisfactorily be explained. There are important strategic motives behind United States aid programmes, and behind United States active intervention in situations such as South Korea and South Vietnam; assistance or intervention in the form determined is apparently considered to be in the interest of the donor State. Aid programmes are designed with the donor's interests in view. Yet there does seem to be disappointment, perplexity and frustration experienced when aid and intervention are apparently not widely welcomed. Similarly, many British leaders find it difficult to understand why the colonial peoples, and the world at large, did not welcome the enactment of Britain's role as a metropolitan State prepared to spend sums in administration and development of under-developed areas long after these had ceased to be useful markets and a source of revenue. Britain, unlike the United States, and probably because it lacked the ability to continue it, was quicker to acknowledge that its role was unacceptable. It withdrew with the conviction that it was the colonies that were the losers. In the sixties the same kind of incredulity and frustration became a feature of French–United States relations, and of Western–Nonaligned relations. The striking feature is that it is not the employment of power, the threatened use of force, or the relatively strong bargaining positions of the great Powers that creates tensions; it is the particular enactments of leadership roles that make aid unacceptable and weaken alliances, despite the general acceptance of them. Similarly, in the relations of the two thermo-nuclear States, tensions arise from unacceptable enactments of their respective leadership roles more than from their opposing ideologies or their strike power.

When States enact acceptable roles, differences in their size or economic power are of no account; units within international society are then acting as equals. The role of a very small State supplying a high proportion of the world's needs in a particular commodity, the role of a neutral in time of war, the role of a small State in an important mediation situation, cannot be rated greater or less than the roles of others. As in a factory, or in a mechanism, each unit, no matter how small, plays a role which is important to the total process. The leaders of the new States of Africa and Asia wish their roles to be so regarded: this is their meaning of equality and the justification for 'one State, one vote' at the United Nations General Assembly. The egalitarian nature of international society is destroyed once unacceptable roles are supported by power; cumulative elements of power enter into relationships, and it becomes unrealistic to describe international society in terms of sovereign equality of States. Aid with strings, discrimination in an export or import role, or intervention in domestic affairs of others, are examples of the employment of power, and the destruction of equality in role enactment.

Role playing by States is a potential source of conflict because of the tendency of States to play their roles to the limits acceptable to international society. However, these limits define themselves, and the restraints are self-imposed. Role enactment within systemic needs is an extension of reciprocity and co-operation; once the limits of agreed authority are exceeded, the player is unacceptable. Indeed, even the original role may then be rejected, as is the case of the total rejection of all aid if some is offered on unacceptable conditions. The restraints on the player of a role are the threatened withdrawal of the opportunity to enact his role.

The concept of roles draws attention to the acceptance by States of the exercise of authority by other States, but not of power. Authority carries with it certain powers, but by definition they are being exercised legitimately, or in an acceptable context. The force–power–influence spectrum can be translated only into policies ranging from national defences, to alliances, to balance of power, to collective security, to world government: at no point along this continuum can problems of peace and security be solved, for along it peace and security can be achieved only temporarily by preventing challenges to the status quo. This spectrum explains only some aspects of world society, and in particular those which are created by power policies. Authority is not at any point along this spectrum, even though it may include force, for the power spectrum depicts unacceptable roles, while authority is limited to acceptable ones.

IV. STATE ACTION WITHIN TERRITORIAL BOUNDARIES

We have so far been concerned with the systemic behaviour of States; their self-protection, even by means of force, is within this field. The protection of boundaries and of territorial integrity, of territorial waters, of ships at sea, and of citizens travelling or engaged in commerce in other States, is the traditionally recognized function of a State: it is within the systemic behaviour of a State, and so governed by widely accepted conventions that serious problems do not usually arise. Reciprocity and co-ordination are widespread in connexion with defence of territorial interests.

Preservation of State interests by action within territorial boundaries is basically the function of protection of society against undesired change, especially change initiated from outside. A stable international society, in which each unit is in a condition of peace with all other units, becomes unstable or potentially unstable immediately any change occurs, at least until adjustments are made. Each State faces options of accepting change and adjusting itself, or of endeavouring to force the burden of adjustment on others. Faced by an altered market position, a State may transfer labour out of an industry, or give protection to labour in that industry. In this sense power is the ability of a State not to have to adjust to change; it is the ability to force adjustment on others. Conflict is not resolved by this exercise of power; a new international structure is created which requires the continued support of power. The roles of exporter and importer become altered, and probably altered in ways unacceptable to some units within the system. Usually retaliation and cumulative self-enforcing trends become established leading to escalation of conflict, and to cumulations of adjustments required in the structure of international society. Ultimately these invite drastic changes in structure by drastic means, this being the alternative to a smooth flow of change and adjustment.

The development of the Welfare State led to government intervention into domestic affairs, including the protection of industries against foreign competition, and the Great Depression of the thirties stimulated this trend. In its initial stages government intervention was almost wholly restrictive, that is it sought to maintain existing structures, to protect against change, and was rarely directed towards facilitating adjustment so that there could be accommodation to altered market conditions in the rest of the world. It was easier to impose tariffs, quotas and embargoes than to transfer, retrain and rehouse men in industries which were declining. In the thirties in Britain, despite a shortage of skilled labour in the developing electrical and transport industries, the policy was to protect contracting industries rather than actively to intervene to transfer labour to new ones. The between-wars period was one of competitive protectionism: each State endeavoured to shift the burden of adjustment to others. Thus the protection of State interests acquired an aggressive characteristic. Even domestic economic policies became a matter of international concern. States least in a position to export their unemployment, or to throw the burden of adjustment on to others, were the main sufferers. After the Second World War the interdependence of States was recognized: the United Nations Charter included an obligation on all States to maintain high levels of employment on the grounds that high consumption levels in the main industrial States were important to exporters of raw materials. GATT introduced principles of non-discrimination, and sought to restrain the tendency of States to take the easiest way out. The problem of economic aggressiveness has been reduced to manageable proportions: one does not today consider the economic policies of particular States to be a major source of international tension.

The protection of State interests by action within territorial boundaries now extends beyond economic interests; those features of the State that a government now wishes to protect are its structure, its culture, its way of life and its philosophies. It is the import of ideology which is most widely restricted, and its export most widely promoted. As was the case with industrial protection, the intervention of governments has not been to promote an understanding of other cultures and ideologies and to facilitate adjustment: the intervention of governments has been to protect existing thought and behaviour patterns. There has been no attempt in East or West to expose ideologies and structures to the competition of foreign products, to allow them to compete by becoming more relevant to the needs of the people, to allow them to absorb some of the foreign product; on the contrary, protection has taken an aggressive form, and attempts have been made to force the burden of adjustment on to others. By propaganda, by subversion, each State that produces a specialized ideological product has tried to destroy at its source the specialized product of other States; failing this, each exporter of ideologies has tried to compete in the world market by offering economic and military inducements.

This aggressive activity is clearly related to the protection of values within territorial jurisdiction: export of ideology is a self-preservation response, an attempt to avoid internal adjustment. Those States that are not in the ideology market, that is, those States that are new and prepared to adopt any structures and philosophies that are suited to their requirements, gain from the provision of inducements. This is a new experience. In the previous period of economic competition their markets were closed to competition, for they were colonial territories and were the losers because they were able to purchase only the dearer products of the metropolitan Power. Now political ideas and advice are being given competitively, along with economic inducements to take them. In due course they too will determine their own political structures and philosophies, and take steps to protect them.

Slowly the restraints which GATT introduced, in respect of aggressive protective devices in the commercial field, are being introduced into political relations. A flow of ideas is difficult to prevent in days of international television and increased travel —no matter how controlled are the vehicles of mass communication. Changes in thinking are widespread, East and West. The lack of success achieved in exporting ideologies, even when assisted by material inducements, and the lack of success achieved in containing ideologies in defined geographical limits, are gradually leading to a reappraisal of costs. To the extent that economic protective behaviour, which was aggressive in the thirties, has not been restrained by reciprocal and co-ordinated activities, it has been normalized. So, too, with respect to ideological protection; there is a norm range of activities, which does not endanger political relations, and is governed by traditional laws of co-existence.

As in the case of role enactment, protection of State interests and values by action within territorial boundaries is not always a serious source of conflict because of the same kind of self-policing influences. The same restraints that govern reciprocity and role enactment generally govern a State's bilateral relationships; any State which arbitrarily alters its trading policies, acts discriminatively, or acts in ways likely to lessen confidence in its administration, does so at certain cost in terms of future relationships of value to it. Protection of ideologies and cultures is still an important threat to peaceful relations; but this form of protection, like the previous economic protection, is related to special institutions and interests, and not necessarily to State interests; it, also, will tend to weaken.

V. THE CONVENTIONALIZATION OF BEHAVIOUR

These systemic behavioural norms have been conventionalized, and are reflected in international customary law. Conventionalization of behaviour is itself a factor contributing to orderly behaviour: etiquette is likely to be observed just because it is conventionalized, and some international behaviour patterns are of this order. It should be noted, however, that the laying down of rules outside norms of behaviour is unlikely to promote observation of them: one of the problems of international law is that a small group of older States has developed norms of behaviour that are not always regarded as appropriate by other groups in the expanded world society of the post-Second World War period. They are not 'norms' in the sociological or systemic sense, and conflict situations have arisen out of attempts by European States to have them observed as though they were.

7

NON-SYSTEMIC BEHAVIOUR

So far we have been examining those influences which render international society as orderly as it is: relations based on bilateral or multilateral reciprocity, including trade and commerce, joint use of resources and avenues of communication, and other relationships of a mutually agreeable nature; relations organized through international institutions, especially functional institutions; acceptable universal or regional roles of States, even those carrying authority, including leadership roles, and *ad hoc* roles such as peacekeeping; the exercise of State power within territorial jurisdiction for the protection of boundaries and the promotion of welfare and values; and the generalized observance of conventions and rules of conduct that emerge in time out of these four processes.

I. THE INEVITABILITY OF POWER RELATIONS

The demise of pure reciprocity is reflected in a bargaining position in which each successive exchange leaves one party increasingly more wealthy than the previous one: salt being essential, terms of trade are likely to be in favour of the coastal trader, and against the highlander. Once this differentiation occurs, the superior bargaining position carries over into relationships outside the exchange: in due course, the issue is not the price of salt in terms of other commodities, but the loss of independence, or land, and the political subservience of those buying salt. In times of drought in a feudal system, the landlord-serf relationship tended to go beyond bargaining over the share of production, into interference with the lives of the serf and his family. These are political processes that arise out of exchange, differentiation of power through exchange, and power bargaining. These and related processes ultimately determine political structures. A similar process operates in international relations, creating structures that favour those with superior bargaining power, leading to processes that increase material inequalities, and placing some States in a dominating political and strategic position.

The point at which what was perceived as reciprocity or a fair exchange comes to be perceived as a bargaining advantage is impossible to determine except in relation to a particular case; but at some point an exchange relationship gives place to what is predominantly a political relationship. At some undefined point the percentage of the crop obtained by the landlord moves beyond that which is perceived as a fair exchange for the use of his land. It is also impossible to determine, except in a particular case, at what point that which was perceived as unfair but nevertheless tolerable political control is perceived as intolerable subjugation and loss of independence; but, at some undefined point, power relationships give place to conflicts of interests. The process that transforms reciprocity into a power relationship, and then into a conflict situation, is hastened by changing social values which tend to reduce acceptable levels of inequality.

Exchange relationships that are unacceptable, and even those that are being tolerated, are stable, therefore, only if they exist within a threat system: some deterrence is required to offset reactions once exchange relations are felt to be unacceptable. Similar processes operate internationally. Whenever in international relations a differentiation of power leads to positions of advantage that are unacceptable, whenever any role is enacted that is unacceptable, the resultant structures are inherently unstable, and rest only upon relative power.

There is an implication here that needs to be made explicit. Any State that has relative advantages becomes more and more powerful. It is not necessary to postulate that it is seeking power for its own sake, or even furthering its interests: there is an inherent inevitability in the acquisition of power once specialization occurs. Furthermore, there may be an inevitability in the employment of power once possessed, in the absence of a clear-cut distinction by authorities between systemic and non-systemic interests. Perception of State interests is a function of State capability. Economic and military power is not just a means of pursuing given national interests; it also helps to determine them. Weak States have few interests that are vital; great Powers have few interests that are not vital. State interests are like the basic needs of individuals; they expand with ability to acquire. Increased (purchasing) power leads to additional needs. Furthermore, existing felt needs increase in value with increased purchasing power; with increased purchasing power more and more needs are promoted to the category of 'vital'. Thus a great Power like the United States, by reason of its capability, has interests in almost every part of the world that are perceived as 'vital'. Any political change anywhere that might appear to be strategically or politically unfavourable, the prevention of which is within United States capability, is a change that is seen to affect United States 'vital' interests. In due course an identification of State with world interests takes place, and a sense of responsibility for the stability of world society emerges. While this responsibility is rationalized and exaggerated to justify the behaviour of powerful States, it has a basis outside the immediate interests of States. Usually there is more than one State in this position, and a community of interest develops amongst major Powers, political stability and the maintenance of existing structures being perceived as one and the same thing. This explains many alliances, attempts to maintain balances of power, and collective security arrangements that are dominated by major Powers. Other and even less acceptable extra-territorial activities come to be regarded as acceptable amongst great Powers; each major State tends to accept the right of others to control the policies and the social and political movements of smaller States within their spheres of influence. Especially has this been the case in respect of the defence of overseas territories, and provision against unrest within them. Bases, overseas forces for the protection of overseas installations and investments, and acceptance of invitations by other governments to render them assistance against internal political threats, have been tacitly acknowledged rights amongst greater Powers. Even these imperialistic and aggressive extra-territorial activities must be regarded as part of a politically inevitable behaviour once a State has acquired power by the ordinary evolutionary process of specialization and exchange advantage. This is especially so of States that, by reason of their political and economic institutions, are subject to group pressures, and are less able to make valuations of longer-term State interests. Indeed, this perspective raises the query whether a powerful State, even one fully aware of the likely aggressive responses that its behaviour will ultimately stimulate, can extricate itself from its power position and, furthermore, from its leadership role and position of responsibility, or whether the possession of power binds decision-makers to behavioural patterns that change only when power relationships change.

II. MOTIVATIONS OF INTERVENTION

The reasons for non-systemic behaviour are many and complex. Capability, which we have discussed, is not a full answer, and would be only if the State were so affluent that it could afford the costs of foreign intervention without sacrifice of internal values—only if, for example, decision-makers regarded every citizen as being so well equipped as to justify expenditure of surplus resources in these ways. This we know is never the position: in 1965 the United States had to employ some of its military capability, even during periods of foreign intervention into strife in other countries, to control its own civil strife created by conditions of poverty. Value judgements are made that place the support of some types of governments in distant lands before the satisfaction of pressing domestic demands. This is explicable in periods of colonization and expansion when identifiable pressure groups were influencing governments: it is less clear what the motivations are in contemporary world society.

The explanations of intervention since 1945 have been in Cold War terms: Communism (or Capitalism) is an actual threat to the independence of all non-communist (or communist) States because Communism (or Capitalism) as a system is aggressive; it must, therefore, be contained at some point. Social and political change is desirable, but in the process of change, power vacuums occur that play into the hands of local and foreign-inspired minorities. It is therefore necessary to help existing governments to maintain themselves in office if they are generally in support, and meanwhile to persuade them to induce changes. Opposition to all forms of Communism (or Capitalism), whether they be aggressive or not, is a responsibility of the United States (or the Soviet) in its defence of the rest of the world; any weakening of its opposition anywhere would both encourage aggression and discourage resistance to it. The United States and the Soviet Union must oppose the alternative ideology even though there is no direct threat to their territories, and even though the nature of the threat were no more than that which arises out of competition in ideas.[1] This is an argument based upon an identification of western or Soviet structures and interests with universal interests.

There are, however, important reasons for intervention in the affairs of others in addition to those stated in terms of political and strategic necessity. Modelski has shown very persuasively that any serious civil strife invites foreign intervention. In any condition of social change there are bound to be parties to an internal political conflict in need of, and anxious to receive outside help, and there are bound to be outsiders sympathetic to the faction seeking assistance because of their interests in social change. He traces through the procedures by which intervention occurs.[2] This is a step forward in international political analysis: a general theory must explain the employment of power in the struggle for participation by factions within States, no less than by States. Modelski has added to existing knowledge valuable insights into the processes that relate civil to international conflict, thus demonstrating further the universal nature of the demand for participation, and resistances to it. But an understanding of the dynamics of intervention is not sufficient for our purposes. It is a matter of observation that great Powers have responded to appeals from governing factions that lack popular support, including governments that in their own view are both corrupt and inefficient. Halpern touches upon this in his discussion of morality, knowledge and power as displayed in intervention, particularly intervention by the United States of America. He pays particular attention to lack of knowledge, and argues that the United States has 'invested much more in power than in the knowledge on which the prudent and effective exercise of power must be based'.[3] The range of choices and the decisions a State can make, he observes, are limited in the absence of knowledge of facts and trends—and, one could add, of theories that help to interpret them. Knowledge is a most important factor; but lack of knowledge does not explain, first, why great Powers are prepared to employ resources in intervention in civil strife in other States, especially strife in countries far removed from them,

---

[1] R. H. Fifield, *South East Asia in United States Policy*, 1963, especially chapters one and two.
[2] G. Modelski, article in J. N. Rosenau (ed.), *International Aspects of Civil Strife*, 1965.
[3] *Ibid.* p. 263.

incapable in any circumstances of posing a direct threat to their territorial security, and, second, why they have chosen to employ power so consistently and deliberately in defence of regimes that within their knowledge are socially and politically indefensible without power.

The policy of any State is a compound of domestic and foreign influences. United States and Soviet intervention may be explained in general terms as a response to a perceived threat to their security and interests. From an internal decision-making viewpoint—and this is the one that analytically is relevant—intervention arises out of a complex of interconnected economic, social, political and even philosophic influences. One could, for instance, postulate pressures from industries interested in armament production, from military interests themselves, from religious bodies, and other pressure groups. One could point to the influence on American and Soviet thinking of years of ideological education by press, radio, television and schools. But these are symptoms of a situation and of attitudes; they do not explain policies. We need to look more closely at value systems that determine distribution of resources between domestic and foreign activities.

It is of interest that Cuba became a preoccupation of America; there was an emotional response to the failure and rejection there of American-type institutions. Soviet sputniks at first shattered illusions about the unique superiority of American private enterprise achievements. Declared policies of Socialism in Asian States and in Britain in the immediate post-war period initially seemed to be perceived as a challenge to successful American political and economic institutions. Nonalignment was at first described as 'immoral' because it implied lack of whole-hearted support for an American way of life, and at least a tolerance of communist values and institutions. These were defensive reactions; that Socialism, nonalignment and Communism appeared to be important threats to American society suggests that it lacked confidence in the stability or morality of its own institutions, or in their social relevance. Similarly, the Soviet reaction to Yugoslav policies and to nonalignment in Asia and Africa was initially of this emotional and despairing character. It is relevant to observe that the United States has those institutions of social privilege, marked inequalities of real income, racial tensions and political unrest, and business–military alliances, that have been associated with the types of regimes it has endeavoured to support in Asia and Latin America. In terms of its own value systems, such as 'democracy', 'morality', 'free enterprise', and 'observation of law', the United States is far removed in practice from its own self-image, and at some press and academic levels it is aware of this. In some respects, not least in the degree of personal involvement in decision-making at local levels, it tests badly against some regimes it opposes. Equally, the Soviet Union has, and previously had to an even greater degree, those institutions of political repression that have been associated with the types of regimes it has endeavoured to support.

Certain propositions are suggested. First, in an age of modern communications, a challenge to political and social institutions cannot be contained within geographical areas; support needs to be given to any factions anywhere that are withstanding the challenge. The elimination of certain institutions in the rest of world society would threaten their survival even within a great State. For example, the demands in recent years for racial equality in the United States have been assisted by the existence of similar demands throughout the world; a president of the United States felt the need to meet the demands for equality in the interests of his nation's international standing. Other demands for equality and social justice within the United States would follow similar demands in other countries. The elimination of restraints on freedom of association and expression in all other countries would threaten their survival in communist countries. Second, a challenge to political and social institutions within a State can effectively be met by identifying those making the challenge with foreign ideologies, thus casting them in a treacherous role. Social reformers have been labelled in the United States, 'soft on Communism'. The political criticisms of Horowitz[1] and Fleming[2] and an increasing flow of critical books on law,[3] reflect an internal disquiet; one way of quelling it is to identify values to be preserved with the values of allies, and the opposing values being advocated with the values of potential enemies. Third, the capability of a State in world affairs, its ability to intervene in the affairs of others, is itself a product of

[1] D. Horowitz, *The Free World Colossus*, 1965.
[2] D. F. Fleming, *The Cold War and its Origins*, 1961.
[3] See for example Friedmann, *The Changing Structure of International Law*.

its social institutions. It has been possible for poverty to exist in the United States alongside great affluence, and this has made possible expenditure of resources in maintaining strategic positions. United States capability overseas would have been greatly reduced had there been greater demands for expenditure on poverty within the United States. The social and political institutions are now so consolidated that a redistribution of income within the United States to improve conditions of the underprivileged, and to eliminate privilege in economic, social and political life, is probably impossible within the existing political institutions. The United States is better structured to export intervention than to divert resources to bring about an egalitarian system. A fourth and related proposition is that the activities of power-groups will seek to ensure that the economy will continue to be distorted, and existing institutions maintained, despite internal demands. Any change in social values in the United States, requiring increased public expenditure on relative poverty, would lead to political reassessments of foreign capabilities, and this could lead to reduced capability in foreign affairs with a suddenness that would create its own problems for the United States and its allies. A reassessment would threaten some existing structures, the preservation of which is regarded, by those interested, as a vital national interest. The unemployed and workers in defence industries, no less than *entrepreneurs*, would resist any cut-back of defence production, even though the purpose were to provide better housing, schools and hospitals. The same kind of pressures, though taking different forms, are probably experienced by communist decision-makers.

These are sociological reasons for intervention in foreign civil strife; those who make policy may not be aware of them. Certainly they do not act with complete cynicism, destroying foreign life and property merely to defend domestic sectional interests. Their conscious motivations are likely to include those they state: a civilizing responsibility, a duty to preserve freedom, and other such justifications of State behaviour. Decision-makers face a situation: they respond to a set of circumstances. The underlying forces creating the situation are not apparent, and would not be considered by the practitioner as relevant at the moment of taking his decision. Yet it is only by revealing these underlying forces, by arriving at explanations of decisions in terms of them, that we begin to understand international politics. Modelski has given us some insights into the ways in which civil strife extends internationally; we need, in addition, some insights into the processes by which States become involved in the civil strife of others.

III. THE CUMULATIVE EFFECTS OF NON-SYSTEMIC BEHAVIOUR

The drift from a position of bargaining power to a position of political control and coercion is a self-enforcing one. International stability, the maintenance of law and order on the seas and in the conduct of international trade, and the preservation, for the benefit of all, of international structures, might be the sincere objectives of authorities in leading States; there may be no intention to interfere in the affairs of other States any more than might be regarded as desirable in the universal interest. Aid, police, and other related roles are costly, and involve sacrifices for the nationals of major States. Nevertheless, even when this is so, even when no specific sectional or national interest seems to be pursued, the policies of great Powers provoke aggressive responses in other States. Agreements for long-term repayments of aid, arranged deliberately to make repayment easier, are likely to be interpreted as devices to tie the recipients to the donors. Collective security organizations, such as the United Nations, can be perceived as a device to prevent the development of new and emerging forces. The failure of great Powers to achieve a goal because of their misjudgement of reactions leads them to increase their activities, including increased intervention into the affairs of other States. Further aggressive responses occur. A threat or sanction system becomes a coercive system, and a coercive system leads to violence. One has the impression that both the Soviet Union and the United States have been dismayed and perplexed at aggressive responses to policies which were designed, on the basis of their own assumptions, to protect and to assist the development of other States. China seems to have experienced the same bewilderment. Even when some unsympathetic responses could reasonably be anticipated, they have proved to be more determined than was expected: this was the experience of the United States in South-East Asia, and of the Soviet Union in Eastern Europe. One is led, therefore, to examine more closely the assumptions on which great Powers operate, and the responses of those that are being controlled.

Relatively satisfied States seek to maintain existing structures, and the protective devices they employ, such as power balances and collective security, tend to do this. They are not seeking to prevent all social and political changes within their own and other States. However, the preservation of existing structures, whether they be communist or capitalist, seems in practice, and for purely tactical reasons, to lead to the prevention of even that degree of peaceful change that would be acceptable within existing structures. The United States has been in continuing dilemma in Asia and South-East Asia, for while it is not opposed to substantial reforms in feudal and undemocratic systems, and in fact advocates them, it has adopted the tactic of supporting anti-communist factions and governments as its means of preserving basic structures. In practice these tend to be opposed to social and political reform. The Soviet Union tended to employ the same tactics with the same results. When a faction is under local political pressure but can count upon the support of a foreign Power, it need not respond to demands for change. Consequently, one of the most serious effects of non-systemic behaviour—even that deliberately designed to contribute to the peace and security of world society—is that basic political and social adjustments which are being demanded by peoples of their governments are not made. There are many recent examples of this, and the consequences are serious conflict. The new States of Asia faced enormous problems of adjustment in this post-colonial age; independence, welfare, freedom from domination by indigenous overlords, political participation and racial equality were amongst the values that were being translated into demands, and this was taking place in an environment that included many accidentally made State boundaries, poverty and underdeveloped public administration. The existence of these problems was undoubtedly a cause of internal unrest, but it was the failure of authorities to adjust to new conditions that caused conflict between them and factions under their control. In Asian societies there have been over the centuries continuing processes of adjustment to foreign influences and to new ideas, and the adjustments required by the emergence of new values after 1945 were not necessarily outside the capabilities of the civilizations that comprised the Asian and

South-East Asian regions. But the adjustment process failed: the adjustment that would have re-established within each community the links between those governing and those governed did not take place. There was open conflict in Malaya from 1948 to 1957, within Indonesia from 1958 to 1962, in the Philippines from 1949 to 1952, and there was the long and destructive conflict in Vietnam. Furthermore, the adjustment process failed in relations, not only within, but also between Asian States; there was open conflict between Indonesia and Malaysia, and also between India and Pakistan. In all these cases quoted above, factions, seemingly favourable to the West, received economic, political and military support, and the adjustment processes were thereby rendered inoperative. To a more limited extent factions favourable to the Soviet Union and China received encouragement and support.

The slow-moving processes of consensus that are typical of Asian communities are little understood by western sociologists, and still less by western decision-makers, though more recent studies are beginning to reveal them.[1] The mere promise or presence of military support to a party to a dispute can disrupt adjustment processes, because it encourages stands to be taken by élites that otherwise would have been required to compromise or to retire. Once a smooth flow of adjustment is interrupted, the adjustment needs accumulate. 'The longer repression succeeds in postponing the political adjustments to the trans-formation of a society's structure and values, the more likely it is that the more extreme and violent elements will gain leader-ship of the opposition.'[2] Equally the mere threat or anticipation of foreign intervention can disrupt adjustment processes. The fear that opposition might attract foreign support is an impor-tant reason why in many new States oppositions have been under restraint. The gap between government and oppositions thereby widens, leading to increased internal repression and increased fear of foreign intervention.

There are, however, more fundamental reasons for the breakdown of adjustment, and we now have some insight into them thanks to the observations of sociologists who have concerned themselves with conflict. Peoples who have been

---

[1] R. Iyer (ed.), *The Glass Curtain between Asia and Europe*, 1965, and J. S. Mintz, *Mohammed, Marx and Marhaen*, 1965.

[2] M. Halpern, article in Rosenau (ed.), *International Aspects*, p. 262.

suppressed by a more powerful State, against which they can offer no effective resistance, find an outlet for their frustrations by turning against factions within their own community group: violence takes place in circumstances in which otherwise there would be political debate and compromise. Experiments have shown[1] that after receipt of an electric shock rats will behave aggressively towards each other, suggesting a built-in propensity to be aggressive, not just for the sake of being aggressive, but as a biological response to certain relevant conditions. Other experiments have suggested that the object of aggression has also to be biologically relevant, and not just any other object. Furthermore, the aggression was found to vary with the intensity of the shock. These rat experiments serve as an analogy rather than explanation of the type of social conflict which interests us; but a hypothesis suggests itself. The British are given credit for being masters of 'divide and rule': these experiments suggest that they did not need to be masters of this art, or deliberately divide and rule, for foreign rule itself was sufficient to cause divisions and conflict. There being no possibility of directing hostility towards the powerful foreign oppressor, it is transferred to a scapegoat within the environment. The scapegoat is not any object, it is a relevant one in terms of interactions within the community, and likely to be related to a religious, racial or political faction. While a partial theory of this nature might help to explain in-fighting under colonial rule, and perhaps immediately after independence, it may not seem to explain continuing conflicts. We know very little about the sociology of communal conflict, but perhaps it is relevant to observe that fighting in Kashmir flared up after the United States postponed aid to Pakistan, that China threatened India after the United States had threatened retaliation if it were to intervene in Vietnam, and that India, Pakistan and China are still living through a memory of western dominance which, in their perception, still affects their economic and strategic relations.

[1] R. Ulrich, R. Hutchinson and N. Azrin, 'Pain-elicited Aggression', *The Psychological Record*, vol. xv, no. 1, January 1965.

IV. AN INTERVENTION CYCLE

Capability is a measure of power available, including force, in relation to a particular goal. It is, therefore, not an absolute: capability has meaning only when related to goals. In any non-systemic behaviour, capability is relative to natural obstacles, such as distance, and to man-made defences or resistances designed to prevent the goal being reached. These physical restraints and resistances that operate upon physical capability are not the only ones, and not even the most important. Concentration by political philosophers and by politicians upon power relationships has tended to blind us to non-physical restraints and resistances that reduce the capabilities of States, even of the most powerful. The physical capability of a State is reduced in practice by the inhibitions of its own people against the employment of power against other States. Escalation towards full employment of physical capability is usually gradual; attempts are made to relate means of coercion to the requirements of the situation so as not to arouse national and international resistances unnecessarily. It is, however, the non-physical responses of those being coerced that most reduce capability. We have been led to believe that power relationships determine the power structure of society; but the responses of peoples and States to the threat and use of bargaining power and force are not a function only of power relations. Coercion to do something, or deterrence against doing something, cannot be measured in terms of physical capabilities to coerce or to deter, and physical capabilities to resist coercion and deterrence. It is far from clear that alliances, collective security systems, or any form of outside intervention can coerce or deter behaviour by a State, even a small State. The assumption that they can leaves out of account motivations and responses that are not less real than the physical capabilities to which historians and political realists have drawn most attention.

Coercion and deterrence are relative to values, senses of injustice and desires to change political institutions, demands for independence and participation in decision-making, and percep-tion of aggressiveness on the part of the State acting outside its territorial jurisdiction. Capability can be rendered ineffective when confronted by resistances of this nature. When, in addition, the State and peoples being coerced have little to lose physically, physical capability is even less effective in coercion. In face of these resistances, no State, however powerful, can indefinitely base its policies on coercive power, or continue to employ power as a means of maintaining the right to enact unacceptable roles. A role of defender of the 'free world' cannot be maintained, despite physical capability, once those being defended no longer accept the role, and once those not directly involved also begin to oppose it. The rules that guide a powerful State are, finally, the rules which guide the trader in his relations with an unknown trading partner in another State; the mutually profitable relationship breaks down once there emerge incompatible values, goals and patterns of behaviour.

The non-physical resistances to non-systemic behaviour have increased since the Second World War. The nineteenth-century policies of imperialism met little internal or external resistance; the only restraints upon States were those of the competition of other States wishing to extend their influence. But movements of nationalism, demands for social equality and political participation, cannot be contained in relations between States any more than they can within States, even by the exercise of force. It is within the recent experience of many States that deterrence by force cannot deter where social movements of protest are concerned; and western influence and education, western communications, and the spread of western values have helped to create these conditions of protest.

Some of the greatest weaknesses in contemporary analysis of world society arise out of the failure to examine the degree to which sociological processes have rendered unnecessary or unusable the military, political and economic power of States, especially in the period since 1945. Of the 120 States that comprise world society, each one with a complex relationship with all others, few have power that can be exercised outside territorial boundaries. Of those that have such power, the Soviet Union in its relations with its allies has experienced the resistances created by unacceptable employment of power. Britain and the United States have no less experienced the limits of power in their alliances, and in their dealings with Africa and Asia. Some 'realists' argue that each State is obliged to pursue its natural interests to the limits of its abilities, including the employment of whatever power seems necessary.

Some would argue that a State has a moral duty so to do, and that in any event it will certainly not limit its activities to acceptable roles. This argument confuses available power and usable power. In practice, great Powers are restrained in the employment of their power to their leadership roles; they are most cautious in going beyond this, and do so only when some pressing circumstances lead them to risk hostile responses. Nuclear power is available but not usable in situations of great importance. Economic bargaining power is available but not always usable in aid programmes. It is this which is significant in the twentieth century; in the pluralist, interrelated international society, power is restrained by non-power factors. The pursuit of State interests is no longer possible by physical capability, even though capability itself helps to determine these interests.

These considerations stimulate a hypothesis about the growth, and the decline and fall of great States. Those State interests that are literally vital, for instance territorial interests, are not costly for a great Power to secure, both for technical reasons, and for the reason that territorial integrity and sovereignty are widely observed; but when 'vital' interests require intervention in the affairs of other States, costs escalate as one step leads to the next. The United States was led to intervention in distant regions because there is no stable position at any point between protection of vital territorial interests on the one hand, and very extensive activities on a global basis on the other. The defence of one position leads logically to the defence of a further position in order to preserve the former one. The Monroe Doctrine is one which in practice has a universal application. Experience has shown that United States 'vital' interests extend to the Middle East, to Europe and to Asia—to the limits of United States capability.

At each successive step the 'vital' nature of the interests is less clear to others, and resistances are encountered. They arise in the main out of local nationalism; the vital interests of other peoples are affected, for the protection of which they themselves are prepared to pay high. The consequence of a constant expansion of interests, in which each further step is more costly than the last, is that eventually the capability of the greatest of Powers is ultimately challenged. Not only are greater and greater foreign resistances encountered, but in due course the costs can be met only by the sacrifice of domestic interests and expectations, thus setting up increased local dissatisfaction with foreign policies. Then there is inevitably a weakening of will by decision-makers to pursue their unpopular power policies. Weakened will leads to a halt in the progressive expansion of vital interests, and therefore to the defeat of peripheral interests, which are no longer protected. Contraction of influence sets in: lack of confidence by others in guarantees and undertakings, and evidence of lack of reserve capability, inspire reactions. Resentments, previously suppressed, come to the surface.

The individual who suffers a contraction in income finds adjustment a complicated process involving choices of sacrifices, and not infrequently certain non-essential consumption habits, such as smoking, are retained, while some essential requirements, such as protective foods, are sacrificed. Like the individual, the State finds expansion of interests an agreeable process, but contraction most difficult. Having previously been in a position to pursue overseas interests and still maintain an expanding domestic economy, States find contraction presents unexpected choices, and the tendency is to place non-essential international prestige aims higher than essential production ones. Both diplomatic and military officials tend to be isolated from domestic affairs and to advise on goals that may not be, or may no longer be, within the range of capability; long-term domestic costs are then incurred that ultimately reduce national capability. Against the combination of industrial and defence interests, consumer interests are likely to be given a low ranking. Education, health, building programmes and essential social services are likely to be impaired, until ultimately social needs demand the sacrifice of foreign commitments. This helps to explain the rise and fall of Britain as the leading world Power; Britain is a modern example of a State that has had to adjust to contracting capabilities. Even yet the contraction is far from complete, and attempts are still being made to maintain positions in the Middle East and Asia which were once related to capability, and therefore could be regarded reasonably as 'vital' to British interests, but have now become a luxury likely to endanger far more vital interests, including Britain's domestic stability and overseas financial position.

There is thus a capability cycle in evidence. Capability extends vital interests by a process which is inherently self-destructive: each successive extension can be promoted only by further extension, and the cost of each successive extension is higher than the previous one. At some point the cost must exhaust capability, and the process of extension is necessarily halted, and the widespread structure begins to crumble. The rise and fall of previous empires can probably be explained in these terms. In the modern world there are additional pressures on resources due to changed values and increased social demands. Because the cycle is a process, we are able to predict from it, and therefore to learn from it.

The process also gives us some insight into the way in which the pecking order of States changes over periods of years. The capability factor is related to an interplay between domestic and international demands on resources. In comparative terms, Britain's economic position could be less favourable than Japan's by the end of this century if Britain persists in playing a foreign role to the limits of its capabilities, while Japan forges ahead with a high rate of increase in production. These cyclical features in behavioural patterns of great States also suggest that the United States, currently the leading world Power, will likewise find itself no longer in that position by the end of the century if increasing costs of intervention are accompanied by increasing demands for social change. In addition, it may be that the Soviet Union and China will avoid entering into this self-perpetuating defence of positions by reason of the nature of their domestic institutions that make constant internal demands on national capability, and thereby reduce foreign capability. The relative capability position of the United States to these other States could change very rapidly if this were so.

There is one twentieth-century factor that could help the United States to avoid the fate of past world Powers. The really vital interests of the United States, its defence and territorial interests, are ultimately secured by a thermo-nuclear capacity. It may prove feasible politically and strategically to fall back to a position of strategic isolationism in which vital interests were more narrowly defined, a position that was not possible for any former imperial Power. British experience suggests that a more likely political response is to pursue interests even beyond the limits of capability: at some point of pressure on resources it might appear expedient to employ overwhelming power in a desperate attempt to eliminate all threats to 'vital' interests.

As was earlier stated, we are familiar with non-systemic behaviour: it is this which is described in traditional studies of power politics. Power politics and power structures are a development from reciprocal relationships based on specialization and unequal skills, resources, demands and needs. We turn now to examine the reactions towards the norm of behaviour, which tend to deter these same non-systemic activities.

8

REACTIONS TO NON-SYSTEMIC BEHAVIOUR

So far we have distinguished, for analytical purposes, two processes, one integrative and based on reciprocity, and the other disintegrative and based on a differentiation of power. Now it is intended to distinguish a third process, which is a reaction against the second.

This reaction has been most pronounced since 1945, especially in the former colonial areas, and where there has been under-development as a result of the bargaining advantages and the power of greater States. Independence movements led to new States, and new States have sought an improved bargaining position. The East–West conflict represented a first overt stage of reaction, and is now being followed by a North–South struggle.

The reaction itself brought its own defensive reaction, as could be expected in conditions in which additional boundaries were being superimposed upon existing systems. In a situation in which new systems emerge within the area of existing and functionally similar ones, there is a conflict of interest between the old and the new: the emergence of the new makes demands on and forces contractions in existing systems. The conflict is a zero-sum type: the gain of the one is the loss of the other. But it needs to be noted that this type of conflict is a systems one, and not one between States. In systems terms it is a process of multiplication. It is a conflict only in terms of interests involved in maintaining old systems, and in creating new ones. States needs were rarely affected. There were needs of some Powers to secure sources of raw materials and markets in Asia and elsewhere. However, means were available by which these could be met within the newly created structure. The United Kingdom interests in the Middle East no longer required that sources of oil be under its control. On the contrary, reluctance to acknowledge the systemic changes was probably contrary to the interests of the United Kingdom.

Reaction to non-systemic behaviour is not a recent development. It has been more conspicuous in the period since 1945, but it has been part of a continuing historical process. The same process of alteration in systems led in the past to alterations in State relations. Commercial, ethnic, religious and ideological struggles in Europe altered relationships amongst the European States that were the creation of these systems, and which once created sought to control them. Alterations in State boundaries, State powers and values, reflected the altering needs and values of systems. When State control of systems does not reflect their needs and values, then there is conflict between States and systems: legitimization is reduced. Ultimately open conflict is likely to occur between States where their interests in particular systems are in conflict, or when some States have a common interest in protecting each other against changes taking place in systems that other States favour. Such a process must occur wherever there are changing values, technologies and cultures. A tunnel under the Channel, the Suez Canal, radio and television, and scientific development of all kinds create conflicts between systems and States. Any State that firmly seeks to resist the pulls of systems, any State that seeks to confine the boundaries of systems to the boundaries of States, is likely to be in conflict with other States.

The contemporary world is one in which conflict is accentuated by reason of the major structural alterations that have taken place: while the political trends towards independence have been accepted, full adjustments to it have yet to be made. At the same time, the adjustment of the new State boundaries to meet systemic needs, and the internal satisfaction of participation demands in the newly emergent States, are processes that have just commenced. Adjustment processes within the old and the new systems are both a source of conflict. Even in the absence of this particular transition, there would be conflicts of interests occurring merely through the constant pull of changing systemic demands on State organization that usually fails to respond immediately to them. No sooner will the former colonial Powers have made adjustments, and the new States have conformed more to a systemic ideal, than a new set of demands will be made on both, for example, the demands of a wider system in international institutions, both private and public. These will also lead to conflicts within and between

States, and within these more broadly based international systems.

It is at this point that we depart from traditional power appreciations of world politics. Power theories are concerned with the net effect of political processes. But it is convenient to distinguish between the use of power to support unacceptable roles, and the use of power in reactions to such role enactment. Such a distinction demonstrates that the differentiation of power, the employment of relative power, and expansionism, are not functions of ideology, personal whim or aggressiveness, but are inherent features of any international society in which specialization and natural advantage are exploited by States. It makes clear that there are some exercises of power that are legitimized and create stable structures, and others that are unacceptable and stable only to the extent that they take place within a threat system: these latter exercises of power provoke reactions in those States, even relatively weak States, that find them unacceptable. If balance of power can be given any useful meaning in contemporary world affairs, it is the balance between the employment of power to support unacceptable behaviour, and its use in reactions to such behaviour: it is a balance between those that have a position of advantage and those that do not have economic bargaining power, between 'haves' and 'have nots', between States with economic and military power and those that have to employ whatever meagre means may be at their disposal to protect their independence, between those endeavouring to maintain existing structures and those trying to change them.

Clearly such a balance of power rests upon influences different from those traditionally associated with power politics: the balance is between States that are powerful in the traditional sense, and those that are relatively powerless in this sense. Consequently attention is drawn to motivations of small States, and forms of resistance they can employ.

I. THE CHANGING PATTERN OF POLITICAL DEMAND

Traditional power theories did not take into account reactions to the use or threatened use of power, because it is only in the last two decades that these have become significant in international society. The contemporary world structure is different from the nineteenth-century one, dominated as it was by Europe, and western ambitions and values. The contemporary world society is one in which a great many States are active as independent units, in some cases seeking foreign intervention and help, in others resisting its effects by any device at hand, and in all cases trying to redress the balance of advantage of major States.[1] We have now the benefit of area studies, descriptions of foreign policies of new and small States, general studies of voting patterns at the United Nations, studies of nonalignment, analyses of cultural behaviour patterns and comparative studies. Arising out of these we have pointers to the main alterations in behaviour patterns. Analysing these involves us in one of the most recent areas of study, that of choice. Anyone who likes the security of certainty will wish to escape the consideration of values. But this is what political relations are about; for example, States have a choice between independence accompanied perhaps by reduced law and order, and dependence accompanied by relative efficiency and stability. Sometimes the choice is between independence and reduced living standards, and dependence with increased welfare. When we have an adequate theory of values, we will know more about defence and aggression, intervention, and non-intervention, and more especially about change and adjustment or resistance to it.

Relative values such as freedom, independence and welfare alter in every age, because they involve not only wants, but also effectiveness of demands. The peoples of India want more food, but these wants have not yet been translated into effective market demands. Peoples want and always have wanted freedom and independence, but these wants could not always be translated into demands—no choices could be made. The feudal serf wants freedom, the African in South Africa wants equality, but he cannot effectively demand it. In the contemporary international environment in which policies of States are now being formulated, wants that previously were only latent demands are now being realistically sought. Choices can be made.

There are evolutionary and sociological reasons for this. International society reflects social behaviour, that is, processes

[1] See K. W. Deutsch, 'The Growth of Nations: Some Recurrent Patterns of Political and Social Integration' in McLellan, Olson, Sondermann, *Theory and Practice of International Relations*, 1960, pp. 29–39.

and structures within States; during this century there has been an important development in the establishment of the Welfare State, in which wants can be translated into demands. The translation of wants into demands in international society arises out of demands within a State. Radio, travel, newspapers and education have stimulated wants by spreading knowledge of possible choices. What had been acceptable for thousands of years in Asia, because no alternatives were considered, rapidly became unacceptable towards the end of the last century when new wants were learned. The Second World War universally, and especially in Asia, provided the opportunity for wants to be translated into demands, demands both for independence from foreign rule, and demands for freedom from the overlordship of local rulers.

These demands are self-expansionist in two dimensions. First, the effective translation of wants into demands in one geographical area leads to choices being made in others: peasants in India are influenced by knowledge of improved conditions in China. Second, the effective translation of wants into demands leads to even wider choices: the Negroes of California are not content with an equal vote, they demand equal economic opportunities. The new States of Africa and Asia are not content with independence, they demand an end to 'neo-colonialism', and even an alteration in their favour of the terms of trade.

These are the demands for independence, nationalism, egalitarianism, political involvement, and values which are universal, and which are characteristic of western civilization. There are, in addition, other demands that are indigenous aspects of these broader ones. For example, demands are made for forms and processes of political involvement that are indigenous and a reaction against many that were imposed by colonial Powers: processes of arriving at a consensus without the western forms of government and opposition, and leadership roles which appear not to be government by the people. Or again, demands are made for indigenous forms of government that relate legitimacy, not to power, but to social support. It is within this world political environment that roles are being evolved and enacted. Any role or specific policy that runs counter to the demands that characterize it cannot be sustained indefinitely, even though supported by force, the threat of force, and a strong economic or strategic bargaining position.

In international society exchange relationships have been offset by the processes of power relations, especially the domination of States by other States; but they are only offset, not eliminated. A characteristic of the contemporary world environment is the weakening of external power-dominance and, therefore, the emergence of previously latent demands for independence and for participation in decision-making. The reaction to non-systemic behaviour may be as important in an explanation of contemporary State relations as power behaviour, with which traditional studies have been most concerned.

Thus we are led to postulate that the international system of States is one in which there is a continuing interplay at national and international levels, between factions and States that are endeavouring to win the right of participation in decision-making, and those that are endeavouring to deny this right to others. The struggle for independence from foreign rule is a manifestation of a universal desire to participate fully in the making of decisions, and in the control of the environment of the individual and of the national group. Freedom from indigenous overlordship, in particular in feudal conditions of land tenure, is a reflexion of the same drive. It is for these reasons that political independence has emerged as a value more highly rated in Asia and Africa than even welfare—one reason why the bargaining power of economic aid is less than donors anticipate. Ginsberg, in the course of discussing the psychological basis of social life, draws attention to the need of people to enter into relationships with others; he suggests the felt need is not for co-operation in common ends, but more especially for response and the opportunity to respond to others. The sense of participation in a relationship is what is sought. Speaking of men in society he points to the change of tactics that appears to be in evidence in contemporary society '. . . from sheer compulsion to more subtle forms of persuasion. . .', and to the '. . . growth or diffusion of intelligence and of the habits of self-determination. . .'.[1]

Theories of conflict between social groups also point to the importance in social life of relationships in which participation is experienced by members. For a long time the existence of social wants and desires that were satisfied was unrecognized; the interest was in conflict, not in harmony. In 1907 a

[1] M. Ginsberg, *Sociology*, 1963, p. 108.

paper before the American Sociological Society contained the following observation: 'There may be many cases where there is complete harmony of interests, but these give rise to no problems and therefore we do not need to concern ourselves with them.'[1] If participation is experienced by members of a society in which there appears to be a harmony of interest, absence of participation is clearly a matter for examination in relation to conflict. Once the interrelations between harmonious and conflict behaviour were perceived, discussion dwelt upon the question whether conflict was an essential aspect of social life with a positive role contributing to social organization, or whether it was essentially disruptive. In international relations the political realists of the post-war period seemed to adopt the Weberian view that conflict cannot be excluded from social life.[2] Changes in thought occurred as sociologists began to look at elements in social structures that assure their continuation, and Parsons drew attention to integrative aspects of social life, viewing conflict as disruptive, with few if any positive attributes.[3] From many points of view he returned to Durkheim's pre-war interest in the forces of cohesion. Lundberg demonstrated an interest in communication and adjustment in the social process; conflict was to him a negative and dissociative phenomenon. Simmel took the view that conflict could have a positive function, but he broke away from the narrower Weberian approach and was able to state general propositions that better described the circumstances and processes of negative and positive conflict. In 1956 Coser[4] took these propositions and further developed them. International Relations studies have moved along lines parallel to sociology, despite little interplay between the two areas of study. The common social environment has had a common effect. Questions such as whether structures are altering under social and political pressures, or whether actors are adjusting to structures, are commonly debated. The thinking of Parsons and Lundberg is closely linked with the communications and cybernetic models of Deutsch in international studies, and with the decision-

---

[1] From a paper read by T. N. Carver, and quoted by Coser, *Functions of Social Conflict*, p. 15.

[2] Max Weber, *The Methodology of Social Sciences*, translated by E. A. Shils and H. A. Finch, 1949.

[3] T. Parsons, *The Structure of Social Action*, 1949.

[4] See Coser, *Functions of Social Conflict*.

making theories of the last fifteen years. The view of Simmel, shared by Coser, that conflict may have a positive role and help to create systems of balance, is shared in International Relations studies by those, like the 'political realists', who believe that a non-war or temporary balance of forces is the only condition to which we can aspire. Beyond this point it is misleading to draw parallels between sociological and international thought. Simmel and Coser recognize that 'whether feelings of hostility lead to conflict behaviour depends in part on whether or not the unequal distribution of rights is considered legitimate'.[1] Changes in legitimacy lead to altered social structures, and new balances. In international society, however, social revolution in one State, even though it could otherwise be conducted peacefully, frequently involves foreign intervention in support of one faction. Legal legitimacy is substituted for social legitimacy, and internal and international conflict result.

The struggle for participation is a characteristic of the conflicts taking place within national and international contemporary society. The West, and factions within States that support western ideologies, regard the existence of criticism and oppositions as a test of democracy; the oppositions are limited, however, to those that accept the framework in which they oppose. Effective participation by oppositions seeking to alter this framework is discouraged. The interest in the West is in participation in decision-making at the highest level of government, that is elections of presidents and governments. The communist States regard, as their test of democracy, participation at all levels, but especially the lower and local levels of government where participation is often enforced, and where criticisms and oppositions are encouraged within the given framework. Participation in decision-making at higher levels, where broad national policies are determined, is regarded as less important in view of more active participation throughout the 'consultative' structure. The new States that have inherited Western philosophies, and which have traditional cultures more in accord with communist means of participation in decision-making, have found difficulty in combining the two. The worst of both worlds sometimes results: domination of decision-making at a national level by a respected leader, without any widespread participation in local decisions, has

[1] *Ibid.* p. 37.

been the most general result, ultimately leading to neglect of local affairs, to despair, to revolt, to repression of oppositions, and to military take-overs. The West and communist States are not in direct conflict; their ideological conflicts are merely defensive or offensive assertions of general relevance, that need affect neither. Where they do clash is in relation to the rest of the world where choices of forms of political participation are seen by them as altering their own strategic, economic and political relations. Nonalignment is an attitude, even a policy; but it does not carry with it any third form of political structure that could be regarded as a continuing one, and sufficiently distinct from the other two to remove nonaligned States from the power rivalries of capitalist and communist States. Meanwhile, demands within these States for participation, and the denial to factions of rights of participation, invite the attention of the rival Powers in the Cold War.

The most widely acknowledged general theories about relations between and within States feature power, an ability to press values and policies upon others. Every power theory includes the existence of political, moral and technical restraints on the exercise of power, even by the most powerful. It would seem that these restraints have increased both within and between States in the welfare-nuclear twentieth century; but it would also seem, as is in evidence in Asia, that the employment of power by and amongst the least powerful is increasing: terrorism and guerrilla warfare, and a refusal to be deterred by the threat and use of great force, characterize many contemporary inter-State relations. The motivations behind the employment of power in Asia by Asians do not appear to be those that have been attributed to European States in traditional power theories; they do not necessarily include aggressiveness or a built-in desire to dominate. They appear consistently to be related to the goals of national independence, social and racial equality, participation in decision-making, increased social justice, and to the pursuit of other values of this order. These were the motivations both of those in colonial areas who fought against foreign control, and also of those who subsequently were prepared to fight indigenous systems and élites that represented to them social and economic injustice: fighting after independence in Indonesia, Malaya, Philippines and Vietnam can reasonably be explained in these terms. Any general theory intended to explain contemporary world politics must take into account these new characteristics of political behaviour. Power theories may be restated in the light of this contemporary perspective. Power is not an end in itself; its function was in the past most usually to impose a system, an administration or a policy upon weaker States. Political and technical restraints have limited this employment of power by greater States; now power is being employed by weak States, and by factions within States, to throw off the systems, administrations and policies previously imposed upon them. One could generalize about political experience and suggest that relations between States can be explained, first, by the drive of more powerful States to secure a determining or dominant role in political affairs, power being one means either to acquire and to defend such a role, or to prevent others having it; and second, by the drive of less powerful States to secure at least effective participation in the making of decisions regarding those political affairs perceived by them as being of immediate interest. Greater Powers are curbed in their attempts to control the political environment of smaller States by their own strategic calculations, and by universal political and moral restraints; smaller States have, especially since the Second World War, succeeded in promoting and exploiting a favourable political climate in which to promote their demands for participation in decisions affecting them. A useful theory of even more generality that takes into account the resultant interplay between greater and smaller States is one that postulates that international society is a continuing movement in which each State employs all available and politically appropriate means to acquire for itself effective participation in decision-making affecting it. Such a theory, which we could conveniently call a general participation theory, is particularly relevant to Asian relations where many States deliberately follow nonalignment or independence policies; but it equally helps to explain even the policies of those States which within an alliance framework are endeavouring either to prevent others having, or to acquire for themselves, the status of full participants in decision-making. It helps to explain the resistance of new States to commercial terms of trade, and to aspects of international law, which in their view have been imposed upon them, and have had the effect of limiting their freedom to determine their own environment.

Such a general theory also helps to explain, as any general theory must, the behaviour of factions within States, for example, French-speaking Canadians in Quebec, Chinese-speaking Malaysians in Malaysia, Greeks and Turks in Cyprus, and Indians in Fiji, who have struggled for the right to participate effectively in the determination of their own affairs.

Thus we are able to add to Waltz's three categories of theory, a fourth that attaches importance, not to Man, the State or even the international system of States, but to the defensive responses of more powerful States to change in international society, especially to demands for effective decision-making in areas in which they have previously held a dominating position.[1] This fourth category differs from the other three in one important respect: it is a condition that is subject to deliberate change. In this fourth perspective, the problems of world order relate to the abilities of States, especially the more powerful ones, to adjust to change by means that are acceptable, and to avoid the apparent need to force adjustment upon others or to prevent change by others taking place. The problems of world order relate to the abilities of States to adjust to the demands made upon them by the world environment, and in particular to demands for equal participation in international society. The management of and adjustment to change is the function of the State. Whereas a power model presupposes that the nature of conflict is a clash between those wishing to maintain existing structures, and those wishing to alter them, and suggests the need for international institutions designed to regulate the ensuing power struggle, these systems models draw attention to the sovereign State as the principal actor in the avoidance and resolution of conflict.

II. CONTEMPORARY REACTION

We have distinguished three processes of international society: integrative processes such as reciprocity, disintegrative ones such as the enactment of unacceptable roles, and reactions against this second mode of behaviour towards the egalitarianism of reciprocity. Each of these processes has been the dominant one at some period in the evolution of world society; but each

[1] See, in relation to this chapter, K. N. Waltz, *Man, the State and War*, 1959.

has been present in all periods. Participation in decisions is involved in each of these processes: complete equality in participation is implicit in and fundamental to the first process; the second is characterized by bargaining advantage; and the third is the process of regaining decision-making status as a first step towards a less unequal power-bargaining relationship. Power in all its forms, including force, is employed in the second and third processes; it is a means, employed by States and factions, of obtaining or preventing others obtaining decisive participation in any decision-making that affects their systems and the environment in which their systems exist. The object of analytical and prescriptive attention is, therefore, the decision-making process of a State.

It needs to be demonstrated that the participation drive is fundamental, and that these economic motivations can be explained within its framework. It may be that with more empirical work and case studies the conclusion will be reached that the economic motivation is the fundamental one, and the drive for participation merely the symptom. Another general concept, better suited to the environment and to our knowledge of world society, must then be adopted. Whether or not a participation drive is an independent variable, and the use of power and other behaviour dependent upon it, is an empirical question. As such it should be conspicuous in empirical studies of behaviour at various political levels. Unfortunately such studies at the international level are still rare. The results of empirical studies reported by Cantril offer some relevant data.[1] Cantril used a 'Self-Anchoring Striving Scale' to obtain from persons their best and worst hopes and fears, both for themselves and for their State. He took samples from four westernized nations, three underdeveloped large States, two from the Middle East, three Caribbean States and Philippines, and obtained a ladder of strivings and satisfactions, and then made some cross-national comparisons. He obtained a pattern of human consensus, mostly relating to economic welfare and security in one form or another. It can be assumed that the existence of wants and fears implies some desire to be involved in decisions affecting wants and fears; but it was not until Cantril made comparisons between the wants and fears of people and political decision-makers that the participation demands were at the surface. He

[1] H. Cantril, *The Pattern of Human Concerns*, 1965.

discovered very marked differences between these two groups. People are more concerned with issues of peace and war than parliamentarians; but the latter are tremendously concerned with independence status. Unfortunately these empirical studies did not cover peoples who were still dependent, and did not specifically isolate people that had a dependent status within their own society, and participation demands were not fully revealed. But it was clear that even in the United States the fear of loss of national independent status was felt to be important. The general conclusions drawn by Cantril could readily be placed in a participation framework.

This third condition of reaction to non-systemic behaviour can, like forms of social reaction, be regarded as anarchical and destructive, or it can be interpreted as the coming to the surface of resentments and frustrations experienced by nations and peoples in subordinate roles or underprivileged circumstances, and in this sense a process that could lead to a new condition of greater stability. It could be regarded as a description of law and order, or interpreted as the process of change that takes place in the absence of means of peaceful change and of willingness of privileged States and factions to accept change. In real terms, the rash of conflicts that have occurred since 1945 within and between smaller States, and between smaller States and great Powers, could be regarded either as a danger to world peace, or as the type of conflict which would eventually lead to even more serious violence if contained and repressed. Within a traditional power or legal framework the contemporary period of world history looks like destructive anarchy. In the framework of this analysis, evidence of the dominance in reality of this third analytical condition could herald a world society of greater security and stability as participation demands are met, and as administrative systems satisfy demands made upon them.

There is, however, a controlling factor which would determine the outcome of reaction even though this analysis were valid. This is whether the violence of the contemporary period were perceived by decision-makers in major States within this framework. If policies were not formulated on the basis of this third analytical condition, if they were formulated on the basis of a traditional viewpoint, they would in practice lead to suppression of conflict, leading to intervention in domestic affairs, and finally to major conflict such as war involving many States.

The policy significance of micro- and macro-analysis is self-evident: a situation is perceived, and State policies are formulated and carried into practice, on the basis of general theories. In any set of conditions, the perceptions and policies of a State whose authorities assume power to be the motivation and objective of other States, will be different from the perceptions and policies of a State whose authorities do not regard States as entities, and are aware of degrees of legitimized status, and sectional and State demands for participation in decision-making.

PART III

Diplomacy

9

THE ROLE OF THEORY IN
DECISION-MAKING

State diplomacy, whether interpreted as merely negotiation, or as policy-making and negotiation, has conventionally been regarded as an art. In the practice of diplomacy there are no generally applicable aims except broad 'national interests'. No clear distinctions are made between group and community interests, or contemporary and future ones. Nor are there objective tests of achievement. Diplomacy is successful or unsuccessful according to the interests and values of the observer making an assessment. Policy-making and negotiation as an art may be regarded as successful even when the consequences are breakdowns in diplomatic relations and warfare.

The argument that lies behind this conception of diplomacy as an art is that in practice the perceived interests of States are incompatible, while some States are more powerful than others. The task of diplomacy is, in these conditions, to achieve what is possible: success is relative to perceived possibilities, diplomacy is the art of approximating the possible. At best the outcome for each State of the practice of diplomacy as an art is the avoidance of those conflicts that are more costly than the value of the interests that might be gained, and the contriving of relationships from which there is the highest possible gain, or the least possible loss, in all the prevailing circumstances. In this view, the art of diplomacy, even efficiently practised, is likely to result in the kind of unstable and power-dominated world society with which we are familiar. Such diplomacy, it is believed, can achieve no more until there is a supranational institution that plays an effective role in the allocation of values and interests of all States, and in the enforcement of its decisions.

If diplomacy were approached as a science its definition, like a definition of medicine or economics, would include reference to the attainment of purposes against which its practice could be tested. Medicine seeks to maintain and restore health; the existence of incurable disease is evidence of scientific inadequacy, and the death of a patient in some circumstances is evidence of practical failure. Economics seeks to employ scarce resources fully and to best advantage in satisfying infinite demands; unemployment of men and resources is evidence of scientific inadequacy or of practical failure to attain this goal. A science of diplomacy would, no less, aim to design and manage inter-State relations in order to attain definite objectives. Amongst these objectives are security, welfare, independence, peace and many others. Usually not all can be sought simultaneously: it may seem necessary to wage war to secure welfare. But war, even to achieve a vital interest, would be evidence of failure in the sense that it is not an objective, but a means States would prefer not to have to employ. Diplomacy as a science would be concerned with the accurate and tested perception of the current and future policies and responses of other States, and the pursuit of current and future State interests and values by means that would attain them with predictable certainty, and with the least possible cost in terms of State resources and loss of other current and future interests and values.

Diplomacy is concerned with the conduct of a State in world society. It is regarded as an art because it is assumed that it is not possible reliably to attain objectives in a world society of States that are in an anarchical relationship: it is the art of the possible to be practised pending an international rule by law. But diplomacy as a science would be based on the hypotheses that with an adequate knowledge of State behaviour goals can be achieved reliably, that a condition of anarchy is perceived not because there is no order but because international relationships are not adequately understood, and that the ultimate aims of international society might be attained within the existing predominantly inter-State structure without awaiting the doubtful advantages of a world State. The student of international politics who holds that a scientific diplomacy may be possible is asking the fundamental question: would perfect knowledge induce peaceful community relationships, or is the character of interactions of States such that there must inevitably be conflicts of interests leading to violence? In short, are the issues of peace and war primarily a function of decision-making or of power relations?

It will be agreed even by those who hold that diplomacy is and must remain an art, that if all States had complete knowledge of their own interests and values, and those of other States, currently and in the future, and absolute efficiency in the pursuit of their goals, many major conflicts of the past might have been avoided. They might not entertain the possibility that an approximation to this condition might be possible. However, a condition effectively similar to one of complete knowledge and foresight is one in which tested general and special theories, and accurate calculations and assessments, determine behaviour. Much of our everyday life—housekeeping, car driving, social relationships—is made possible by acceptance and observance of rules of behaviour evolved and scientifically tested by others in other circumstances. Behaviour in complex situations is always influenced by superstition, myth, some notion or theory. It is the purpose of science to provide tested theories and rules to guide decision-making, and in this way progressively to overcome problems involved in decision-making in particular instances in which perfect knowledge is not possible. With knowledge of relationships, what once appeared to be unmanageable except by trial and error becomes subject to predictable action and response.

The question that is posed by the political scientist is, therefore, given adequate explanations of world society and rules of behaviour based upon them, would States be fundamentally in a society relationship in which relative power was the governing influence, or in a relationship in which each acted in ways which led to an allocation of interests and values such as those that occur in a community?

This question immediately raises another: are adequate explanations of world society, the most complex of all behavioural relationships, in practice possible?

It is being argued in this study that there is a body of theory concerning world society that could serve as a basis for the scientific practice of diplomacy, and therefore for the formulation of commonly observed international rules of behaviour. Like all scientific theories it needs more development and testing to make it adequate for more purposes; but it is at a stage when it can serve as a valuable guide to practice. As is the case with medicine and economics, it would become increasingly more advanced and useful as a consequence of its application.

Because the practice of diplomacy is concerned with the

precise determination of present and future State interests and values, the accurate assessments of the present and future policies of other States, and the pursuit of State goals in ways that attain them reliably, clearly it requires the guidance of a belief, a faith, a notion based on experience, or a theory. The decision-maker has to be in a position to say, as does the practising businessman, the farmer, the doctor and the engineer, 'within the limits of my knowledge and experience, and in the circumstances as perceived by me, it would seem I should do so-and-so; but the situation is complex, and future responses by others are involved. Folklore, tradition, or theory and tested propositions indicate that I must do such-and-such if my goals are to be achieved: rather than rely upon my inadequate knowledge I will be so guided.'

In the practice of diplomacy the available theories have been poorly developed. Indeed, it is not always appreciated by practitioners that their decisions are always guided by a notion or theory. Some set of values, some conviction about the rights and duties of States, some theory or conception of international society, or some expectation of the behaviour of other States, is at the back of every decision taken by the practitioner of international politics. It is also behind every judgement made by a scholar. Differences that exist amongst practitioners, amongst scholars, and between practitioners and scholars can frequently be traced to different theories or hypotheses that are being employed—usually unconsciously. What political science tries to do is to bring to the surface, to reveal to the subject, assumptions and theories that are not consciously recognized, and to examine and test them, and to find ones that better explain political conditions and interactions, and are better guides to purposeful behaviour.

The role of theory cannot be stressed too much. Whether we are interested in explaining an event, a situation, a policy, or even in studying a branch of International Relations like International Institutions, a theory is in the background. It determines what will be observed, and how what is observed will be interpreted. For this reason it needs to be held consciously, and be subject to critical testing, and not held as an unstated assumption.

Machiavelli, some five hundred years ago, expressed his ideas about how the head of a State and his advisers should behave in order to achieve his policy objectives, and later thinkers such as Rousseau, Kant, Bentham and James Mill were all concerned with goals and how best to attain them. All put forward interpretations of history, and guide-lines that governments should follow. Today, historians, political scientists and decision-makers have in their minds conceptions of contemporary international society, of national interest, and of what is generally required to be done in any particular situation. There is today a widespread consensus of conventional wisdom about international society, international tension and conflict, how a State must behave in its own interests, and the place of international organization. It is a consensus that cuts across political, cultural and ideological boundaries: the Soviet Union and United States disarmament proposals contain suggestions for a disarmed world that are essentially the same. This commonly shared wisdom is derived from the same type of experiences of State behaviour that Machiavelli had observed from his point in time and space, and from the same kind of consideration of values and historical trends that philosophers discussed some two hundred years ago. The agreed reasons for international tensions and conflict relate to the ambitions of leaders and States, to fear, to the psychological make-up of the human race, to the scarcity of resources that it can exploit, to the different behavioural patterns of races and political systems, to the structure of international society based on States, and to other persistent features of human behaviour and social structures.

All these explanations of international society that enter into decision-making have been supported and criticized over the years by their advocates and opponents; the practitioner, along with most other people, attaches at least some importance to each of them. Each may both be supported in part and invalidated in part by reference to history, to sociology, to psychology and to philosophy. No one of them provides an adequate explanation of the behaviour of States, or of international society. All together take into account a mass of variables and perhaps if they could be synthesized they might provide an adequate explanation of international society. In their present form they do not provide a useful explanation, one that can be translated into prediction and policy.

Consequently the view is widespread, especially amongst experienced practitioners, that no guide-line theory of behaviour of States is likely: events and decisions must be regarded as having a large random element that is not subject to explanation and prediction. Furthermore, irrational decisions are frequent, or if not irrational, then ones based on short-term political considerations of little relevance to the problems being faced. Diplomacy must, in this view, always be an art in which experience and the lessons of the past remain the only guide to the behaviour of other States, and to one's own policies.

The belief that international politics are indeterminate has far-reaching implications. If the future is indeterminate, if there can be no predictions about changes in the world environment, and about the responses of other States to these changes, then the policies of States must be day-to-day responses aiming to achieve, as well as possible at each moment of decision, some broadly stated goals. When there is no reliable prediction possible, the cautious assumption must be made by each State that the behaviour of some other States may be aggressive. Policies based on this assumption themselves appear to others to be aggressive, and provoke aggressive responses, which when perceived seem to validate the original assumption. If there is any one theory that has, more than any other, dominated relations between States, it has been the theory of aggressiveness of others; and this is a theory which may or may not be valid, and which has been directly promoted by the need for caution in the absence of a theory of behaviour. Thus, the types of explanations of the behaviour of States that have been traditionally acceptable, and the belief that there can be no prediction of the behaviour of States, both caution the same defensive policies, with the same consequences.

Despite this concept of indeterminate world political relations, practitioners are aware of a high degree of order in international society, some consistency in their own behavioural patterns, and generally in that of their allies. In practice they do try to predict, perhaps on the basis of known personalities, and upon the consistent enactment of a particular role by a State, in ways which make possible some integrative policies. They are aware that the behaviour of States is effectively conditioned by structural, physical, environmental, cultural and other determinate features that restrict the freedom of decision of decision-makers; they are aware that it is possible to predict the broad outlines of the policies that other States will follow over long periods of time by reference only to these features. But they are not largely concerned with the longer-range view; national interest, welfare, security, are subject to day-to-day decisions, and it is uncertainty, and the apparent indeterminate nature of international society in this short-term range, that counsel cautious decisions. Longer-range policies are, in practice, directly dependent upon the sum of day-to-day decisions; the latter determine the former, unless day-to-day decisions reflect some general theory. Usually the general theories of practitioners tend to reinforce rather than to modify the cautious and defensive decisions taken from day to day.

It is clear that theorizing—either its presence or absence—has an important place in the decision-making process, despite the frequent denial of practitioners that they are concerned with it. It enters into their policy-making, whether they are aware of it or not, and it determines to a large degree their perception of the behaviour of others. But theory of the kind described is at a primitive level: it is a generalization of experience at different points in history, in different States, in different environments, by different persons, untested and untestable except by historical experiences of aggression—and these are created to an indeterminate extent by policies which have assumed they will occur. It is theory at the myth level, based on assumptions that are validated by its application, and perhaps only by its application. Rarely do practitioners act upon integrative theories of society; it is an unstated assumption that States are engaged in a contest in which the gain of one is usually the loss of another.

Because policies of States have universally and throughout time been perceived by others as potentially aggressive, there has been a continuing interest in international means of control that might help reduce conditions of conflict, settle conflict when it occurs, and in the last resort control the behaviour of States. But there were amongst the earlier philosophers, and there are amongst contemporary thinkers, those who have argued that structures of control like power balances, collective security and an international supra-State, frequently must be unacceptable to States because of ways in which their interests run counter to participation in these structures. They have observed that balances and collective security in practice are largely power politics in disguise in which the greater Powers dominate, thus provoking attempts to upset these controls. Furthermore, some philosophers and political scientists have argued that these structures are not even desirable, even though they were practical. They restrain a smooth flow of change, though an important need in international society is for change and smooth adjustment to it, and they interfere with separate national, cultural and institutional developments. Thus conventional wisdom condemns the human race to an existence without any basis for peace, and with no conviction that even a non-war situation can be maintained.

Philosophic thinking and ideologies that condemned the human race to wars from time to time were once acceptable: wars were accepted as part of the natural order of things. But we are now in the nuclear age. Traditional thinking may be based on sound assumptions; perhaps the human race must adjust to a continuing non-war existence, breaking down from time to time into limited, conventional and even nuclear wars. However, contemporary thinkers are not prepared to accept this conclusion, at least without first re-examining the assumptions and logical development of the arguments which gave rise to it.

The processes by which philosophers came to their conclusions, and by which a general consensus on State behaviour has developed, are the ordinary and everyday processes of human observation and experience. They have been refined by means of systematic recording of experiences and by historical analysis; but basically consensus has been the outcome of observation and experience of different persons, at different times, and in different conditions. It is the same processes of observation and experience that have enabled us to generalize about the seasons of the year, and about the stages of growth in children. The same processes have led peoples to the view that crops are better when prescribed sacrifices and taboos are observed, and when the seed is planted while the moon is full; that certain races are more aggressive than others; that people with red hair have a hot temper. We enact our daily social and political lives on many generalizations of this order; some seem more reliable than others. In each case the generalization is derived from observation and selection of data, and from interpretation of the selected data. What the observer perceives, and what he fails to perceive, are determined very greatly by his expectations. If he believes, perhaps because of a generalization previously communicated to him in conversation or in fiction, perhaps because of some experience, that redheads are hot-tempered, his experience will tend to confirm his belief; he will tend to note those that are, and also interpret the behaviour of redheads as hot-tempered in circumstances that would appear normal to others. The observer, even a trained one, tends to perceive within a framework of a preconceived notion or theory of behaviour.

These are simple cases of generalization based on social myth or inadequate sampling; there are more complicated and more serious examples of false perception due to false, and unconsciously held theories. That Chinese, Indians and Jews tend to be traders and concerned with money-making, is a proposition that could be confirmed statistically in some localities. The reason could be that they are immigrants, and therefore a selected sample operating in special environmental conditions. It could be that they have been excluded from other occupational pursuits. But an observer tends to transfer generalizations derived from one situation to others in which they may have no application. That Germans are aggressive is a generalization that could be made by reason of histories of aggression; it could be that circumstances imposed by the environment, including all other States, predisposed aggressiveness, which once enacted was further predisposed by conditions that followed defeat. The observer, even the trained observer, in making generalizations cannot easily distinguish between persistent and accidental reasons for behaviour patterns.

Arguments about everyday things in which two people throw facts at each other, and lose tempers because the process fails to convince, mostly arise out of different theories of behaviour by which facts are selected and interpreted. Employers and employees have conflicts in which both parties suffer losses; they cannot agree on the facts or the history of disputes, and discussion frequently increases the area of conflict and the height of tensions. The image each party has of the other reflects different social theories and attitudes; both sides attribute motives that colour interpretation of events, and no accumulation of facts can alter the unstated and often unrecognized assumptions each side is making about the other. Children are born into a political environment and become little Liberals or little Conservatives. Each new experience or observation of social life tends to confirm attitudes acquired within their early environment; these are confirmed by every new observation because every new observation is already conditioned by them. Supporters of the politically left and the politically right can rarely find common ground in relation to a particular situation, even after detailed arguments from both sides. Teachers of International Relations struggle in their first year to overcome prejudices that prevent students absorbing data that do not comfortably mesh with their preconceived notions. A question to be asked in an argument or dispute is, first, what are the essential facts; but no final answer can be given to this until a second question is asked and answered, what are the theories and images each party is employing in looking at a situation, and in selecting and interpreting the facts?[1]

We may find here reasons why historians, early philosophers and practitioners have faced us with the inevitability of conflict, and the dismal prospect of regulating a non-war condition. In the past we have been guided by experience, and have arrived at generalizations about behaviour of States that are probably no more reliable than primitive mythology, which asserts that rain follows sacrifices. When we consider the number of points at which prejudiced observation and selection of data enter into the process by which conventional wisdom is acquired, our failure to understand and control international politics is no surprise. Decision-makers observe on the basis of some unstated and unconscious prejudices; they state their policies in terms calculated to justify their actions and win support; their actions and public statements and the events associated with them are observed and selected by contemporary reporters on the basis of their unstated theories; and in due course an historian makes, on the basis of his unstated theories, a selection of the speeches, acts, events and reports, and interprets the selected data, again on the basis of unstated theories. Explanations of international politics arising out of a process of this kind might be useful as hypotheses; but, no matter how great is the accumulation of facts and events on which they are based, they have no status

---

[1] These introductory remarks to observations on diplomacy draw attention to the relevance to International Relations of studies such as the following, in other disciplines: Abercrombie, *Anatomy of Judgment*; G. W. Allport, *The Nature of Prejudice*, 1954; M. Rokeach, *The Open and Closed Mind*, 1960; J. M. Thyne, *The Psychology of Learning and Techniques of Teaching*, 1963; M. D. Vernon, *The Psychology of Perception*, 1962.

other than that of working hypotheses. They are in all respects like the working hypotheses associated with fertility ceremonies and rain-making. Like these latter hypotheses they can be tested negatively and positively; negatively we know that the traditional policies of States based upon traditional explanations of behaviour of States do not achieve their objectives of peace and security, and positively we know that there are causes of international conflict other than those implicit in conventional wisdom. However, as in the case of fertility ceremonies, traditional thinking and policies continue despite reason, at least until clear-cut explanations and plausible alternative policies can be demonstrated.

Similar criticism can be made of policies based upon examination even of contemporary events. Data are more accessible, and modern means of communication, observation and reporting make possible more detailed accounts; nevertheless, most observers select and interpret data according to a theory or prejudice: no two accounts of Suez, Cuba or Vietnam are the same. Consequently we cannot come to an understanding of international society by this type of case study, whether drawn from history or from current events. Descriptive case studies may be useful in giving colour to a theory, or to explain one, but reference to them cannot prove any propositions.

If we want to scratch beneath the surface in International Relations, to discover the nature of international society and of conflict, and to check on traditionally held assumptions, we must examine the behaviour of States and the interaction of States. This includes the perception of State behaviour by other States. Whether we are examining the behaviour of States as they appear to the sociological observer, or the perception that States have of each other, we face the problem of observation, our own observations as scholars, and that of States by States. Consequently, theory or prejudice is central to our studies, both the theories we have as observers, and the theories States currently act upon.

The two sets of theories are not at this stage of our academic and practical knowledge the same; the theories that States hold are part of the data of the scholar. What International Relations seeks eventually is to find that prejudice, that preconceived notion, or that theory, which will enable scholars to select and to interpret contemporary observations accurately. Theory that reliably explains the international behaviour of States, and theory on which States can base policies that reliably have the results intended, are one and the same thing. The test of accuracy is reliability in prediction by the scholar, and the reliability of achievement of policy objectives by the State. The scholar interested in the theory of International Relations is attempting to improve upon the practitioner's mythology, and to validate and to disprove aspects of it, and to provide a guide to empirical studies. He is doing this in the belief that if there is a general explanation of the behaviour of States then, subject to differences due to tradition, culture and other variables unique to each State, State policy can be based on a theory that will reliably attain its goals with the least possible cost in terms of other goals and of unforeseen consequences. If amongst the goals of a State peaceful relations rank high—even if only because of the costs of conflict—then the achievement by each State of its goals would create an international condition of peace.

A general theory is meant to apply to the whole field of behaviour that is relevant to relations between States. As such it has an application in international society and its sub-systems, in national relationships that impinge upon international society, in religious and racial relationships that cut across State boundaries, and in every other relevant aspect of behaviour. Its primary purpose is to assist in selection and interpretation of data; it provides a deductive system of thought which is applicable to particular situations, no less than to explanations and predictions concerning the behaviour of States and groups of States generally. It serves to indicate choices and consequences of policy.

Many contemporary theories, some of which purport to be general, appear little less 'bewildering in their variety and contradictory qualities'[1] than were the theories of the political philosophers. Power theories have been criticized, but they do have the virtue of providing one central concept. A question arises as to whether we should seek, or even expect to find, a general theory which is sufficiently general to cover all systems for all times, while being at the same time useful analytically. A good deal of scholarly time and thought may have been misdirected in the search for general theories that know no time limits. Systems develop in an environment and for a purpose;

[1] See Waltz, *Man, the State and War*, p. 12.

in due course the immediate goals are achieved, and the explanation of their continued existence is found, not in a past environment, but in a present and altered purpose. The reasons why systems survive now may not be the reasons why they survived in the past. Power may have been the organizing factor in one age, communications in another. In the present age a general theory might relate to the struggle for independence, and in the future it could be the deliberate endeavours of States to assist other States adapting to their environments. Many organizing forces operate, some more at one time than another.

General theory in International Relations is different from general theory in psychology, anthropology and sociology. It is concerned with behavioural patterns that are relevant to States. While other behavioural patterns may give leads, they cannot be more than analogies; individual and group responses are different in character from the responses of States. In attempting to find a general theory there has been a tendency to examine behaviour at a level not relevant to relations between States. There has been a concentration upon, and unstated assumptions about the behavioural patterns at the small-group and even individual level. This was the approach of most early philosophers, especially those like St Augustine, who were for religious reasons concerned with individuals in society; and the same nature-of-Man approach has coloured most thinking since, especially that of the political realists like Niebuhr and Morgenthau in contemporary times. The nature of Man has been treated as part of the explanation of international politics, and not merely as analogy to explain the behaviour of States. This confusion of analogy with actuality led to some logical and psychological difficulties that side-tracked thinking in the postwar period: is Man the actor in world politics, is the formal decision-maker who can agree to the use of nuclear bombs the same psychological unit as the humanitarian in private life, can analyses of Man or of the group be applied to the behaviour of States? A general theory of individual behaviour clearly needs to explain the nature of human behaviour, and the continuing endeavours of Man to survive in a hostile environment, to co-operate in various social forms such as the family, the community group and the nation; but a general theory of systems and State behaviour is more limited, and if not limited is misleading.

Sociology, which is concerned with the behaviour of groups, is more relevant to relations between States than is psychology, which is most concerned with the behaviour of individuals; but even sociological analysis can be treated only as analogy. International Relations is concerned only with the behavioural patterns of systems that are relevant to its purposes; it is not concerned with the systems of the family, tribe or trade union, except in so far as these, as systems, have features in common with wider systems that enter into international politics. Being not concerned does not mean that it is artificially limiting its field of inquiry; it is not concerned because to base explanations of international society on an analysis of the behaviour of these groupings would be misleading.

In practice, while general theories purport to be general in time, in fact they serve to interpret the past and to predict the future on the basis of a theory that seems to satisfy contemporary conditions, with suitable allowances for observed and anticipated environmental changes. Each successive generation of historians reinterprets history in the light of contemporary theories, and each successive generation of political scientists predicts in the light of contemporary theories. This is as it should be; but because theorists are not always consciously aware that they are doing this, because they claim to be stating truths that are universal and timeless, they see value in making reference to small social units, and events in history, to prove as well as to demonstrate their theories. This is not to deny continuity in social evolution, and a consequent continuity in political thought. On the contrary, theories that seek to explain contemporary conditions rest heavily upon trends observable in history, and upon evolutionary theories of society that explain differentiation of power. Continuity in thinking arises out of the fact that many aspects of the contemporary environment can be traced back through the history of civilization. But each phenomenon observed alters in significance in time, and changes in form, and each aspect of the environment alters with an alteration in others. Freedom and independence have always entered into political thinking; at some times they were more valued than at others, and the particular connotation of these concepts has varied with time. We can be precise in the formulation of a general theory only by cutting free of concepts evolved in different environments, and by determining the nature of the environment in which contemporary systems operate, and in which contemporary theorizing is to take place.

The attraction of general theories that are timeless is that they are simple. If one is prepared to be sufficiently fundamental, and to trace all evil to the nature of Man, easily understood theories of politics emerge—theories that have been understood since Genesis was written. They can be applied at all levels of behaviour. This has been the attraction of power theories; they seem to explain, in terms of some of our personal experiences, behavioural patterns outside our experience. No alternative general theory, so simple and so directly related to experience, is likely: no substitute is likely to emerge that will be equally concrete and attractive to practitioners engaged in political relations between States. The challenge to contemporary theory is to find a simple concept that directly, and not by analogy, describes and explains the behavioural patterns of States. No simple concept will suffice for purposes of theoretical analysis; but without a simple generalization about the behaviour of States, suited to the contemporary environment, science can contribute little to diplomacy. If the traditional concept of power as an organizing force is inadequate in the twentieth century, how should it be modified, or what should take its place? At the micro-level of analysis, legitimization of authority seems to be a key factor. At the macro-level the struggle for independence and self-expression, that is the struggle to prevent and to acquire effective participation in decision-making, is, in the contemporary political environment, more fundamental than the struggle for power which is but one means to this end.

Waltz would rightly observe that this is merely substituting one single-solution concept for another. There is a very great number of variables relevant to any sociological phenomenon, and selection of any one is open to criticism, despite any practical political advantages. However, this criticism is more formal than real. Experience in the investigation of a situation is that only a small percentage of variables is relevant. In an inquiry in the United States of America by an oil company into why some service stations made a loss while others made a profit, many variables were isolated. Complicated mathematical calculations, with the assistance of computers, took all of these into account; but the results were inconclusive. Weighting of the variables was clearly lacking. As a consequence one variable, the time taken to give service, was selected. Many other variables, such as distance from road to pump, were disregarded as sub-variables. Reliable results were produced. Power theorists have used power as a single variable, in relation to one phase of history with some success; participation in decision-making can be treated in the same way.

How do we arrive at this scientific prejudice or general theory? There are several means; they are interrelated and often employed simultaneously. For present purposes they can be described as though they were independent.

First, there is what is in a sense a negative approach, and that is to examine critically existing concepts and terms, and to destroy them or reshape them as is required. The simple concepts which have been so widely employed for so long, for instance 'collective security', 'balance of power', 'the nation', 'national interest', 'power' are, upon analysis, seen to be too vague and mostly misleading. Also, unstated assumptions, such as that Man or the State is the central cause of conflict, need careful re-examination. This first approach of contemporary studies has been adopted by many scholars since the fifties, with useful results: it is an attempt at intellectual brainwashing, so that a new scientific start can be made with whatever remnants of traditional thinking remain after this critical examination.[1]

A second means of evolving a theory is to examine persistent features and trends that affect relations between States. History can, with some accuracy, point to continuing features and long-term trends. Population changes, tendencies towards independence of States and resistances to forms of imperialism, persistent improvements in communications, and a wide range of static and dynamic data, can be observed through the proper use of history. Persistent features and trends can be observed also by sociological analysis; anthropological and evolutional studies demonstrate the continuing existence of integrative processes, such as exchange systems, and the progressive differentiation of power once reciprocal exchanges are destroyed by specialization and bargaining advantages.

A third area of studies is within the field of decision-making; partial theories—many of which can be tested—give insights into perception, responses, feed-back and adjustment, the

[1] Especially Waltz, *ibid.* and Claude, *Power and International Relations.*

influence of pressure groups and consensus, the origins of civil strife and the way it becomes international conflict, the role of the military in new States, the nature of racial tensions and responses to acts of discrimination. Propositions concerning a wide variety of aspects of international politics are now so numerous that some mechanical means is required by which everything that is relevant to a particular situation can be brought to attention.

A fourth approach, and this is becoming increasingly important in contemporary studies, is systems analysis, by which the behaviour of a particular system is examined in the total environment of all other systems, thus revealing the responses of the system, feed-back into it and its consequent adjustments. This provides an orderly means of analysis that helps the scholar to observe all that is relevant, and to trace through processes that might otherwise not be apparent or appear to be relevant.

A fifth approach, known as simulation, concerns the generation of data, the enactment of an artificial situation in order to gain insight into behaviour. The same process can be employed to test hypotheses. An adaptation of simulation is the method out of which the study arose, that of controlled communication.

General theorizing emerges from these studies. It is arrived at deductively in the sense that it is suggested by an examination of persistent features and of partial theories, and not inductively from an examination of history and raw data. It is inductive in the sense that the persistent features and partial theories may be derived from empirical observation and testing. General theory itself provides a deductive means of analysis, and it can be tested only by reality-testing, by actual application to a situation, and not by reference to subjectively interpreted past or current events.

In summary, contemporary thinking in International Relations is different from classical thinking, and different also from contemporary practice, in that it breaks the traditional reliance on history in the formation of policy. Policy based on observation and experience can achieve its objectives only if the unrecognized prejudices that control observation happen to be reliable ones—which is not likely in the light of the ways in which prejudices are created and communicated out of context. Contemporary thinking seeks to evolve a deliberate prejudice or preconceived notion that will guide observation; prejudice or theory is now seen as central to thought and to policy.

The starting point of these introductory remarks to a consideration of diplomacy was the observation that conventional wisdom and the policies of States rest on the assumption that the human race must continue, even in the nuclear age, to be content to regulate conflict by structural devices which many philosophers and scholars have shown to be impossible and undesirable. Contemporary thinking, by recognizing the central role of theory, is beginning successfully to challenge the idea that a condition of non-war is the only one that is within the range of men and States, and it is beginning to throw light upon a condition of peace by determining State policies that reliably achieve their stated goals. It is this which is making International Relations studies not merely challenging, but also rewarding.

10

AN ALTERNATIVE SYSTEM
OF THOUGHT

No official or formal decision-maker with responsibilities in the field of relations between States, and certainly none in the administrative systems of the greater States, can rest content with his current image of world affairs, with his interpretation of the behaviour of States, or with his procedures for obtaining and interpreting information. Responsibility invites a continuing learning process. Deutsch has written an interesting account of thought processes;[1] he shows how international society has been perceived at various stages in terms of maps, balances, organisms, and now electronics, to mention just a few of the images of thought. Such a history provides a useful reminder that the approaches made are on the basis of models or analogies. As Haas[2] has pointed out, we tend to take the dominant metaphor in use at the time—whether it be the thread of history, the wheel of fortune, the balance of power, the power vacuum—as more than an aid to description. We give to it the status of theory or explanation. We tend to require of States that they behave in accordance with our metaphors. 'Balance of power' tends to become metaphor, explanation, theory and then policy. From the vantage point of the middle twentieth century, when the dominant metaphor is a communications or cybernetic one, the classical period of balance could be redescribed in different terms, pointing to different essential features and to different policies.

When a decision-maker thinks and plans in terms of balance of power or power vacuums, he needs to remind himself that these are merely analogies, thought to be useful at one time as a means of explaining, and like the wheel of fortune, in due course found to be inadequate. To assert without any theoretical support that power balances or power vacuums explain international society or its failings, and to base policies on such an

---

[1] K. W. Deutsch, *The Nerves of Government*, 1963.
[2] See Haas, *Beyond the Nation-State*, p. 5.

assertion, methodologically is not unlike witchcraft or superstition. Reference to long diplomatic experience is no justification; attitudes and policies have the habit of being self-
perpetuating, and experience may be nothing more than the
effects of policies. When A assumes B is aggressive and takes
counter-measures which provoke B's aggression, A has not
proved B to be aggressive—he may have merely rendered B
aggressive.

I. THE GREAT DEBATE

A major transformation in any discipline or area of thought
takes place over a period of twenty or more years as new
generations of scholars adopt fresh concepts and methods.
Within the field of International Relations there is still a major
debate between those who follow classical or traditional
approaches, and those who favour analytical and behavioural
ones. This historically important debate has already been well
described.[1] Those who adopt the classical approach are in
greater affinity with practitioners than with contemporary
theorists. The change that is taking place is not one merely of
emphasis on the importance to be attached, for example, to
power as opposed to restraints on power, to the role of values,
and to the significance of communications. Contemporary
theory does not offer minor criticisms of traditional systems of
thought. Its methods, assumptions, hypotheses, its field of
inquiry and the areas of special interest, together create a
system of thought which is in important respects a separate or
different one, and not a modification of a previous one. In the
analysis in Part II three systems of thought were outlined. They
may be described as featuring, first, primitive reciprocal
relations, second, power politics, and third, the cybernetic and
communication processes that characterize behavioural studies.
Each is especially relevant to a particular historical period
or stage of evolution of international society; but each has some
relevance at all stages, growth being a transition rather than a
series of discontinuities. Each system of thought is separate and
self-contained; attempts to blend them by modifying concepts

---

[1] See H. Bull, 'International Theory: The Case for a Classical Approach', *World
Politics*, vol. xviii, no. 3, April 1966, p. 361; and M. H. Banks, 'Two Meanings of
Theory in the Study of International Relations', *The Year Book of World Affairs*,
vol. xx, 1966.

lead to theories of such generality that they have little utility. Consequently, these separate systems of thought are not rivals; they become rivals only when claims are made for them that exaggerate their relevance as an explanation of the stages of society for which they were not constructed.

It is in this perspective that traditional and contemporary theories need to be seen. Schwarzenberger has constructed a system of thought which spans international politics and international law.[1] It is wholly consistent throughout. It is, indeed, the system which has been and is prevalent amongst historians, lawyers and political scientists, and it is the basis of thinking amongst practitioners. Criticisms have been made of emphases and of methodological aspects, but the critics themselves accept its terms of reference.[2] Broadly, this system of thought, based upon a synoptic account of history, is one which features power politics; world society is governed by power politics or power politics in disguise, and tends toward more and more centralization of power. Behaviour in a community context is different from behaviour in the context of a society: men and groups respond differently in the different circumstances. Various observations can be made based on this system of thought: inter-State conflict is inevitable unless contained by balances or by some other threatening device; smaller Powers must finally meet the requirements of the greater States; neutrality, nonalignment and alliances are functions of power relationships.

Some political scientists and many lawyers, less forthright and more reluctant than Schwarzenberger to argue logically within this system of thought, have been led to advocate 'solutions' to problems of world politics, such as disarmament, the elimination of sovereign States, world order through world law, world government, and world government of peoples once States are eliminated. These are the hopeful, but illogical responses of scholars who would otherwise be led to predict catastrophe by the logic of the system of thought in which they operate. Each tries both to claim to be realistic, and yet to justify such excursions into the realms of wishful thinking. One must not allow these to detract from the logical consistency of

---

[1] See Schwarzenberger, *Power Politics*, 3rd ed., 1964 and *A Manual of International Law*, 7th ed., 1967.

[2] See, for example, E. E. Harris, *Annihilation and Utopia*, 1966.

the central theory. The destruction of one of these 'solutions' does not destroy the system of thought.

Not only is this system internally consistent, but the methods employed were those relevant to the development of a theory designed to explain the behaviour of States in the past. The selection of cases in a synoptic account of history is open to methodological criticism: it is not always clear whether theory is derived from the evidence of history. There is probably an interacting process. Any attempt to explain the past must encounter these methodological difficulties. Confusion and academic argument are engendered once too much is claimed for the conclusions reached; once, that is, claims are made that contemporary events can be explained, or that prediction can be based on these historically derived theories. The application to the twentieth century of a power theory, derived primarily from an examination of a past span of history, needs to be made with a full appreciation of the transitional nature of society. There is an application; but a claim that twentieth-century society could be explained wholly or even largely in terms applicable to the international society that, for example, Machiavelli knew, a society that accepted warfare as the primary means of change, could not be sustained.

Contemporary phenomena, because they are contemporary, can be examined, and hypotheses arrived at, tested, and if necessary changed, by sociological methods, and by inter-disciplinary analyses: a behavioural system of thought, and the accompanying methods, are possible and appropriate in an explanation of contemporary society and its trends. However, the credibility of another system of thought, as distinct from a modification of an existing one, is difficult to establish. Societies are in transition, and there are always sufficient data to support theories that were more relevant to past periods. These data are used in all disciplines to justify the attitudes of those who find unlearning and relearning processes unacceptable—and this includes most of us over the age of thirty and not professionally engaged in exploring fresh ideas. It was observed earlier that a great debate in the academic world continues for at least a generation or two because it is usually only young and uncommitted people, people who do not have to unlearn and therefore do not have to relearn, who are in a position to absorb a new system of thought. In international politics we are dealing with notions that have been transmitted for generations in history, law and politics, and with which individuals are often politically, and therefore emotionally, involved. Moreover, international politics is still regarded by many historians, lawyers, and other social scientists as being within their preserve. Not having the time and opportunity to specialize and to be informed of contemporary thinking—there has been a flood of literature in the last fifteen years—some tend to argue from within the system of thought with which they are familiar. This makes communication difficult, and the same problem arises in communication between practitioners and contemporary theorists.

Furthermore, the behavioural pattern of thought seems to contradict many time-honoured and firmly established notions, the destruction of any one of which seems to undermine what little security and hope the individual in modern world society enjoys. Destroying any part of an acquired system of political thought, even only some of the 'solutions' that are not really part of it, is as damaging to the individual as the removal of an important tenet of religious faith, and is no less resisted. The unlearning and relearning process would be more acceptable if it were clearly understood that contemporary theory does not seek to destroy any other system of thought: it seeks to introduce another which seems to have a relevance, and not an exclusive relevance, to twentieth-century and future conditions. The following are examples of some of the hypotheses that emerge from a behavioural system of thought, and which may be wholly unacceptable to anyone accustomed to any other system. Sovereignty and nationalism are benign features of international society, and internationalized power is both impracticable and undesirable (though international institutions as voluntary functional organizations are useful means of co-operation between States). Collective security and alliances, and any other structures that thwart change and preserve an existing order, are potential sources of conflict. The international system, the existence of sovereignty, the aggressiveness or power motivations of States, ideological and other value conflicts, are not a major source of conflict. The source of conflict is in internal politics, in failures by States to adjust to altered conditions, and in the struggle of States to defend their internal value systems by supporting equivalents elsewhere.

The settlement of conflict by the intervention of Powers or of international organizations merely represses conflict; its resolution can take place only by processes involving communication, devoid of 'noise', between the parties. This behavioural approach dismisses the inevitability of doom, and postulates that insight into the operation of world society enables a flexibility in State decision-making based on goal-changing and cybernetic processes, making possible the enactment of roles that attain national interests without provoking hostile international responses.

Some of the implications of this approach are unacceptable to traditionalists, for example, the likely, and in some respects the desirable, spread of nuclear weapons; the unlikely, and in some respects undesirable, spread of regional unifications; and the impracticability, and in some respects the undesirability, of world government with enforcement powers. Someone committed to disarmament and world government as a primary goal will wish, on the grounds of this commitment alone, to reject this alternative system of thought—strangely enough in favour of the traditional power system which includes these goals only as an illogical extension. Contemporary theory rejects many widespread hopes and aspirations, and introduces as positive values some of the main objects of traditional attack, such as sovereignty and nationalism. It may appear at first glance an extreme form of realism in that it seems to push aside many goals difficult to achieve, merely because they are difficult, and to treat as benign many present features of society which have been regarded as causes of conflict merely because they exist. But contemporary theory is neither idealistic nor realistic: it attempts to explain State behaviour.

Once perceived as a whole, the behavioural mixture of apparent idealism and apparent realism will be seen to be an integrated system of thought, one that is capable of being tested, and positive in offering alternative 'solutions' or policies that are a logical part of the system, and not merely wishful extensions of it. Its acceptance should not be difficult for scholars and practitioners who interpret politics in the broader context of their social experience. This alternative system of thinking is not new: it is new and an alternative only in relation to international politics. Contemporary international theory, which is essentially behavioural theory, is related to politics, sociology, psychology and psychiatry, cybernetics and many other related disciplines. Even the pattern is not new: the general principles of legitimacy, participation, and social interaction, determine it. It is our experience within a State that society cannot be maintained by force; authority must be legitimized, many social conflicts cannot be settled by judicial means or by enforcement, unacceptable roles cannot be maintained, power can be maintained only if it serves the society over which it dominates. It is this common experience which contemporary theory is applying to international politics. This behavioural approach to relations between States, being more in accord with our contemporary social experience than a power approach, offers an alternative system of thought which should readily be acceptable, provided one does not make an arbitrary distinction between social relationships within and between States, which traditionalists tend to make, and which a systems framework tends to eliminate.

Behavioural approaches are not divorced from traditional thinking: they clearly stem from it. Hence, there is a relationship between traditional and contemporary theories of international politics. If the two systems of thought are developed logically—that is, if they are shorn of the excursions into problem-solving which are not an integral part of them—the similarities and differences become clearer, and the hypotheses that require testing, and the assumptions that have not consciously been recognized, become precise. What is revealed is that there is a power theory that has served well as an explanation of international society during a stage of exploration and development. It serves no useful purpose to try to restate it to fit it to altered conditions. There is also a wholly consistent behavioural theory which better takes into account aspects of the world society that is emerging. It serves no useful purpose to try to restate it to fit it to past conditions. It is important consciously to state assumptions, and the framework in which one is operating. In a power system of thought logical components are alliances, power balances, the special role of more powerful States, the rule of law, and international institutions to organize power. In the behavioural system, which tries to explain State behaviour in conditions in which the employment of power provokes its own opposition, the analytical interest is in State capacity to alter policy goals, to adopt alternative means and to make internal adjustments to external events; and consequently the study of relations between States is primarily concerned with processes of decision-making. Both systems of thought are logical and relevant to aspects of international society; but in the making of any judgement, observations and hypotheses about a particular situation need consciously to be related to the one system or to the other. In comparing events in different historical periods it is even more important that frames of reference should be stated. In respect to the question, what is the value of behavioural studies of international relations?, the answer suggested by the one system is, very little; the answer suggested by the other is, very great. In answer to the question, what value has neutralism to a new State? similarly, the answer is, very little or very great, according to the system of thought. The answer to the question, should relations between States be broken off as a means of coercion? is yes, or no, according to the framework being used. Is internal political conflict an important source of international conflict?, is personality of leaders an important influence?, is State sovereignty a source of conflict?, are international institutions with enforcement power desirable?, and most other questions in this area, will receive one answer on the basis of one system of thought, and another from the other. Both may be supported logically, and it is an obligation of political scientists to state clearly their hypotheses. Both answers cannot, however, be wholly valid in a particular case. It is, therefore, also an obligation of political scientists to test their hypotheses. One feels that in the nineteen-sixties International Relations should be emerging out of the great debate, referred to above, into an era of empirical studies and research, and that the practitioner could co-operate with the scientist to make this possible.

Rarely is there any evidence that diplomacy has moved beyond traditional approaches or noted the altered systems of thought of Political Science, and of International Relations in particular. The nature and role of diplomacy has altered under pressure of progress in communications: it has altered little under the far less directly exerted pressures of academic progress. Resistance to change in diplomacy is still justified by reference to the apparent nature of inter-State relations. The view still prevails that, while it might be useful to have knowledge of interactions of States, of decision-making processes, and of the more subtle behaviour of States, in actual practice relations are determined, finally, by the threat or use of economic and political power. This argument seems not to give sufficient weight to contemporary restraints on the use of power, and the need to achieve goals without the costs of coercive force. It is an argument relevant only to greater Powers that are in the contemporary world a small minority, and not necessarily the major source of conflicts.

II. DIPLOMAT AND SCIENTIST

Those responsible for the foreign policy of European States have throughout the years engaged in bargaining and power balancing, scheming and negotiating to achieve the best possible result from their national point of view. Within the limits of the art great skill and insights have been demonstrated. A diplomatic literature has flourished. Inevitably there have been failures; there have been occasions when sought-for goals have not been obtained, and indeed occasions when situations to be avoided have unwittingly been brought about. Failure has led to the destructions of war. War has been a means of important change in the international structure; change there must be, and for this reason diplomatic failure and war have been acceptable. Now war between major States is no longer a politically acceptable or useful instrument of policy. Diplomacy in the modern State is required not to fail, not even in promoting change. It is required to achieve intended results reliably. Diplomacy is required to be scientific, that is, to have predictable results; diplomacy as an art is a luxury no major State can now afford.

The progression from art to science in foreign policy-making is being forced by the logic of nuclear relationships; but it is a progression which was to be expected in any circumstances. The art of diplomacy, not matter how skilled, could never avoid the self-defeating features inherent within a world society that relied upon war as a means to important change. On the contrary, despite experience and skill, policies of alliances, of balancing, of negotiation from strength, of prepared defence against the possible, have reliably brought about the situations they were designed to avoid; diplomatic history provides the evidence. Scholars observed this, even before the nuclear age: even if there had been no nuclear weapons, they would have endeavoured to find a theoretic basis for policies which would reliably achieve stated objectives. In the years immediately before the last war, the academic study of international relations began to develop from the study of languages, history and aspects of economics and politics, into a specialized sociological discipline.[1] Before this it described and reflected the attitudes of the practitioners, and shared their assumptions, and sometimes indulged in 'oughts' and 'coulds' and simple solutions to complex problems of peace and security. Since the fifties it has been especially concerned with examination of assumptions, with analysis, with theories, with experiment and with prediction, in much the same way as in the case of other social and natural sciences. Stimulated by the dangers to all States of the existence of weapons of mass destruction, and hastened by scientific developments in other social fields, there has now developed a body of theory concerning relations between States, and there are certain hypotheses which can guide makers of policy. These sometimes imply revolutionary changes in policy, and even reversals of traditional policy, to achieve the policy objectives of States.

While rapid advances have been made in this new science, there has been little exchange between those in academic and those in diplomatic work. Further useful advances in the science are being hindered by the absence of opportunities for testing which only the practitioner can provide. On the other side, the practitioner is being denied something of value— something which could be vital to us all. Ways need now to be found by which the makers of policy can assist scientists, and by which scientists can assist decision-makers, few of whom have any knowledge of theory, and most of whom are steeped in the traditional art of diplomacy.

Unfortunately, the gap between the theorist and the practitioner is growing—as is the gap between contemporary and classical theorists.[2] The decision-makers and the scholars concerned with world politics have traditionally worked upon the same assumptions and held fundamentally the same theories:

[1] See Schwarzenberger, *Power Politics*, 1st ed., 1941.
[2] 'Classical' is the term used by Bull to describe traditional approaches. See 'International Theory'.

both have held that nation-States tend to be expansive; that their relations are governed primarily by relative power possessed; that each must seek its security by its own defence, by alliances, by power balances, and if possible, by wider collective security. Both have observed the inherent dangers in all of these organized power relationships. Both have, therefore, given support to alternative means of organizing power, such as federations and international institutions designed to set a course toward world government. Over the years political scientists have advocated, and decision-makers have agreed to negotiate, agreements on disarmament and arms control as a means of reducing dangers of war and tensions. The twentieth-century weapons of mass destruction have attracted even more attention to the precarious balances and self-defeating elements of the threat system. Consequently there has been more advocacy of, and support for these same alternatives. In response to the realities of nuclear weapons, there has been greater caution in decision-making, an increased sense of responsibility on the part of leaders, tacit agreements such as mutual deterrence, and an increased willingness to accept and to support the existing world structure and distribution of power. But the same nationally based power approach has remained. The power approach to policy, and these alternative means of organizing power, have persisted throughout the years, and still persist in the nuclear age because there appear to be no clear alternatives. Research initiated by the decision-maker is concerned with improving his art within a power framework; most of all it is concerned with improved techniques of defence and deterrence. The position of the decision-maker in the second half of the twentieth century poses a dilemma: he cannot experiment with popular ideas, such as unilateral disarmament, or contracting out of alliances. Nor can he immediately follow the contemporary theorist and experiment with policies that seem to involve short-term risks for a long-term pay-off. Until there is a clear alternative he must adhere to a traditional power approach, despite its dangers, relying upon experience, responsible leadership, deterrence and improved communications.

Faced with the same political realities of the nuclear age, the theorist has more recently sought to find, not alternative means of organizing power, but whether or to what extent power is the governing or organizing factor in world politics, whether there are other factors, and to what extent these can be encouraged. In his quest the theorist has been led to reconsider basic assumptions and to re-examine traditionally accepted notions: are States inherently aggressive, or is apparent aggression a consequence of the absence of an effective mechanism for peaceful change? Are not power balances and collective security inherently unstable and self-destroying? Are nationalism and sovereignty sources of conflict, and should policy therefore be designed to discourage them; or are they the basis of an international decentralized community, and should policy, therefore, be designed to secure them? May not defective State decision-making be the important source of conflict: to what extent and under what conditions is perception false, to what extent is there failure of information and failure to adapt policies to altered conditions? May not non-legitimization and domestic political conflict be the main source of international conflict? Theorists are becoming less and less concerned with analysis of non-war situations—situations in which open conflict would take place in the absence of some deterrence—and, therefore, less interested in schemes for international enforcement, in the power policies of the Powers, and in systems of deterrence generally. They are becoming more concerned with a theoretical condition of peace, the factors that create it and those that destroy it, and therefore more interested in the relations of politics at the domestic and international levels, the whole process of foreign policy-making, demands for change and means of adjustment to it, the development of policies designed to avoid alignments and power relationships, and, generally, the policies each State must pursue if it is to remain in a peaceful relationship with other States.

The decision-maker and the theorist are thus moving in different directions. Such a separation of practice and theory has both fruitful possibilities and grave dangers. If the theorist achieves some major breakthrough which eventually appeals to the decision-maker, then the temporary separation will be fruitful. If, as is likely, the theorist is engaging in reassessment, rethinking of fundamental propositions, and time-consuming research in subjects which may seem remote to the decision-maker, the temporary estrangement could lead to an era of both unrealistic theories and fatal policies.

The work of theorists will be more irritating to decision-makers the more it progresses. In world politics, long-term policies could endanger a State in the short term unless adopted universally and simultaneously. There is little prospect of such policies being adopted until they are widely understood. The theorist's scientific approach, therefore, is likely to embarrass the decision-maker, especially the decision-maker in the more academically advanced States where the thinking is taking place, by undermining public confidence in his art, thus forcing upon him compromises which are neither the logical extensions of power politics, nor viable alternatives. Settlement of a conflict is, traditionally, a function of power relationships, with threats, bargains, persuasion and mediation playing a role. Facts and history are employed by all parties to support their case. In the disputes involving Cyprus, South Africa, and India and Pakistan, in the race riots in the United States, in the conflicts in Vietnam and between Malaysia and Indonesia, all parties had a case, and could justify it on grounds of justice, legal rights, self-interest and common interest. But the contemporary approach to conflict is not primarily concerned with the history or with the apparently relevant facts of a dispute. It is concerned with attitudes, prejudices, perceptions and images, mutual understanding of stances as a means to resolution of conflict, and the operations of the international system as a whole. If behavioural scientists were invited to intervene in the kind of dispute which existed in Cyprus in 1961, the approach would be fundamentally different from the bargaining settlements that were proposed— which were intended to give a kind of justice, but which did not touch upon attitudes that condition perception and reception of any proposal. The new States of Africa and Asia are likely to be the location of racial, religious, ideological and other conflicts. The decision-maker in the stronger States looks upon each of these in power terms, giving support to one side or to the other as seems to be expedient. The theorist argues that, if the goal is peace and stability, conflict must be resolved, and not merely settled. He is interested in the sociological influences which have fed on race and religion, and which are a basis of conflict. Investigation of perception of the motivation of others, desire for independence, race, nationalism, a sense of justice, equality of treatment, transferred aggression and elements of this order, are regarded by the theorist to be more useful and relevant than collection of facts, historical analysis and institutional devices designed to control conflict. Hypotheses are being stated, and little by little they are being examined. They range from the obvious to the surprising, from the simple to the most involved aspects of human relationship. The relevance of each to particular types of conflict is usually clear. The theorist is not introducing mysterious, supernatural elements. [Attitudes, for example, can be discerned, and even measured, they can be induced, directed and redirected.] But none of this is useful to the decision-maker handling a situation in which conflict has already advanced to a point of open combat, or in which open combat is being deterred only by the threat of force. The decision-maker is faced, thanks to academic pressures, with a dilemma—if available power is not used in appropriate measure a national interest will be prejudiced, if it is employed there could be a widespread political reaction. The scholar is a cause of embarrassment, while supplying no practical alternatives to power policies. The United States government faced this position in 1966 over Vietnam.

The problem before us is not so much what kind of academic research is of interest to the decision-maker, for academic research cannot be guided; but by what means can the widening gap between decision-maker and theorist be bridged. Constant contact by means of seminars and discussions is one means; postgraduate courses for recruits to policy departments is another. But one precondition of effective contact is for the theorist to clarify his concepts and to simplify his exposition so that what is at present the thinking of 'frontiersmen' can quickly become conventional wisdom. This academic process will require a far greater concentration on research, and some actual field research where conflict exists. A tremendous body of theory developed over the last fifteen years has yet to be assimilated. Propositions and principles of an inter-disciplinary nature still require clarification and testing. The decision-maker can today be advised that an alternative to power politics, an alternative which is more than an alternative organization of power, is theoretically possible. But this is not immediately helpful to him. Before a specific and acceptable alternative is discovered, and 'made commercial', large-scale testing is required. The theorist argues that the pay-off in terms of peace and security is likely to be greater from research investment in this virtually unexplored area than from further investment in the traditional and well-exploited fields of power and organization of power.

A second precondition of co-operation between practitioner and theorist is for the former to understand his own limitations. These arise out of the day-to-day nature of his decision-making, his specialization on some aspect or region of international relations, his narrow or short-term national approach to problems, and his unawareness of some of the interplay between domestic and foreign politics. More than anything it arises out of an unfamiliarity with recent achievements in sociological method and the way science supplants art. As long ago as 1950 Harold Guetzkow wrote of decision-makers in unflattering terms with which even decision-makers could not readily disagree:

Top foreign policy-makers probably feel they live in too urgent a world to concern themselves with the theories of modern social science. They devote little, if any of their organizations' resources to theoretical studies which have no immediate bearing on day-to-day decisions. Yet, in making decisions, statesmen use assumptions about social behavior which they learned early in life and which may be valid only with reference to one ethnic group or not at all. As a result, their actions and policies are often self-defeating and their solutions to problems are severely circumscribed. In most cases the policy-maker is no doubt unaware of his assumptions about group behavior. It may be this unawareness which makes him content with inadequate and un-workable theories of international relations.

This article contends that the surest and quickest way to world peace is an indirect one—the patient construction over the years of a basic theory of international relations. From this theory may come new and unthought-of solutions to end wars and to guide international relations on a peaceful course.[1]

[1] H. Guetzkow, in *The American Perspective*, vol. IV, no. 4, 1950.

11

THE RESPONSIBILITY OF STATES

This study attempts to relate political science to practice, the discipline International Relations to diplomacy. For this reason it has been appropriate to look at world society from a point within a State; the point from which the practitioner operates. There are scholars and many informed and thoughtful people who react against a State orientation of International Relations. Some argue that the contemporary State system has to be eliminated or internationally controlled before major problems of world order can be solved, and that nationally oriented studies perform a disservice. This attitude reflects a misunderstanding about the relationship of States to world society. It has unnecessarily prejudiced co-operation between scholars and State practitioners.

I. THE STATE LEVEL OF ANALYSIS

That traditional International Relations has been nationally oriented is a charge constantly made, and probably correctly. Machiavelli gave advice to the Prince as to how the latter could best preserve and protect his personal and national position; later philosophers adopted broader humanitarian approaches, but the predominant theme was the interests of the State. Many of the twentieth-century 'political realists' have seemed to be concerned with improving the power position of major States as a means to the development of a world community. The area of strategic studies has been predominantly State oriented. But the reason why national interests have been a feature of international studies has not always been because scholars and practitioners have been nationally oriented. Whether a scholar or a practitioner is internationally or nationally oriented (and motivated) does not necessarily determine whether he approaches international problems from an international or a national point of view. He can be an 'internationalist', not identifying with any State, and look down upon world society as an outsider, but nevertheless draw attention to power clusters, and to collective security arrangements designed to protect the interests of nationally oriented units: this is a State-interest and power approach. On the other hand, he can look at world society from a point within one of the States which comprise it, and identify with one of them, and yet direct attention to a flow of opportunities to alter national goals, and to alter directions in arriving at these goals, as part of the process of achieving State interests by peaceful and non-power means: this is a world society approach. In short, one might identify with world society, yet be nationally oriented, or one might identify with a State and yet be internationally oriented. In academic terms, the difference is between, on the one hand, nationally oriented studies such as the history of the policies of Powers and the nature of alliances and other devices designed to provide State security and, on the other, the national processes of goal-seeking that are efficient nationally to the extent that they avoid tensions and dysfunctional conflict within world society.

World order by the elimination of States seems impracticable, and no less importantly, it seems undesirable because of the implied centralization of decision-making over extensive areas of different cultures. In any event, we live, and will continue to live for many generations at least, in a world society that includes States. There is a challenging academic task to see to what extent State goals can reliably be reached, without the costs of conflict with other States, and without creating conditions which make more difficult the attainment of these goals. If it can be assumed that peace, security, welfare and independence are amongst the values of States, then by determining which goals are the most important in the national interest, and by finding means of attaining them reliably, we may also find the means to a peaceful world order. It is analysis at the State level that is relevant. As Deutsch once commented, 'The most promising next step towards increasing the capabilities of the international system may well consist in first improving the capabilities of its national components'.[1]

The difference between those who adopt a State level of analysis, and those who prefer to commence with an inter-State or world framework, is a difference at an ideological or prescriptive level. The strong tendency since the early fifties

[1] In *Conflict in Society*, p. 315.

amongst political scientists concerned with analysis has been to concentrate upon the State as the main actor in world society, not with a view to increasing the power of particular authorities or States, but in order to examine the role of the State in a world society in which systemic relationships that cross State boundaries are becoming increasingly important. It is a tendency that reflects a judgement that States have increasing responsibilities in the allocation of values and resources to meet the needs of what is already a highly integrated world society. Associated with, or implied in this concentration upon micro-studies of State behaviour is the belief that final responsibility for peaceful conditions is and will remain with each State. International institutions endowed with enforcement powers, and the magic of maintaining peace and peaceful change, are seen as a wishful creation of a past age in which each powerful State held that its own policies were almost beyond reproach, and that it was the policies of other States that needed to be restrained by international organizations which it dominated. A less parochial view that accords with political analysis is that each and every State, and not just the 'aggressor' State, is responsible for international conflict. 'Aggressor' States seem to be States that feel themselves limited in their freedom to control their own affairs, exploited, hemmed in, deprived of markets or in some other way threatened by others. In international society, as in national society, there is a correlation between those who are law-abiding, and those who formulate, administer and benefit from law; and also between those who are endeavouring to defy convention, and those who have little effective role in decision-making. Sociologically, the latter are no more aggressors than those who employ their power and force to maintain existing structures and relationships. States wishing to maintain their favourable economic, political or strategic positions will not add to their security by conducting their affairs as though others were aggressors; they, by their own decision-making processes, need to meet certain demands for change by peaceful means. No international institution could solve world problems unless it were decentralized into units of local authority such as States, and the basic problems would therefore remain.

An analysis of world society at a State level implies the need for international institutions through which independent States can voluntarily co-ordinate their activities. Contemporary theories have not ignored these. On the contrary, alongside an analysis at the State level have gone studies of functional arrangements; the domestic and international institutional aspects of State decision-making are treated within the one communications framework.[1] However, unlike more traditional and popular approaches to world government, functionalism does not assume a world authority with coercive powers, or an extension to world society of the concept of centralized law and order associated with a State. It leaves responsibility for the conduct of world society with independent States.

There is a second, and perhaps even more fundamental sense, in which the State may be regarded as being finally responsible for conditions of peace within world society, and this has also attracted the attention of scholars in recent years.[2] The possession of shared values, the legitimization of authority, skill in management, and other features associated with a developed and flexible welfare State, provide a sense of security: in these conditions external threats are not exaggerated, and accommodation to environmental change even in ideas takes place without imposing burdens upon other States. Ultimately the main sources of international harmony or conflict may be found to be the degree of integration that exists at the State level. International studies have tended to be more and more directed toward domestic political and economic problems that affect the international behaviour of States. Cross-national or comparative studies are beginning to provide basic information which will show the conditions in which States are most likely to be involved in conflict.[3] For this reason a model of international society based on the concept of nonalignment is a useful analytical one, not because there is a widespread adoption of nonalignment amongst the new States, but because it gives some insights into the behaviour of States generally. Alignment is not the preferred policy of a State; on the contrary, States seek independence, for it is only then that they are participating fully in decision-making that affects them. Alignments are reluctantly resorted to by States as a means of defence. Because they help to create a political environment that forces States to

---

[1] See Haas, *Beyond the Nation-State*.   [2] See Rosenau (ed.), *International Aspects*.

[3] See A. S. Banks and R. S. Textor, *A Cross-Polity Survey*, 1963; and B. M. Russett (ed.), *World Handbook of Political and Social Indicators*, 2nd ed., 1965.

continue in them, and to escalate defences still further, they cannot provide security, and they tend to be self-perpetuating and also self-defeating. States struggle to be free of alignments, because they limit independence, and because they do not add to world security; but most States can find no viable alternative. In this present study an attempt has been made to draw attention to the relationship between systems and States, to the legitimization of authority, to those activies of States that do not endanger peace and security, to those other activities of States that are designed to impose an environment upon others, and to those activities of States that might endanger peace and security, but which are designed to win independence and full participation in decisions that affect them. The relationship between internal struggles for participation in decision-making, and international strife, is clear in this last type of State activity. There is also an implication that there is an alternative to alliances once aligned States acknowledge that the apparently aggressive drive of other States is for independence, internally and externally.

The study of world society has passed through stages of growth which are parallel to, and reflect the stages of growth of other behavioural studies. Generalized thinking about behaviour has given place to detailed analysis based upon the examination of individuals. Psychology employed the simple stimulus–response formula to explain individual behaviour. It has had its equivalent in political studies: the input–output formula employed by Modelski.[1] It was a formula that did well enough to describe the behaviour of powerful States at a period of State development in which decision-making was a simple process, and one which took place within a power framework. Altered environmental conditions, including altered values, political influences and strategic possibilities, rendered a simple power-oriented input–output behavioural pattern politically impossible, and therefore analytically inappropriate. Decision-making is now more complicated, and developments in psychology and sociology have made possible an analysis of this more complicated process. Stimulus and input in the modern world relate to images and perceptions of great complexity, and these are themselves the object of analytical attention. Output is no longer a final distribution and employment of power; the testing

[1] In *A Theory of Foreign Policy*; and see Text-fig. 3, on p. 64.

of responses, feed-back from the environment, and altered decisions about tactics and goals, are an important part of diplomacy and State behaviour. A power element remains; but it is a support for decision-making. Like the gold at the reserve bank, it provides an area of manoeuvrability, and its use is evidence of failure in adjustment processes and in decision-making.

The formula that expresses this more recent approach includes the process between stimulus and response, between input and output. The formula is stimulus–decision-making process–response. It is this black box of decision-making that holds the secret to an understanding of international politics. Within it are influences which determine perception of the stimulus: whatever the stimulus is in objective terms, for example, a passive or an aggressive action by a foreign State, the reality in international politics is how it is perceived. The black box determines this. Equally, the decision-making process determines the quality and the nature of the response or output: it varies from a once-and-for-all decision to achieve a goal by the use of force, to a continuing process of goal-changing and internal adjustment to the foreign environment. The majority of reactions are between these two extremes.

The response process in the modern world is best understood by reference to cybernetics or steering models, just for the reason that even the most powerful States are limited in their capabilities by value systems and other influences within the black box, and within the decision-making processes of other States. The study of international relations and of diplomacy is, therefore, essentially the study of the decision-making process of the State. There are no aspects of international relations, including those dealt with in a power framework, that cannot be analysed within this framework. International relations is an abstract concept: whatever interplay there is between States is finally recorded and enacted within the decision-making process of the State.

Taking the black box of decision-making to pieces, either in a general model or in a particular case, is an extensive behavioural study. Geopolitical influences, constitutional frameworks, political pressures of all kinds, resources, traditions, levels of knowledge, levels of dependence, personalities, and many other features are relevant. The decision-maker is a process: the task is to analyse this process, and to describe it. At the motivation level the process is dominated (we have postulated), by the drive for participation in decision-making. Other perceptions by a State of the motivations of other States, for example, perceptions of aggressiveness, result in stereotype defensive responses. To the extent that theorists and practitioners have postulated power as motivation, they have contributed to self-fulfilling power policies that invite aggressive responses. The simple input–output formula, which takes no account of complicated decision-making processes, itself conveys an image of international society as being power-dominated. But each separate State denies that it is so dominated. The image each State has of itself is the complicated and flexible stimulus—decision-making —response image, and the image it has of others tends to be the simple power-motivated input–output model. Contemporary theory endeavours to demonstrate that all States have similar motivations and similar decision-making processes, and that an accurate perception of these enables States to conduct policies that avoid confrontations and crises by goal-changing and internal adjustment, without loss of State needs and interests.

Analysis of a crisis is relevant to situations that have already escalated to high levels of political tension; the more important problem of diplomacy is to handle events in such a way as to prevent this escalation, and to establish continuing conditions of peaceful relations in circumstances of change. With adequate knowledge, foresight, theories, and efficiency in executing policies, States could avoid conflicts that would become dysfunctional. However, decisions are in practice taken in the absence of these ideal conditions and mistakes occur. Strategic and defensive policies continue to be required as a precaution, and their study is valuable in helping to make deterrence effective. But conditions of deterrence cannot always be guaranteed because strategic policies are frequently self-defeating. Consequently, study of crisis management is also important. Practitioners face problems of strategy constantly, and enormous sums are spent by governments both upon actual defence and upon research. Crisis management is within the day-to-day experience of States because it is crises with which governments customarily deal. But decision-making about future events and less important issues takes place at lower administrative levels, or without adequate consideration because of the competing demands of crises. In the world society of modern States the great bulk of diplomatic relations concerns day-to-day affairs not in themselves likely to escalate into a conflict situation. But even these normal trading, cultural and political relationships can and do lead to cumulations of tensions, each successive one feeding on a preceding one. Far less attention has been paid to non-strategic, non-crisis decision-making, yet it would seem from our analysis so far that it is this decision-making which is finally responsible for the need for strategies of deterrence, and for crises. A failure to make an appropriate adjustment to a market change, an attempt to pass the burden of adjustment on to another political system, a move to enlist the support of one community in a colonial area as a defence against another, an attempt to deny to a State a right to enter a market or a world council, may seem at the time to be an internationally harmless means of meeting an immediate domestic demand. But each subsequent response by other States, each subsequent decision, sharpens the conflict of interest, narrows the range of choice, until crisis and dys-functional conflict seem inevitable. The origin is not the last decision or the last but one; it is a whole series of decisions taken at various levels over a period of time. Japanese aggression and Germany's plans for domination did not originate in the coming to power of Tojo and Hitler: their origins, in terms of alterable factors, were in decision-making processes in those two countries and elsewhere at much earlier dates.

It is not possible to pinpoint a date or an event as the starting-point in any conflict; but in the analysis of a conflict or of inter-State relations it is necessary to treat decision-making as a process. Each decision within the total process is part of the origins of harmony or of conflict. It is only general theories and specific propositions that can be a substitute for perfect knowledge and foresight about the future consequences of decisions. The colonial administrator in Fiji found it expedient to buy time in various ways, and sentiment dictated giving Fijians a constitutional power over the more numerous Indians. But if theories of participation and legitimization, or some general propositions tested in other cases such as Cyprus and Malaysia, demonstrated that preference to Fijians and their employment as police to control Indians would have set up conflict in due course likely to be dysfunctional to both the communities, then these would have been regarded as policies to avoid.

Assuming that the problems of world society arise out of the problems each State faces in determining and pursuing its interests without dysfunctional conflict, an ideal world society is one in which:

each State is unified, that is, shares common values and is organized by legitimized authorities;

each State is flexible in its responses to the environment;

efficient decision-making processes in every State permit accurate perceptions, reliable anticipation of the responses of others, and relevant reassessments of values and costs of policies; and

co-ordination of reciprocal State activities is facilitated through international institutions.

These four ideal conditions can be translated into detailed operative terms by reference to the studies of politics, economics, decision-making and international institutions. It is to these studies of State behaviour and functional co-operation (from which diplomatic history, strategic studies and plans for world order through world law have for so long diverted attention) that a systems analysis of world society directs attention. There is no single solution or temporary expedient that can promote a peaceful world society. Education and industrial training to promote flexibility of response, the satisfaction of communal needs for participation in decision-making, and every aspect of State organization and management have a bearing upon international politics. These all involve long-term planning at a State level, and this requires informed decision-making supported by a widespread awareness of the nature of inter-State relations.

II. DEFENCE STRUCTURES

There is a special problem of a technical kind that faces States to which attention is directed by a decision-making analysis of State responsibility. This relates to the organization of defence and its effects upon foreign policy. No matter how flexible are systems within States, how accurate is perception by authorities of the environment, the traditions and interests of administrative structures can seriously restrict and control decision-making.

A particular example serves best to demonstrate this problem —though the problem itself is general amongst States. The

United Kingdom is a relatively integrated and flexible economy, with a relatively mature, experienced and legitimized administrative system in control. It has extensive obligations throughout the world consequent upon its former position as a colonial Power. It has also assumed, more than most States, obligations to protect the interests and lives of British people in many regions of local unrest. It has accepted an obligation to assist authorities it has established that may be threatened by 'insurgency', as, for example, in Malaya. While acceptance of obligations was being limited in the sixties under the growing economic pressures of the Welfare State, defence expenditure in 1967 was approximately £2,250 million, or £87 per head of employed population. £104 million was absorbed in nuclear defence, £184 million in operations in Europe, £700 million in general navy, army and air purposes, £240 million in research and development, £209 million in training, and the remainder in supporting production, acquisition and services.

The authorities at the time endeavoured to make marginal reductions in the budget, and to reduce overseas commitments. The interesting question is what determined the level of defence expenditure, was it a reflexion of political appreciations, or did defence allocations determine foreign policies?

Every State can, if it has the capacity, assume overseas responsibilities. The United States and the Soviet Union assume them, even though they were not previously colonial Powers. Smaller States might like to assume a civilizing or authoritative role. In practice a level of defence expenditure is determined by values attributed to this form of activity in relation to other values, such as domestic welfare demands. The £2,000 to £2,500 million of Britain in the mid sixties was a traditionally determined level: whether British 'interests' would have been better served by adding £1,000 million or by reducing the amount by £1,000 million was a calculation which seemed not to be possible.

The structure of defence planning makes such a calculation unlikely. Returning to the example of the United Kingdom in the middle sixties, the defence ministry employed over 20,000 people, and in addition there were armed services, and the public and private production establishments. Defence planning was up to ten years ahead as it took this time to plan and to acquire new equipment. But political prediction ten years ahead was not possible: the assumption was that political conditions then would be similar to those of the time. Hence the only effective control on defence levels was a budgetary one: conventional wisdom and tradition determined what the State could afford. The interests of elected authorities who are in office for limited periods were not greatly relevant to the longer term behaviour of this structure: they had little option but to conform, imposing whatever ceilings or minor reductions they could. Even when Britain in the middle sixties urgently required manpower in industry of the age groups and skills of men in the services as a means to combat inflation and balance-of-payments difficulties, the manpower structure of defence underwent little change.

A policy not to have conscription imposed a control in Britain that does not always apply. Budgetary provisions for expansion of defence services can be made only if manpower is available. Manpower limitations are a particularly effective control of defence structures because they limit procurement of equipment. In the United States conscription made possible greater defence structures, and equipment needs were limited only by the willingness of authorities to finance them.

The effect of these traditional defence structures upon the making of foreign policy is extensive. In theory defence policy is subordinate to foreign policy: a State has certain objectives, and the function of defence is to assist in achieving them. Civil authorities in theory remain in control of policy; the defence services, the military leaders, order their strategy accordingly. But in practice defence planning tends to condition and to control longer-term foreign policy. Defence policy is conceived within a traditional power framework: it seeks to provide for all possible contingencies within a budgetary limit established for it. It therefore sets the limits of foreign policies that are conceived within a power framework: it is an important factor in determining, and even in limiting the extent of possible non-systemic behaviour. In Britain in the sixties the defence ministry seems to have taken the initiative in reducing British commitments overseas to bring them within the limits of capability set by a budgetary figure.

Furthermore, in practice there can be no sharp division between immediate policy objectives and strategic means of achieving them. A State may wish to help maintain a foreign government in office. The military strategies involved require certain steps progressively to be taken, and little by little more and more intervention in domestic affairs occurs. The original political objectives become less important than the strategic requirements: the ends become lost in means. Foreign authorities that are strongly in support of some ideology, but which have limited popular support, are accorded support for strategic reasons in preference to oppositions that could ensure stability by reason of their support. Politics as well as strategy become the province of the military, with the foreign office trailing behind as ineffective advisers.

III. THE ROLE OF PREDICTION

The forecasting of political conditions has become of importance to contemporary defence planning for two interrelated technical reasons. First, modern defence systems tend to be instruments designed for special purposes. Second, the time lag between planning and operation of defence systems is up to ten years, during which period their specialized relevance is likely to be reduced by political change. It is probable that little can be done either to design weapons of greater flexibility, or to reduce the gap between planning and operation. On the contrary, greater specialization and an increase in the time lag may occur with the introduction of even more complex missile and anti-missile systems.

These technical influences have wide implications. In so far as forward planning of specialized equipment must be in relation to a particular enemy or set of conditions, it tends to freeze a present political circumstance, and to institutionalize public and official attitudes despite political change. Foreign policy tends, in these circumstances, to be formulated within a framework of defence planning, and not vice versa. The more widespread throughout the world these conditions become with the further spread of technological developments, the more inflexible inter-State relations will become.

Forecasting is also of importance for domestic political reasons. Costs of defence create a serious political problem in the modern Welfare State in which there are increasing demands for educational, medical and other services. In most communities there is little disagreement in principle that there should be provisions made for defence; but the absolute levels of expenditure, and the levels relevant to education, health and other services, involve value judgements. The allocation of values is a political function, and the viewpoint of government is unlikely to correspond with that of people who are direct consumers of welfare services, and less aware of defence needs. The political difficulty experienced in allocating and justifying resources for defence is becoming increasingly acute because of the nature of modern defence systems. Defence systems are more highly capitalized than most other service industries, and most of the capital goods that comprise them are more prone to obsolescence. Defence systems of States are in direct competition, unrestrained by the market conditions that control rates of technological development in other service industries, and relatively un-inhibited by value judgements such as make possible the continued use of outmoded school or hospital buildings. Indeed, an objective of the defence policies of major States is to render obsolete the defence systems of other States by research and development that create obsolescence in the State's own defence system. Obsolescence of unused equipment also arises out of the nature of the service being provided. Defence systems, like police systems, are themselves designed to create conditions that render their use unnecessary. Furthermore, the objective of State policies is to avoid conditions which would require the operational use of defence systems. It is the success of State policies, and the effectiveness of defence systems, that lead to idleness of men and to obsolescence of equipment still capable of service. These wastes of idleness and obsolescence are the unavoidable costs of the service provided by defence systems. There are also cumulative costs of defence that occur by reason of self-fulfilling consequences of defence policies. Innovation in defence breeds innovation and increased strike capacity breeds increased strike capacity. No separate calculation of the cost of this element is possible: it is an inevitable component of defence systems. Superficially there appears to be no limit to defence needs, and, in the absence of war no perceptible return, for large amounts of defence expenditure, whereas less expenditure on other government services has tangible benefits.

At first glance political prediction would seem to be the most promising means of reducing both inflexibility in foreign policies and costs of defence. To the extent that the future could be predicted in detail and with certainty, the most advanced and appropriate defence systems could be planned to be operative at the appropriate time without the wastes of idleness and obsolescence.

Prediction relevant to defence and foreign policy concerns forecasting in many fields, including technological change, changing social values within States, demands by dependent peoples for participation in decision-making, struggles against the exercise of non-legitimized authority and power, racial and other communal conflicts, changes in efficiency in public administration and decision-making within States, the future of international organization, and all other influences of international concern.

However, generalizations at a macro- or micro-level about future trends in world society cannot be sufficiently specific or accurate to alter significantly the problems of defence planning. Even with all present knowledge of such generalizations, the view would persist amongst decision-makers that a State such as Britain must continue to plan to meet all the contingencies that it can within an acceptable allocation of defence resources. Consequently, while the theory of prediction is that forecasting of world events offers an encouraging prospect of reducing defence costs, in practice predictions about world society of a type that would be regarded as useful in defence planning are probably impossible.

So far we have been dealing with the prediction problem within a framework of all-purpose or unspecified defence needs. The problem has been discussed in the absence of stated goals, or precise descriptions of situations in which defence systems would be brought into operation. In determining levels of government expenditure on any public service two factors are involved. Firstly, there are goals to be achieved, and, secondly, there are provisions that must be made currently to achieve these goals in the changing conditions of the future. In education and health each community has defined standards: school leaving age, numbers in classes, and listed hospital and medical benefits. Provisions for the future can be made by reference to predicted alterations in size and composition of populations. The problem is of the same kind in defence. Once goals are set, prediction in relation to these should be possible. It is relevant for the research worker who is asked to predict political conditions relevant to defence, to ask what precisely are the types of situations toward which defence systems will, as a matter of policy, be directed. The prediction problem is then to predict the likely occurrence of such situations—a very different problem from predicting every change that affects international relations. The problem of defence planning may appear to be a problem of political prediction; in practice it is probably far more a problem of policy-making on the basis of which probabilities of certain situations occurring can reasonably be made.

The difference between defence planning with an all-purpose objective, and planning to meet defined conditions is clearer when placed in an historical perspective. The traditional means of determining levels of defence were by reference to available resources and capabilities. This was an approach which was appropriate for greater Powers in an era in which State interests were pursued within a power framework, and therefore conveniently defined in terms of power or capability. It was an approach relevant to a period of discovery, political expansion, imperialism and colonialism. Perceived State interests reflected State capacities to achieve interests: industrial, economic and military power were not just means of pursuing 'national interests', they also helped to determine them. Weak States had few interests they could defend; but great Powers had few interests that they were not prepared to defend. But in the contemporary world society there is no such clear power–goal relationship. The most powerful of States is not always capable of pursuing goals by military or power means. New influences are present such as altered values attached to independence, to human rights, to participation in decision-making, to welfare, and these are spreading rapidly within great States and elsewhere thanks to the spread of education and technological advances in communications. Whereas once a great Power could freely intervene in the affairs of another State, or accept an invitation to intervene from a faction within it, now it is restrained by many pressures and by increasing costs. Whereas once a great Power claimed rights to protect properties of its nationals in foreign countries, it is now less free to do this. In these contemporary and changing conditions, the relevant question to be asked and answered annually by a government is *not* what commitments and defence expenditures can be added to or must be subtracted from an existing defence budget to bring defence costs into line with available resources. It is what commitments can and should, and cannot and should not be undertaken as a matter of political policy.

The difference between the two approaches is not merely a procedural one. It is the difference between determining levels of defence by reference to national or alliance capability, on the one hand, and on the other by reference to assessed needs based upon specific policy decisions on the uses to which defence systems will be put. The first procedure requires first and foremost calculations of balance of payments, and of government revenue and expenditure. The second requires these also, but is primarily concerned with specific policy decisions and political judgements concerning conditions in which defence systems could and would be brought into operation. In short, in so far as there is specific defence planning based upon specific policy decisions in respect to specific conditions, then the prediction problem is the more limited one of assessing the possibilities of occurrence of these defined situations in which, as a matter of policy, the defence system would be called into operation. Is it intended that there will be defence of any government that alleges it is suffering from aggression? of any government that sees a possibility of aggression? of feudal governments that are threatened by indigenous forces? Is it implied that the force would be designed to prevent 'insurgency', and if so, how is this defined? Is it proposed that forces will be used to protect one race against another in a communal conflict, or some minority government against demands made by an ethnic majority? Governments are reluctant to commit themselves in advance even on matters which seem to be ones that can be determined within a given philosophy. But it needs to be stated that prediction relevant to defence becomes possible only when policies are defined: it is an evasion of the main problem, and a futile academic exercise, to cast around for some means of predicting likely defence needs in the absence of precise defence and foreign policies.

Political prediction relates to foreign policy-making. Consequently, the academic who is asked to predict political conditions within a defence context is also being asked to state a basis for foreign policy-making. But political prediction that challenges basic assumptions, philosophies and policies is unacceptable to governments. Looking back over the last twenty years, the surprising features have not been the events and trends of the period, but the failure of governments to take any notice of their existence, or to do other than to control them by coercive means once they have occurred. Probably the greatest costs of defence, and the greatest mistakes of foreign policy, have been due to a reluctance of administrations and political leaders to accept statements of analytically arrived-at probabilities, especially when these are, by implication, critical of past policies, when they cast doubt on political philosophies and judgements, when they imply that men and resources have been or are being wasted, and when local administrations and interests would be upset by the changes required to avoid a predictable situation.

The prediction that is relevant to defence planning includes the predicted consequences of past and present foreign policies. Policies contribute to future events, many of which are predictable in the light of these policies. Part of the reason for huge defence budgets is the consequences of current policies, and the absence of policies, that predictably help to create situations that require high defence budgets. In this sense the problem of predictability is part of the problem of policy-making, and not a separate problem.

One is led to query whether it is prediction that is the important problem in defence planning. If governments were prepared, first, to take policy decisions that realistically and in terms of their political philosophies defined situations of defence interest, and second, to acknowledge when formulating policies the reality of observable trends and testable propositions, the prediction problem would not be seen as a justification for large contingency budgets, and all-purpose defence systems.

(This subject of political prediction in relation to defence is of special relevance to Britain. Currently the foreign image of Britain is of a Power greatly weakened industrially and financially, and therefore forced to contract out of responsibilities once undertaken in Asia and elsewhere. This image is projected by defence planning that takes place within some budgetary figure. This is a false image. Welfare demands, altered values and attitudes, acknowledgement in Britain and elsewhere of the right of other peoples to determine their own futures, have led a Britain that is much more wealthy than ever before to contract out of a great Power role. As a matter of policy this same contraction could and probably would have taken place in due course even if Britain were in a better financial position. A different image of Britain would be projected if defence planning were seen to be based, not on capacity and budgets, but upon specific policy decisions regarding conditions in which defence resources would in the future, as a matter of deliberate policy, be employed. The probability is that the defence budget could then be greatly reduced—if the obvious resistances could be overcome. Status once depended upon military power. In the contemporary world status rests far more upon policy leadership; Britain with a small defence budget and clearly defined policies that reflected the values of world society could have a greater status and influence in world affairs than it has at present with a defence expenditure of £2,000 millions.)

These considerations serve to underline the need for diplomacy to have general theories and tested propositions of international politics that are not the conventional ones that guide defence planning; otherwise, in effect if not in appearance, the foreign office remains the servant of the defence department. The role of the State in world affairs then becomes the Machiavellian one, and not that which is required to meet the needs of systems within and crossing the boundaries of States.

12

ON DIPLOMACY

The *Oxford English Dictionary* defines diplomacy as 'the management of international relations by negotiation; the method by which these relations are adjusted and managed by ambassadors and envoys; the business or art of the diplomatist'. Nicolson, in his study of the subject, adopted this definition on the grounds that it was important to make a distinction between the role of the decision-maker and that of the diplomatic corps: it seemed to him that such a distinction was in accord with the nature of democratic institutions in which elected representatives are the decision-makers.[1]

This is not a definition which is meaningful in practice. Earlier it was found necessary to refer to administrative systems that included both political holders of office and permanent officials, and that had the functions of making and executing policies, on the grounds that the political appointees in practice had the role of interpreting the values and interests of the whole community and responding to all pressure groups, and not merely those that elected them. It is especially so in the field of foreign affairs. Values and interests concerned are widely shared within the administrative system and the community. Furthermore, the administrative machinery of defence and foreign policy-making is vast, and forward planning, especially in modern defence, is necessary. The occupants of elected positions cannot radically affect this. Even on a day-to-day basis, decision-making and administration cannot be separated. The formal decision-maker is frequently a negotiator; thanks to developments in travel and communications he can leave his base and still retain full control of his office. On the other hand, the permanent official in foreign, commercial, financial and defence departments of administration is frequently in a decision-making role: preliminary negotiations that tend to determine final decisions are conducted at technical levels. In some circumstances there may be a distinction to be made between a representative of a State serving in a foreign country,

[1] Sir Harold Nicolson, *Diplomacy*, 3rd ed., 1963, p. 15.

and the home-based adviser; but they are exchangeable and in close communication. It is doubtful whether the narrow concept of diplomacy that excluded policy decision-making was ever a meaningful one: the making and execution of foreign policy were never entirely separate. In contemporary conditions of highly developed permanent civil services and improved communications the term diplomacy is best used to include the whole process of managing relations with other States and international institutions, including the complicated processes of perception of the environment from a locality or from a central office, assessment of immediate and longer-term interests, balancing of internal and external pressures, testing of likely responses to proposed policies, final implementation, and perception of the environment once again—in a never-ending sequence.

I. TRADITIONAL DIPLOMACY

Diplomacy originated within a limited world society of expanding feudal States. It was an instrument fashioned and generally accepted amongst States on the commonly held assumptions that each State then made regarding the nature of other States, their propensity to expand, their aggressiveness, and their readiness to employ force either to preserve an interest or to pursue one. Certain diplomatic rights were mutually accorded. The period of traditional diplomacy was one in which the major decisions affecting international society were taken by a limited number of powerful States—European States in the main. When the responses of other powerful States were relevant, diplomacy included the important art of local persuasion, and the imposition of a policy if possible without recourse to the threat or use of force. Diplomacy was an instrument of power politics. Morgenthau analysed it as an important element of national power; even diplomatic ceremonial attracted his special attention. In his view, the task of diplomacy was fourfold: '1. Diplomacy must determine its objectives in the light of the power actually or potentially available for the pursuit of these objectives. 2. Diplomacy must assess the objectives of other nations and the power actually or potentially available for the pursuit of these objectives. 3. Diplomacy must determine to what extent these different objectives are compatible with each other. 4. Diplomacy must employ the means suited to the pursuit of its objectives.'[1] In these terms, traditional diplomacy was the art of the possible, the art of accommodation, and the art of coercion. Diplomacy was the means of pursuing a power policy to the limit, but avoiding where possible the use of force. It was the means by which threats and counter-threats were communicated, by which evaluations were made as to the substance of threats and of the force supporting them. If diplomacy revealed the existence on one side of a willingness to use superior force, then violence might be avoided. If the diplomatic combat failed to 'demonstrate a clear position of military or economic advantage on either side, the issue might be resolved temporarily by an acceptable compromise. If the diplomatic combat left each of the contestants convinced that it had the advantage, then an actual test of force might be the result. In the circumstances an important part of diplomacy was to convince others that one's State was more powerful than other States—even though this might not have been the case, and be known by one not to have been the case. Secrecy, bluff and counter-bluff, espionage and counter-espionage, prestige displays of military might and nationalist propaganda for foreign consumption, were all part of this diplomatic procedure. The diplomatic process rested finally upon an assumption that a State could measure its power and the power of other States by reference to forces, industrial potential, population, location and other power factors: wars were evidence of misinformation and miscalculation.

Traditional diplomacy was an instrument fashioned to meet the needs of States in the context of the following propositions:

Man was by nature aggressive, at least when behaving in international society;

the quest for power was universal and a fundamental drive;

States, being led by and comprising men, were aggressive and sought power;

some States were more aggressive and more inclined to seek power than others because of variations in needs, human qualities, social institutions and philosophies; and

each State was in these circumstances obliged to organize its defences against the potential aggressive designs of others.

[1] H. Morgenthau, *Politics Among Nations*, 3rd ed., 1960, p. 539.

These five propositions logically led to the assumption that conflict of 'vital interests' between States could be contained only within a threat system, and, if not contained, could be resolved only by violence. The device of power balances, and the organization of collective security to which its failure gave rise, were the operative means of containing violence. They were designed to preserve existing power relationships. Any alterations that took place were those that these arrangements could not contain; changed relationships could come about only by the exercise of force or the threat of force.

Once these propositions and the operative assumption to which they gave rise were accepted, once they formed the basis of State policy and practice, a sequence of events was likely to occur:

each State perceived the defence preparations of others as potential defence against change it sought, or as potential aggression in the pursuit of change it sought to avoid;

no State enjoyed security standing alone in conditions of greatly differentiated power, and each tended, therefore, to seek alliances;

even though these alliances were defensive and designed deliberately merely to create power balances, they stimulated other alliances;

power balances evolved into attempts at securing favourable balances, and arms competition was established;

breakdowns in the balance system, due to the failure of States to give pride of place in policy to maintaining balances, due to attempts by dissatisfied powers to alter conditions, and due also to miscalculation of power balances, led to war;

war settlements led to wider, even universal collective security; and

the collective security instituted after wars was a favourable power balance under the cloak of international institutions, and this led to subsequent challenges by dissatisfied Powers.

There is evidence to suggest that this mobilization system, in which threat and violence were the main means to change, was generally accepted as inevitable, at least until the weapons of violence were nuclear. At this point intellectual confusion became widespread:

breakdowns in collective security had traditionally led thinkers to advocate some form of world government with a monopoly of power, on the analogy of the internal development of the modern State;

but such a world government needed to be preceded by, or accompanied by disarmament and the creation of an international monopoly of force;

however, disarmament was contrary to the needs of the perceived conditions that originally persuaded States to adopt national defences and alliances;

hence, the starting point seemed to be the elimination of States;

apart from the fact that the world system is one of sovereign States, and that the basic problem is the defence of these, few governments or individuals favoured a world imperialism, or the substitution of a civil war for international war; consequently,

the introduction of the nuclear weapon seemed to require that the theoretically impossible be pursued as policy.

Experience pointed to some inadequacy of theory and practice as evidence appeared of self-defeating elements within any power approach to relations with other States: there were certain obvious dilemmas in seeking both peace and security when the means to national security either posed a threat or were interpreted by others as a threat. The diplomat in these circumstances was an artist, aware that he could have only limited success in achieving his goals of peace and security, aware that he was likely to be defeating his own ends; he continued his activities because there appeared to be no alternative. In recent years States have continued to conduct their diplomatic affairs within this traditional and self-defeating power framework, despite altered conditions. The United Kingdom demands on Egypt which preceded the Suez crisis in 1956, and the United States demands on Cuba which finally led to landings by exiles in 1961 and to Soviet intervention in 1962, and the Soviet intervention itself, were examples. In the absence of any clear-cut policy alternatives, the political form of this confused thinking has been to seek arms control where possible, to reduce political tensions where possible, to make mutual deterrence more efficient, and meanwhile to continue the traditional art of diplomacy.

The assumptions of traditional diplomacy led to confused thinking and self-defeating policies; they were conspicuously irrelevant to the conditions that developed simultaneously with and through technological advances in communications. Nuclear restraints, pressures of political consensus applied to authorities within States and from world society, and the altered values that emerged with the growth of the Welfare State, led to a weakening of the power framework in which States had traditionally operated. Diplomacy in its decision-making and implementation evolved within a power framework, on the basis that relations between States were perceived as power-dominated. The same diplomatic process continued to operate in circumstances in which force was clearly not a useful instrument of policy, even as a last resort, and therefore in circumstances in which policies, goals and means needed to be reviewed and altered in the light of unanticipated responses by others. In the altered conditions of the nuclear–welfare age, power and diplomatic practice were no longer effective substitutes for knowledge, or a relevant compensation for an inability to adjust policies to changing circumstances.

Perhaps the conditions for which the instrument of power diplomacy was evolved existed at one period in the history of inter-State relations; perhaps, on the other hand, the fashioning of the instrument was due to assumptions that were not valid, but were made valid by its creation. This problem of past self-prophesying policies may never be solved. But the employment of an instrument fashioned for conditions that no longer apply invites operative failure. Contemporary world society is characterized by threat relationships in conditions in which warfare is unacceptable, and in which threat and deterrence are no longer credible or effective means of forcing States and communities to sacrifice their goals and values. Greater Powers are less and less able now to determine the behaviour of small States, either directly or indirectly, as their interventions in South-East Asia and the Middle East have demonstrated.

It is not fully appreciated that diplomacy as still practised is frequently destructive of relationships, and creates misunderstandings and tensions. Within a traditional power framework diplomacy does not provide communication; it does not enable

States to perceive accurately and to know the real intentions of other States. Diplomacy injects 'noise' into communication systems. It is calculated to prevent efficient decision-making. In the course of 'controlled communication' research reported in the companion study, there were occasions in which parties involved in discussions met third parties within a normal diplomatic context. Subsequently they reported that there had been conversation but no communication of any fact, attitude or policy, whereas around the academic table there was almost uninhibited communication. Exchanges within this controlled communication pinpointed instances in which authorities that had been in diplomatic contact had failed to communicate information and intentions that would have radically altered perceptions, and perhaps avoided conflict. Assessments of situations made on the basis of personalities, mutual assumptions that each side is seeking to deceive the other, reporting of diplomatic party hearsay by representatives that have little direct contact with decision-makers, are merely some of the sources of 'noise' that prevent communication and lead to false perceptions and irrelevant responses.

Other instruments of the bargaining or power framework of diplomacy are mediation, arbitration and conciliation—the whole area of negotiation. There are few important differences of interest amongst States that are negotiable because most involve values. Reperceptions of intentions and attitudes, and the revelation of choices is possible by accurate communication, but not by bargaining and the usual processes of diplomacy. Apparent differences of interests between States present problems to be solved; but diplomacy is primarily an instrument of contest, not of problem-solving.

II. DECISION-MAKING IN PRACTICE

The concern with State decision-making, which is now reflected in most contemporary writing in the area of international politics, draws attention to the common belief or assumption that decision-making processes of politically developed States are efficient. The foreign offices of European States are amongst the most experienced, and in terms of conventional diplomatic procedures amongst the most sophisticated. But this is not evidence that these States are efficient in terms of attaining their goals. The First World War was not immediately due to conflicts of interest that could not be resolved. It was due to false perceptions, faulty and inadequate information, failure to adjust and alter unattainable goals, and finally faulty costing of war in terms of goals sought. The Second World War was associated with settlements of the First, with unemployment in Germany and lack of markets for Japan; but there was no unavoidable conflict except in so far as western decision-making failed to perceive the consequences of western economic policies, and of depressed conditions and the remedies then pursued, and in so far as decision-making in Italy, Germany and Japan was overwhelmed by internal conditions. Given the circumstances, these wars were inevitable—at least they occurred; but amongst the circumstances was inefficient decision-making in respect of internal and external policies. International institutions with enforcement powers can help powerful States patch over their own reluctance or failure to adjust to internal and external politics by helping to suppress dissatisfied States; they cannot of themselves promote conditions of peace.

This realization of State responsibility has focused attention upon decision-making theory, upon the use of force as evidence of failure in decision-making processes, upon cybernetics or steering, goal-changing, feed-back and adjustment. This is the advance in contemporary thinking over thinking in any past age: States are now being forced to introspect, to re-examine their own roles, in the endeavour to find sources of conflict. Empirical research is persistently raising questions such as whether perception by States of other States is accurate, information is reliable, processing is efficient, feed-back is leading to adjustment, or whether there are blockages in the information, decision, and implementation processes—whether national decision-making is as efficient in terms of its goals as is ordinary industrial management.

It has been argued that the task of diplomacy is wider than representation in foreign States; it is the whole decision-making process. In practice it is even wider. The foreign decision-making process is part of a whole: the interplay of domestic and foreign influences renders a foreign office ineffective unless it serves to combine all relevant influences in its decision-making processes. Even in the nuclear age, no politically responsible person would agree that all domestic policies should be subordinated to the requirements of peace; equally, in the nuclear age, a politically responsible person must agree that domestic policies, and more particularly domestic pressures, cannot be allowed to endanger peace. Foreign offices of European States were apparently powerless a century ago to prevent policies of 'imperialism', which in retrospect appear not to have been in the national interest, and were advanced because of group interests. One could as readily argue now that the cause of tension in international politics is that many authorities are not masters in their own house. It is in this sense that even the most sophisticated foreign offices, however efficient in diplomatic protocol, are inefficient in their decision-making processes. Decision-making is influenced by popular images and stereotypes, by educational systems, by procedures of recruitment, by mass media, by a host of factors that are important in the modern State. Diplomacy is a profession, and like the medical and other professions, it has a status that reflects the ignorance of those outside it of the knowledge and skills required to practise it. Indeed, despite the absence of any specific professional training, diplomacy has a high professional status, due perhaps to a degree of secrecy and mystery that its practitioners self-consciously promote. It is less awe-inspiring the more that is known of it. In practice it is quite unprofessional in any scientific sense, and grossly inefficient in most of its functions outside the routines of diplomatic protocol and administration—where it usually excels. Other professions have an input from a science: professional diplomacy has traditionally been learned by practising the art, by apprenticeship. There has been no new input from any science.

Some of the problems of diplomacy are due to the sociological fact that responsible persons are usually those who ceased to learn, in a formal sense, some twenty years previously. Different concepts and methods seem to be complicated and inconclusive merely because they were not part of one's general education: those who have not the required training react against the use of mathematics in various branches of social science. This is a serious problem in the formal study of International Relations even at the teaching level; there are those in academic work who prefer to hold to what they know, rather than to grapple with the complications of contemporary theory. Today, teachers of International Relations, and particularly textbook writers, are still often persons educated in a pre-war and pre-nuclear era. Most were not trained in the relatively new discipline, International Relations: they are historians, economists or students of politics. They tend to approach international relations from the viewpoint of the discipline from which they came, and rarely have they been able to acquire a special knowledge of any other discipline. Furthermore, they understandably tend to interpret world events in the perspective of the world they knew at the point of their active thinking. They tend to assume that what they know, that those things with which they are familiar by experience, are the most simple for present-day students to learn; for instance, the history and problems of power balances, collective security and international institutions. They are not always aware of the extent to which students today are thinking in different terms due to their different experiences at the time of their most active thinking. Analogies with electronics are now being exploited in current endeavours to understand relations between States, because electronics help to explain self-regulating processes. The undergraduate of today is able to absorb contemporary interdisciplinary theory, and also the challenges that are being made to our traditionally held assumptions and theories. The more recent thought is more meaningful, more relevant, and therefore more readily understood, than the simple explanations of relations between States that were current before 1950. Contemporary 'jargon' of which traditionalists complain—'feedback' and 'cybernetics'—is more meaningful than the traditional 'jargon'—'power balances' and 'power vacuums'.

Senior practitioners, and the makers of foreign policy within States, are today those who have equally been educated in a pre-nuclear, pre-independence period, and decision-making continues to reflect this. The western decision-maker, in many cases acting in the cultural background of a former colonial Power, cannot easily identify with those peoples who choose independence rather than to continue to live in a condition of relative public order. Nor can they easily think about propositions other than that power provides an adequate explanation of modern State relationships, and an adequate guide to policy.

The effect of communications upon diplomacy is not merely related to the point at which decisions are taken and who takes them, but more importantly, to the complexity of decision-making. The diplomacy of the pre-communications period required the appointment of ambassadors and staff who represented the viewpoints of their ruling monarch or government. The education they required, over and above a general education, was in the languages and histories of the countries to which they were accredited. As far as great Powers were concerned, these countries were predominantly European even as late as last century. In this century, greater variations in constitutional processes, the rise to positions of importance of States that have non-European languages and unfamiliar histories, the emergence of functional institutions, a vastly increased interdependence amongst States in all aspects of life, a greater emphasis than in any previous age on internal welfare, have helped to alter the tasks of diplomacy. Language and history are no longer sufficient as equipment. The most experienced practitioner cannot hold in the focus of his attention all the interrelated factors that must be taken into account if policy is to be conceived in such a way as not to defeat itself. The traditional procedures of interdepartmental consultation and advisory opinions of specialists are not sufficient to meet the difficulties. Practitioners now require, in addition to their traditional skills, some basic propositions and theories to ensure that nuclear age decision-making is at least as efficient in the field of peace and war as it is in the field of factory management and production.

Diplomacy involves the study of all those aspects of world civilization which bear upon relations between the independent States which comprise world society; every event, development, change in attitude or external appearance of change which takes place within a State and which affects the behaviour of other States, falls within the study of diplomacy. One must today go even further. There are matters which, as we are reminded by the United Nations Charter, are essentially matters of domestic jurisdiction. These were to remain outside the scope of discussion and decision within the United Nations, unless they could be related to threats to peace. Nevertheless, from the point of view of the contemporary decision-maker, any event, development or change which takes place within any State, or even within a national group whose boundaries are within but not identical with the boundaries of the State in which it lies, must be regarded as relevant: the relations of all racial, language, cultural and religious groups are of increasing concern in the wider field of relations between States because they affect these relations, even though they may be claimed by State authorities to be matters of domestic jurisdiction.

Defined in this way, diplomacy is interdisciplinary in that it is concerned with recent extensions of many social studies such as economics, psychology, anthropology and geography. It is also interdisciplinary in a second sense. Diplomacy involves the study of the behaviour of States. A State, a large group, a small group, a corporation, a voluntary society, a person and an animal, each has its own special characteristics which enables each to be differentiated from others. Each has its own behavioural pattern, its own distinctive responses. A science developed in relation to the behaviour of one may throw some light upon the behaviour of others, but finally the distinctive behaviour of each must be examined. Diplomacy needs the support of its own specialized behavioural studies; while it draws upon psychology, it also requires special psychological studies in so far as the actors on the international stage are men and small groups playing special roles, and in so far as the study of the behaviour of States is not part of general psychology.

In most countries diplomacy is still commonly regarded as an art, and the training of the diplomat is in the Arts; but there is now a literature, a discipline and a scientific method of relevance to it. In terms of university curricula it includes the theory of institutions and of functionalism, decision-making, the interplay of politics at the domestic and international levels, the interplay of economic and political relations, conditions of world order, the problems of peace and security, and other aspects of relations between States; more formally it deals with the total behaviour of States. It is a matter for discussion whether the analysis of, and theorizing about, international society is still an academic occupation remote from the practice of diplomacy; but there is little doubt that every State will in the future be giving attention to the academic and scientific aspects of diplomacy. In the competitive world of the twentieth century there is a premium on diplomatic skill which increases as capability to employ force recedes in importance under strategic and political pressures. The State that succeeds best in achieving its goals will be the State whose practitioners understand best the operation and management of relations between States:

less and less will power compensate for deficiencies in decision-making.

In so far as common goals of States are peace and security, it is not sufficient for only one State to be skilled and to succeed: the skill of managing relations between States must be widespread amongst them. Diplomacy is not a zero-sum game: the more skill other States have, the more and not the less likely it is that each State can achieve its purposes. Indeed, the policies of the most skilled States, seeking only those national interests compatible with a universal interest, can be defeated and lead to conflict if the decision-making processes of other States are defective. False perception and false images, failure to assimilate available information, inflexible procedures, committed viewpoints and even breakdowns in simple administrative processes, can lead to aggressive policies in a State that otherwise has no aggressive intent. A universal understanding, at a decision-making level, of the operations of the international system, is not a too-fanciful expectation: it will occur when theorists and practitioners work closely together, just as it occurred in the field of international finance in the late thirties when economic scientists and treasuries almost universally co-operated in the handling of depression unemployment.

While the foreign offices of States cannot be held wholly responsible for foreign policies, being only one element in a total decision-making process, they are the focal points of formal decision-making in the field of foreign relations. They must be deemed inefficient—regardless of the excellence of their administrative procedures—in so far as they fail to determine national interests, perceive accurately the policies of others, and formulate policies accordingly. As an efficient administrative machine they are no more than the servants of commercial, political and strategic pressure groups. Indeed, they have this role, and this role only, unless they have a theory so persuasive and relevant that it can influence these sectional interests.

III. A PROBLEM OF ADMINISTRATION

The traditional approach to international relations, which rests upon history and analysis of contemporary situations, has its administrative counterpart in the structure of foreign and defence offices. In a typical foreign office, input regarding a situation is fed into regional divisions, where there are specialists in certain areas and countries who endeavour to integrate and to interpret new information. The detailed information that is compiled is fed to more senior officials with wider responsibilities who seek to sift out the more significant facts. The end of this process is a submission to a formal decision-maker which is intended to be brief and to the point. At each successive level of the decision-making hierarchy, details are sifted out by arbitrary means; no two people would sift out the same facts. Defence procedures are similar, and equally aim to produce a boiled-down appreciation of a situation.

Even thus treated, total input is likely to overload decision-making, and the formal decision-maker is likely, in these circumstances, to adopt the most clear-cut policy, such as the use of force to prevent social change. Once such a tentative step has been taken, others, not necessarily intended, follow automatically. With more time for thought, with a different sifting out of information, different recommendations might be made and different decisions taken.

A breakdown in decision-making, which is what the employment of force usually signifies, traces back to a fault in administration, and this in turn can be traced to a misconception about the administrative processes of decision-making. Clearly there is a need for the regional 'expert' with a full knowledge of local features of a situation. But the official who is sifting the facts requires a different training: he need not have knowledge of the facts, but he does need to be in a position to ask the appropriate questions of those who do. An arbitrary sifting of what appear to be relevant facts usually draws attention to personality and ideological features, the aspects that press reporters might find newsworthy. A sifting on the basis of a framework or theory would call attention to a different set of features. It would warn against some decisions that run counter to tested or derived hypotheses, it would at the same time point to other means of achieving stated policy goals, and even to alterations in these goals. It would protect decision-makers against stereotypes, and against conclusions based on preconceived ideological notions.

Here we face a serious practical problem of administration. Even the older and more experienced foreign offices of today contain few, if any, officials who are aware of contemporary systems analysis or who have a theoretical framework in which to operate—except a traditional and rather crude version of power, power balances, power vacuums and zero-sum conceptions of international relations. Knowledge of languages, a great deal of specialized local knowledge and 'experience' in handling diplomatic relations is widely possessed. The only qualification apparently required to be a sifter of facts is the additional qualification of seniority. There are gatherers of information, juniors; and sifters and co-ordinators, seniors. To insert a line of trained sifters is virtually impossible because in a hierarchical structure in which co-ordination and sifting are treated as superior functions, there would be resistance. The specialized sifter would have to serve his time as a regional specialist, and first of all acquire language and other qualifications to be admitted to the structure at this level. By the time he became a sifter he would be out of touch with theoretical thinking. It took time for graduates to be accepted into public services; it will take time for specialist graduates to be accepted. The foreign office of the United Kingdom still recruits from the administrative class: no professional qualification is acknowledged despite the existence of graduates who have completed specialized degrees at government expense. What is required is an understanding of the interplay in decision-making of inductive and deductive approaches. The regional specialists are required in large numbers at junior and senior levels, and they are the central pool from which the foreign service is staffed. But the specialists in analysis are also required at junior and senior levels, though in smaller numbers, and they should constitute the continuity of central administration, and provide special missions in relation to current situations. The training required is different: no one person can be up to date as an international relations specialist and also as a current affairs specialist. Neither is 'superior' to the other; each requires the other.

There is a more detailed aspect of this same problem. Foreign representatives of business and governments are usually required to report at regular intervals according to procedures laid down: a State requires regular reports from its representatives on leading political personalities, trade and financial indices, and matters of this kind. Techniques of analysing and reporting a total political situation, as is required in a situation of conflict, in which large numbers of variables are relevant, have not been developed. There are some communication and administrative reasons why this is so. In the days before instantaneous communication, and when international relations were confined to the relations between a small number of predominantly European States, the means of reporting were carefully considered despatches which in many cases were copied, distributed and even read by advisers and decision-makers. There were thorough descriptions of personalities and circumstances, and though in the light of contemporary theory they may not have drawn attention to many significant features they did convey a background in which seemingly reasonable decisions could be taken. In the contemporary world, diplomatic reporting is virtually confined to short and regular cabled reports of events, little different from, and frequently merely to confirm, press reporting. A thorough analysis sent by despatch, on the rare occasions when it is made, is unlikely to be seen except by a few junior officials who have the time and inclination to read it. The new conditions, in which short telegrams are thumbed through by decision-makers who rely upon advisers to draw their attention to any significant messages or important passages that might have been missed, provide the opportunity for the free play of individual preconceived notions and prejudices. The short telegram highlights an aspect of interest to the official drafting it, its handling upon receipt in the foreign office reflects notions there, and the selection of material by officials at lower levels for consideration by officials and formal decision-makers at high levels are determined by interest and prejudice. In short, the older style of reporting, which at least gave a full picture according to the perceptions of the diplomatic reporters, has been replaced by briefer reporting and severe selection, unaided by any system of analysis designed to ensure that essential features are being noted. Whether it be despatch, telegram, or summary analysis, a knowledge of what to look for is clearly essential if reporting is to divert attention towards significant, and not merely superficial features of a situation.

The administrative problem is basically one of education. The solution is probably a general theoretical and analytical training on which to build reporting and analytical functions. The education that practitioners receive has been a general one. Supported by intelligence and the cultural background that is deemed desirable, they adopt a 'common sense' approach to problems of diplomacy. But there is a difference between a common sense frame of reference and a scientific theoretical system. Within a scientific framework what previously appeared to be common sense frequently turns out to be nonsense. A power approach to politics is a common sense one, so is the judicial or coercive approach to disputes. The punishment approach to learning and to crime were once thought to be common sense.

All too often, those who adopt a common sense approach see the problem in traditional ways and fail to abstract the key factors. As a consequence, the solution is likely to be an inefficient one. For example, in an area torn by racial dissension, a playground director may 'solve' the problem of gang fights between boys of different races by allotting different playground hours and days to the various gangs. This may 'work' in the sense that the fights are avoided. However, since it fails to grapple with the causes of tension and this outlet for it, the solution is inefficient and very likely helps to maintain the existing situation.[1]

Within the fields of education, economics and public finance, and more recently in the field of sociology, governments have been able to turn to specialists for advice on policies and to help solve problems, very much as they have been able to enlist the technical assistance of those concerned with health and engineering; but in foreign relations, while advice has come from historians, lawyers, economists and others with a general interest in world affairs, little contribution has been made by scholars that have made International Relations their special field. In the largest foreign offices there are few, and, in some important cases, no officials that have had a specialized training in International Relations. Whatever were the reasons for this, it need not be the position in the future; there is now available an integrated body of literature on international relations on which to base teaching courses, advice, and techniques of conflict analysis and the resolution of conflict. There is a body of theory that can be translated into guide-lines of policy. Foreign policy decision-making can now be transformed from an art into an applied science, and new instruments of communication can now be fashioned.

Once it is accepted that the ideal we seek is State integration, and not international supra-State control of disturbed States,

[1] W. J. Goode and P. K. Hatt, *Methods in Social Research*, 1952, p. 37.

once it is accepted that steps towards this ideal are progressive improvements in decision-making, including capabilities of adjustment to changes in the environment by means that do not provoke non-passive responses in others, there are immediate fields of co-operation for practitioner and scientist. The first is the field of training in international behavioural studies that will provide skills in perceptions, in interpretation, and in choices of goals, in cost analyses of alternatives, and in the promotion of integration in the national State and in other States. The second is in the field of investigation and advice, especially at a stage before relevantly trained scholars are available for policy work. The third is the field of research into behavioural aspects of relations between States that can be studied only in existing conditions. The fourth is the field of conflict resolution. As Deutsch commented in relation to similar proposals, 'This is a very modest programme, but in the age of nuclear energy it is, perhaps, a programme worth pressing'.[1]

[1] In *Conflict in Society*, p. 316.

Masonic
Propaganda

PART IV
Guide-lines

13

INTERNATIONAL GUIDE-LINES

In a previous chapter it was suggested that decision-making in international politics required the guidance of faiths, creeds, myths, superstitions, theories or rules to overcome the problem created by a great many and variety of altering behavioural interactions. Most applied sciences are based upon rules and tested procedures; what is sought in international politics are some that can be used as reliable guides in the making and carrying out of State foreign policy.

There are four possible sources of guiding rules. First there are the past common practices of States. The analysis already made of the nature of world society causes us to reject these. States operate in an environment of States and an infinite number and variety of systems, each having their own needs and interests: it is the purpose of States to defend interests they represent, and sometimes these are the interests of administrations and of sectional interests. State policies tend to be self-defeating of longer-term goals such as security and peaceful relations because they tend to create conflict between States and the wider systems within which they exist, thus promoting conflict with other communities and States. Protective tariffs, reserved markets, control of foreign resources, discrimination, denial of participation to others, foreign bases, control of information, non-recognition—these and many others are practices of States, and each in its own way is calculated to break up political, economic, cultural and related systems, and to control the influence of systems on States. Each is a defensive response to changes in systems that are wider than States. Other States involved in the same systems respond, some favourably, some unfavourably. Practices such as these all require power support, and power escalation is inevitable. Conflict situations are created and they tend to become dysfunctional. It is just because State behaviour has this capacity to be self-defeating that it requires guide-lines for its day-to-day decisions: past State practices cannot be a helpful source of guiding rules of behaviour designed to prevent past patterns of behaviour.

Even treaties and contracts, which provide a more precise expression of State practices, cannot be accepted as guides to purposeful behaviour. They are the outcome of the endeavours of authorities to seek State and group interests, and these may not reflect the systemic needs and interests of all other communities and States involved in common interests. A test-ban treaty may secure the interests of some States at the expense of developments of systemic importance to others. Many trade treaties are non-systemic in character, and create conflict between States. These are merely the final and formal product of the State relationships and practices that we have already rejected as a guide to State behaviour. As far as treaties and agreements are concerned, it is only those that comprehend the totality of relevant systems that can serve as a guide to policy, for example functional agreements that are universal in application and include all States. In practice they help to guide State policies: States accept the decisions of these organizations for the reason that the boundaries and values of the totality of States are identical with the operational areas and values of the functional systems concerned. There is total legitimacy. There is no conflict between State and system, and therefore none between State and State. State practices are in these cases guided by the needs and values of a system common to all. (There can be conflict within a functional organization over matters outside the systemic relationship of the functional system concerned, for example, conflict over membership. This merely signifies the existence of conflict between States within a different system of relationships.)

A third possible source of rules of State behaviour is experience —not the experience of States severally and together, but the experience of world society as can be perceived by historical accounts. Experience, if accurately recorded, should indicate where and how State practices have failed, and behaviour that is and is not self-defeating should be discernible. History has been able to record the evidence of failure—history is predominantly a record of failure in State relationships—but it has been less helpful in ascertaining the reasons for it. Where interpretations have been made they have inevitably reflected the theories of the historians, and, in any event, the records have not been sufficiently detailed for analytical purposes. 'Content Analysis' of history as more recently developed is beginning to describe State behaviour and interactions in ways that might in the future provide some specific rules for decision-making.

A fourth source is the needs and values of systems and States, and in the perspective of the analysis of this study these seem to be the logical source. The pull of systems that extend beyond State boundaries ultimately controls sub-systems and State behaviour. The ideal condition is one in which State and internal and external systemic needs and values coincide: if State authorities wish to achieve goals reliably, then they must pursue policies that conform with the needs and values of the systems concerned. A society becomes a community when the units comprising it have shared values: world society has some community features, and these increase as States perform the role of bringing systems within their exclusive jurisdiction into a relationship with the wider system of world society.

It would seem logical to argue that whatever rules are suitable to guide States in their independent behaviour within a world society that includes other States are also the rules against which to judge whether the behaviour of a State on a particular occasion is in the interest of other States within the some world society.

This view has not been possible in International Law because it has been assumed that State interests—outside limited areas of co-ordinated activity and co-operative or reciprocal behaviour —are inevitably in conflict: law has traditionally concerned itself with regulating conflicting relationships. International collective security institutions had the same purpose: they attempted to enforce decisions held to be in accordance with law. But this traditional law is predominantly the law of non-systemic behaviour. War and dysfunctional conflict of all kinds are 'legal', and attempts have been made to define legally the 'aggressive' and 'defensive' uses of force.

[The difference between the two approaches can be seen in the distinction made by lawyers between co-ordinated and power behaviour. It has been legally convenient to make this distinction because agreements can be made and are observed in a reciprocal context, but not in the political context, thus seeming to point to the success of a legal approach in some areas and the need to extend international judicial procedures and control where power relations are involved. From a political science point of view reciprocal and co-ordinated behaviour is systemic behaviour: State action that coincides with the needs of the relevant systems and therefore the needs of other States within them. Power behaviour is non-systemic behaviour, and it is self-defeating. The remedy is not to introduce an outside agent or set of 'normative laws' to control such behaviour, but to provide States with the theories, insights, and rules that enable them to achieve their goals without running into the self-defeating conflicts inherent in non-systemic behaviour. It is not international coercion that is primarily required, but State decision-making based upon knowledge, or theories and rules that are a substitute for it. If such guide rules were to be translated into international legal terminology, and thus provide States with a normative standard that had the psychological support which the 'rule of law' sometimes attracts, then this could be helpful in inducing States to maintain this standard.

There are examples of systemic rules already in existence. For example, rules about the training of pilots and safety measures are required by each State in the protection of its own people, and because of the international nature of air systems, these obtain a universal character. The boundaries and values of the totality of States and of the system are identical: the rules are enforced at the State level, and without conflict. There are all manner of similar rules in the areas of health, communications and trade practices that apply in the same way. Sizes and powers of States are not relevant: what is relevant is that State practice accords with systemic needs.

It is apparent that these functional arrangements deal with matters that have little political content: values are not involved. System and State needs are no longer identical when political content is introduced: power tends to determine the outcome of relationships. But the normative standard against which power relations must be judged still relates to systemic behaviour: it cannot be found within the non-systemic behaviour of past practices of States, which it is the purpose of systemic rules to eliminate.

This becomes clearer by progressing toward State practices that are more and more non-systemic, that is from reciprocal to power behaviour. Standards for pilots are agreed. More difficulty would be experienced in instituting rules governing the training of foreign office officials—though a functional organization concerned with diplomacy generally, and with standards of entry and training in particular, might be welcomed by governments as a means of offsetting political and social pressures that they sometimes experience in the making of appointments. Difficulty has already been experienced in drafting and having ratified conventions relating to conditions of work. Group pressures outweigh perceived systemic needs. Even more difficulty is found in the drafting of agreed rules of State behaviour when States are intent upon the protection of non-systemic needs, such as declining industries, and in maintaining preference systems within alliance groups. This has been the failing of GATT and UNCTAD. Past State practices are then a convenient justification; but they cannot afford any normative standard. The only normative standard is the needs of the relevant economic systems; these relate to theories of economic development and the political consequences of economic backwardness, and not to past State practices.

Moving even further into the area of political and power relations, State practice seems to justify the giving of assistance to a government of a State by another when the former seeks this in the absence of a legitimized status. United States intervention in Vietnam was no different in this respect from hundreds of other instances, many in Asia since 1945, when governments, which could not maintain themselves because of changes in social, political and economic systems, appealed for support. In systemic terms, the threatened governments had no legitimized role, and foreign support merely enabled temporarily the pull of systemic changes to be resisted. Equally, intervention by subversion can succeed only to the extent that systemic needs and values are thereby being satisfied. Normative rules based upon systems would in these cases run counter to normative rules based upon past State practices: they would bar intervention that was designed to give power support to administrations and policies that were incompatible with systemic needs and values.

The traditional legal rule postulates that if you do so and so, such and such will be the consequence. Rules founded upon systemic needs and values carry no moral, coercive or threatening implications. They merely say certain goals are attainable in certain ways, some tactics will be self-defeating, some can be attained only at dysfunctional cost, and some cannot be attained even by the use of force. This is also the basis of the behaviour of the individual in society, and of the social conventions formulated for his guidance.

A first step in arriving at systemic rules of conduct is to state the results of theoretical analysis of systems in proposition form. Once these are restated in operational terms and tested, they are the raw material of the State rules of the diplomatic game. The formulation and testing of guide-lines is a process that invites the closest co-operation of political scientist, diplomat and lawyer. Co-operation is possible only on a common basis. Traditional diplomacy, traditional law, and the assumptions on which they rest, do not offer one. Political and social sciences offer a basis upon which systems, States, diplomacy and rules can be discussed in a common language, in a behavioural framework that makes no arbitrary distinctions between State and inter-State behaviour, and by methods that reveal the inner structures of units and their functional interactions.

14

RESTATEMENT AND PROPOSITIONS

In any field of scientific inquiry

first there is doubt, a barrier, an indeterminate situation crying out, so to speak, to be made determinate. The scientist experiences vague doubts, emotional disturbance, inchoate ideas. He struggles to formulate the problem, even if inadequately. He studies the literature, scans his own experience and the experience of others. Often he simply has to wait for the inventive leap of the mind. Maybe it will occur; maybe not. With the problem formulated, with the basic question or questions properly asked, the rest is much easier. Then the hypothesis is constructed, after which its implications are deduced, mainly along experimental lines. In the process the original problem, and of course the original hypothesis, may be changed. It may be broadened or narrowed. It may even be abandoned. Lastly, but not finally, the relation expressed by the hypothesis is tested by observation and experimentation. On the basis of research evidence, the hypothesis is accepted or rejected. This information is then fed back to the original problem and it is kept or altered as dictated by the evidence.[1]

In this study some general hypotheses about the motivation of State behaviour and the nature of conflict and conflict management have been formulated. Some of the feed-back process has occurred already and is reflected in the hypotheses put forward.[2] It is now possible to state some propositions about the motivations of international society, dysfunctional conflict and policy, and these should help to clarify the original hypotheses.

The formulation of propositions and stimulating observations relating to conflict is an exercise with a long history. It has not always been rewarding, and one reason is that propositions have been constructed without sufficient thought as to the systems levels to which they are related. 'Real threat causes in-group solidarity' is a commonly stated proposition, but it is not always clear to which systems levels it is thought to apply. It may be true of a small group, it may not be true of a State comprising several nations. 'Crisis decision-making is characterized by failure to consider all possible choices' may be true of the

[1] F. N. Kerlinger, *Foundations of Behavioural Research*, 1966, p. 16.
[2] See J. W. Burton, 'The Analysis of Conflict by Casework', *Year Book of World Affairs*, vol. XXI, 1967.

individual in society, but it could be that the kind of crisis a State faces leads to concentrated attention upon it, and far more consideration of choices, than is the case with day-to-day decisions. There have been very large numbers of propositions stated[1] which might seem to have a bearing upon international conflict because they relate mostly to individual, group and social behaviour. With most of these we are not concerned. Most cannot logically be applied to States. An attempt needs to be made to construct logically developed propositions at systems levels that are applicable to international society. Below is a connected sequence of observations and propositions, some of which have a clear practical or policy implication.

I. SYSTEMS AND STATES

There are four sets of values being pursued simultaneously by any one administrative system: the political values of those who seek or occupy scarce positions, which relate to their endeavours to attain or retain their positions; group values, only some of which are represented by those in administrative positions; community values; and systems values which frequently extend beyond State boundaries.

The political process is such that the priority accorded to these values tends to favour those of administrations over those of groups, group values over community interests, and community goals over wider systems needs. The degree to which this tendency prevails is influenced by the institutions and political philosophies within each State: a 'Welfare State' tends to give a higher priority to community values than to group interests. Thus every State is to a degree in a condition of internal conflict, and also in a condition of external conflict to the extent that control of wider systems by any one authority affects the interests of another.

Two initial propositions are suggested:

1. *Conflict within States exists to the extent that values of administrations and groups take precedence over community values.*

---

[1] See, for example, those of R. W. Mack and R. C. Snyder in *Journal of Conflict Resolution*, vol. I, no. 2, 1957, p. 218; Coser, *Functions of Social Conflict*; R. A. Dahl, *Modern Political Analysis*, 1963; D. T. Campbell, in D. Levine (ed.), *The Nebraska Symposium on Motivation*, 1965; R. C. Snyder, H. W. Bruck and B. Sapin, *Foreign Policy Decision Making*, 1962.

2. *Conflicts between States exist to the extent that values of administrations, groups and communities take precedence over the values of functional systems that embrace more than one State.*

These two general propositions require qualification and elaboration to take into account related variables. In a systems framework they are the two propositions upon which others are constructed.

II. LEGITIMIZATION

The form of authority, and the means by which it attained power, are not the test of legitimization: the test is the degree of support authorities receive, measured by electoral processes, by the absence of protest, or by the absence of any need for coercive restraints. Whatever the political process involved in the filling of scarce power positions—electoral, military, hereditary or any other—authorities have or have not a high legitimized status according to the degree to which they reflect the values existing within the systems within their control. 3. *Legitimization of authority rests upon performance in the satisfaction of values, and not upon the political processes of attaining office.* It follows that: 4. *Power-derived legitimization of authority is possible provided felt needs and values of the political system are satisfied.*

Authorities create systems, and thus create values. It is thus possible for power-supported authorities, that is those having a politically inadequate legitimized status, to create systems that support them. There are examples of European authorities that might have been capitalist or communist, and had initially to be maintained by force, but which with the rise of a new generation attained a legitimized status. 5. *To the extent that power-supported authorities can create additional systems and values, and eliminate incompatible existing ones, they can attain a legitimized status.*

However established, and whatever the political institutions, the support authorities receive within their area of jurisdiction can never be complete. Opposition is greater, in absolute terms, the larger the number of systems within the State, even though authorities give the highest priority to community interests: an allocation of values must prejudice some interests. 6. *The more, quantitatively, are the values to be allocated, the more will be the interests prejudiced.* Because legitimization can never be complete, the struggle to participate in decision-making is continuous, not merely by activity associated with the filling of scarce positions of power, but also by activity designed to influence or even to eliminate authorities in office. Demands for participation, and resistances to them, have features that are characteristic of circumstances: independence movements, demands for constitutional reform, strike action, riots, sabotage, revolution, partition, acquisition of property, propaganda, moral pressures, boycotts, embargoes, sanctions and war.

It is to be noted that there is a distinction being made here between sociological, and normative or legal studies of behaviour. Participation demands are being treated as the independent variable; they lead to administrative changes when alterations take place in values, and in powers of coercion to prevent change. In normative terms these demands lead to 'illegal' action, while resistance to them by the same or similar methods is 'legal'. Normative rules in practice favour politically unstable systems: socially legitimized administrative systems do not require the protection of law and enforcement. That some participation demands are violent is not a justification, at least in a systems framework of analysis, for their suppression.

7. *Participation demands take different forms, depending upon the stage of development of political institutions, and degrees of legitimization of authorities.*

III. MULTI-NATIONAL STATES

Communal relations based upon ethnical and religious values are merely special cases of relationship and no different from ideological or political relationships. They may be more difficult for authorities to control because while ideological values are subject to influence by propaganda, religious values are more persistent, and ethnic characteristics are not subject to any change; but the nature of the relationship is the same. It is not the existence of different communities that leads to conflict between them, or between some of them and the authorities, but the failure of the administrative system—which in practice is dominated at a decision-making level by one of them—to satisfy participation demands. 8. *When, in any State, the demands of one community are satisfied, and others perceive discrimination by authorities against them, there is a condition of communal conflict.* Even attempts not to discriminate are likely to be misinterpreted, merely because full and equitable participation has been denied to some members of the society. It is no less applicable to international society: the 'North–South' conflict is an example.

Where there are distinct communities, especially minorities, failure to achieve expectations tends to be attributed to one ethnic group or political faction; there tends to be a scapegoating process. The real conflict is probably between the State and its environment, but frustration becomes directed inward. Conflict between Hindus and Moslems in India before independence may have been partly due to external domination. It could be that the explanation of conflict within China leading to the 'cultural revolution' was a response to setbacks occasioned by western containment policies: the United States 'imperialist' could not be attacked, but it was possible to find scapegoats within the State. 9. *When any administrative system fails to satisfy expectations, there will tend to be conflict between communities within the State.* There are many special examples of this proposition due to some transitional features of the contemporary world society. Potential conflict is accentuated from time to time by contemporary circumstances arising out of a past period of history. Law and order, as maintained by colonial or foreign rule, consolidated conflict situations, inhibited the flow of adjustments between communities, and thus created situations of open conflict once authority was withdrawn. Furthermore, the requirements of law and order led colonial administrations to enlist the support of élites. These, because of their official positions, tended to move away from the people whom they were supposed to represent and to govern, and this led to increased tensions between the colonial administration and the people, as well as between the élites and the people. Where the colonial administration employed members of one faction for police or administrative duties, because of their greater loyalty or special abilities, and in circumstances in which the administration faced unrest or independence demands, this faction was identified with the administration and conflict outlasted the independence fighting. Many contemporary conflicts owe their origins to the frustration of participation demands made in previous generations.

Under these pressures within States, a trend in world society is toward independence of unitary communities, evidenced in demands for independence from colonialism, and for national autonomy within States once they become independent, and by resistance to foreign influences. Both systems analysis and empirical observation would suggest: 10. *Under pressure of participation demands, and especially in conditions in which administrative systems do not satisfy the interests and needs of separate communities, separate entities evolve.* It follows that any reversed tendency, that is movements toward stable federal structures, is a development that must be based on already integrated units, each having interests and needs satisfied within one administrative system. In practice, the formal constitutional act of federation follows upon the practice at the social level of federation.

IV. THE SPREAD OF INTERNAL CONFLICT

A community within a State that is not satisfied that its legitimate demands are being met has three choices: the seeking of guarantees against discrimination, violence or revolution to gain control, partition or separate organization. All three are likely to involve the seeking of foreign assistance. This is especially so in contemporary conditions in which so many State boundaries are the result of economic or military relations between States that had no interest in local ethnic relationships. Whether the community or faction is a religious, ethnic or political one makes little difference: there are likely to be other States, or communities and factions in other States, that have an interest in responding to appeals for assistance. Any general condition of unrest and lack of popular support for authorities is likely to give rise to appeals for foreign assistance, and finally to conflict that is international. 11. *When communities within a State system, whose effective demands are not met by it, are not eliminated or controlled, or do not achieve a separate sovereign status, the resultant conflict will become international.* A more general statement of the same proposition is: 12. *The existence of legal governments that lack legitimized status is a source of international conflict.* It would follow that: 13. *States that are politically disunified are more likely to be involved in international conflict than those that are united.* This proposition directs attention to the internal conditions of States and their decision-making processes as a fruitful area of inquiry, rather than international organizations and institutions as a means of avoiding international conflict.

The ability of governments that are 'legal', in the sense that they might be recognized by some other authorities, to obtain foreign assistance would, in systemic terms, depend upon their legitimized status. 14. *Intervention that is not aggression is action by and in support of legitimized authorities.* But it is an empirical fact that authorities that lack this status seek and are accepted into alliances, and obtain support; and traditional international law—being based on State practice—seems to sanction this. 15. *The less legitimized are authorities, the greater is the possibility of intervention that is non-systemic.*

Alliances and support of some States by others are not arbitrary or chance relationships, or groupings determined by personalities or even ideologies and types of State administrations. There is an explanation in terms other than strategic expediency why Hitler and Stalin could be allies and then enemies. Germany and Russia were both States whose internal decision-making had been threatened or controlled by the policies of other States. The reason why in the early sixties the United States and the Soviet Union could be closer politically to each other than either to China was that their systemic interests were similar; they sought to protect their freedom of action and their influence on other States, whereas China sought to regain its independence and freedom to participate in world society. There is an explanation why the United States chose to support regimes such as those undemocratic ones that existed in China, Korea, Philippines and South Vietnam, and why Chinese support was accorded to their oppositions. There was a reason why Japan supported the allies in the 1914–18 war, and the enemies of the allies in the 1939–45 war. It is frequently observed that the new States of Africa and Asia have nothing in common except their poverty and their anti-colonialism. What is not always understood is that religion, tradition, and ideologies are secondary influences, and that systemic ones determine policies. The very different new States of Africa and Asia have had a common systemic need to alter an international environment which they perceive as oppressive in terms of the inferior economic bargaining power they have. 16. *Participation and systemic demands, or resistances to them, in one State attract support from those making similar demands or resisting them in other States.*

V. STATE BEHAVIOUR IN WORLD SOCIETY

Each State within international society, being a cluster of systems organized by an administrative system responding to and behaving within an environment, seeks to influence other States which comprise its environment. The means of influence vary with circumstances and capabilities. There appear to be internal pressures, especially within highly industrialized States, that lead to the exercise of whatever power is available in extending influence. This suggests that States may not be capable of adjusting their behaviour to meet the systemic needs of other societies, and therefore of international society. This certainly appears to be true of highly developed and extensive industrial societies in which pressure groups operate; it remains to be seen whether included within the capabilities of powerful communist States is the ability to adjust to the systemic needs of other States. It can be postulated that: 17. *The role of each State in international society is determined by its capabilities (including its cultural traditions), and its environment.* It needs to be noted that short-term conditions, such as the personality of leadership, do not determine State behaviour. Role behaviour is, by definition, a continuing phenomenon: it is the behaviour other States expect by reason of traditional behavioural patterns. These are not usually subject to sudden change, except in the case of revolutions, and even then changes immediately perceived are continuous when viewed historically.

It follows from propositions dealing with values and participation demands that: 18. *Unacceptable roles create responses that can be controlled by threat and force, but only in the short term.* Attempts by the Soviet Union to integrate Eastern European economies led to increased demands for independence, United States attempts to control Latin American politics have given power to the factions it seeks to curb, alliance domination leads to alliance disintegration, aid offered on unacceptable conditions promotes responses the aid was designed to avoid, attempts by outgoing colonial Powers to leave behind a government favourable to them promote hostile political movements. 19. *The enactment and defence of unacceptable roles is destructive of their purposes.*

The systemic motivation of States in seeking to influence others is not that vague and alleged primitive urge to have more power and to dominate more people; it is the systemic need to influence or control decisions affecting relevant wider systems. In practice the distinction may not be clear; a State need may require it to manipulate the environment (that is, other States) so as to reduce required responses to those that are within the adjustment capability of the State. Thus in the thirties Japan at first made passive attempts to persuade other States to alter their trading policies, and when these were frustrated it embarked upon what appeared to be a classic case of aggression. The struggle of this century has been the endeavour of foreign-controlled States and communities to be free to determine their own responses in an environment that does not discriminate against them, and of the controlling States to maintain their positions. After the Second World War GATT endeavoured to introduce principles of non-discrimination in commercial matters in order to avoid frictions that arise out of policies that could be imposed by economically stronger States; in so far as it was successful it tended to satisfy the systemic need of smaller States for participation in decisions affecting them by removing the power of other States to decide on policies that adversely affected others. Attempts by underdeveloped States to alter terms of trade are attempts to alter their environment; they organize amongst themselves to expand their ability to influence other States. UNCTAD experience is that powerful States are not readily persuaded to give up abilities to control the behaviour of smaller ones, and a condition similar to the apparent Japanese response, but on a larger scale, can be anticipated. 20. '*Aggressive' actions are not because of aggressiveness, but reflect systemic needs which are capable of satisfaction only by the policies of other States.* (It is not implied that these other States necessarily have the capability of acting in accordance with these needs.)

It does not follow that for a condition of peace to exist all change must take place freely, and adjustment to it be made by others: a systems analysis does not lead to a pacifist doctrine. Given an alteration in production techniques or demands, it may be easier for one State to react by commercial policies that place the whole burden of adjustment upon others. A shortage of agricultural land can be met by invading the territories of a neighbour, and this may be easier than industrialization and the purchase of primary products. Acquisition of neighbouring coal and steel resources may be easier than intensified development of existing industries and the purchase of manufactured goods.

Some means of forcing States to solve their own problems are clearly required in an international system of separate States: there is a systemic need for bargaining power and national forces to ensure that other States undertake some of the internal costs of change and development. 21. *The systemic need for force in world society is to induce States and systems within it to carry out internal adjustments to change before attempting to force the burden of adjustment upon others.*

In practice, however, State forces have a limited ability to induce other States to make their own adjustments; on the contrary, States with powerful forces are also the economically powerful, and they endeavour to force the burden of adjustment on to others, as the Soviet Union did in its post-war relations with Eastern European States, and as the United Kingdom did when it was in a position to do so. Economically powerful States can export unemployment, and defend social institutions by maintaining them in foreign countries, despite the possession of forces by smaller States. In practice the use of power is not for the systemic need of inducing other States to carry their own burden of adjustments; it is to force adjustment upon others. A systemic need is thus created for increased power, or for new techniques of resistance, by the less powerful to prevent the burden of change and adjustment being thrown upon them. Hence the drive for industrialization and security forces in underdeveloped States, and increased resistance to economic penetration of all kinds, and to what is termed 'neo-colonialism'. Systemic needs relate to freedom to adjust to the environment, and to ensure that the demands of the environment are within the capability of the State system. 'Aggression' against any State that prevents this freedom is in systemic terms a vital response of a State; in systemic terms the policies of States that provoke these 'aggressive' responses in others are dysfunctional. In systemic terms, therefore, defence of existing structures may be destructive of the interests of international society; but it is these that are supported by normative rules. The failure of communication between East and West, counter-accusations of aggressiveness, and charges of double standards, arise out of the differences between systemic and traditional legal requirements. 22. *Defence and aggression are distinguishable by reference to systemic needs, and the distinction so drawn is the reverse of one based upon traditional normative rules.*

VI. INTER-STATE CONFLICT

We have focused attention upon three sources of international conflict: the activities of State authorities that inhibit transactions across boundaries of systems that include other States; the non-legitimized activities of authorities that prejudice interests within their boundaries to the extent of stimulating them to seek foreign assistance; and the activities of State authorities that give power support to transactions across boundaries. In one way or another each of these sources relates to State authorities; each relates to the abilities of States to adapt to internal and environmental change, to the differential ability of States to force adjustment upon others, and to the ability of the international society of States (operating through international organizations) to avoid imposing on any State an adjustment burden or option that it cannot accommodate. Where there is change, adjustment is required. Society is in process of constant change. There are conditions in which change in the environment is absorbed by the adjustment of a State, and others in which States respond non-passively. For example, a crop failure in one country may mean starvation in another, and there will not be an aggressive response directed against the supplier. A deliberate export embargo with far less serious consequences could, however, lead to an aggressive response. The response of the State depends upon its abilities to adjust, and its abilities to force adjustment upon others. This applies as much to ideological change as to commercial change: a State that cannot absorb new ideas has to ban them and then attempt to eliminate them at their source. Power is used to accomplish this, and its purpose is to remove the freedom of decision-making of others: change, participation and power are operationally related. 23. *A condition of conflict is change associated with systems failure to absorb or adjust passively to change.* Empirically one would expect to find a high correlation between the abilities of a State to adapt to change and its success in remaining in a peaceful relationship with other systems. One would also expect to find a higher incidence of inter-State conflict during periods of rapid ideological or technological change. 24. *Greater Powers are a source of conflict to the extent that power is employed as a means of forcing the burden of adjustment to change upon others; smaller Powers are initiators of conflict to the extent that they react against an environment that impedes their progress.*

The burden of change falls heaviest upon, and the benefits are greatest for, group interests, that is particular functional systems within States and world society. Group interests are closely allied to political interests in most States, and are not necessarily related to community interests or wider systemic interests. They are special interests promoted and transmitted through State processes. Examples are the defence of private investments and installations in foreign States, and maintenance of spheres of interest and prestige positions, and interests that persist despite changes that render them non-systemic, such as the occupation of foreign bases and protection of sources of raw materials that could be obtained in the usual course of trading. Imperialism was responsible for many clashes that could not be regarded as originating from wider systems and State needs. Industrial pressure groups, capital and labour, have an interest in defensive preparations that invite escalation of conflict. 25. *Conflict between States arises out of the pursuit of non-systemic needs and values.*

VII. DYSFUNCTIONAL CONFLICT

Whether conflict is functional or dysfunctional from the point of view of a State is determined by costs in relation to the value of the goal sought. It is necessary to eliminate the use of 'functional' meaning 'integrative': conflict leads to a new situation but it cannot be said to be integrative in an evolutionary sense. The costs of conflict include not merely the direct costs of competition, or of waging conflict and of damage sustained, but also the costs of political consequences in relation to other goals, the attainment of which is prejudiced by the conflict. The more detailed the knowledge of States of the direct and indirect costs, and of means of achieving goals without incurring them, the narrower will appear to be the range of functional conflict, and the less will appear to be the integrative benefits, if any, of conflict. In an ideal situation of complete information and efficiency in decision-making, States would avoid all dysfunctional conflict: they would not be involved in a greater expenditure of resources than was justified by the values sought. 26. *Whether functional conflict becomes dysfunctional depends upon decision-making processes.* An objection to this proposition immediately suggests itself: is it not possible for a party that is pursuing a conflict which is functional to it to involve another party in conflict which to it is dysfunctional? In the Goa conflict, which appeared to be functional from the Indian viewpoint, a decision had to be made by the Portuguese whether costs of resistance were worth the values at stake: clearly they were not. Dysfunctional conflict was avoided.

This consideration, however, raises a second. If a conflict is functional for one party while dysfunctional for another, the implication is that the latter offers no resistance to demands made upon it. There were special features that made this possible for the Portuguese in the case of colonial Goa: Portuguese territorial interests were not threatened and the Goa sub-systems could adjust readily to the transfer to Indian systems. But where values are threatened that are held to be vital to State or community, there will be resistance no matter what the cost, as in the Vietnam case. In these circumstances conflict tends to become dysfunctional for all parties, even for the more powerful ones. A tentative conclusion is that: 27. *Any conflict between two parties which is or is likely to be dysfunctional for one party will be dysfunctional also for the other.* (It is only States not directly involved that may gain from a conflict that is dysfunctional.) Hence, both the origin and the avoidance of dysfunctional conflict relate to decision-making processes, and the proposition is that: 28. *In conditions of perfect knowledge, States avoid conflicts of interest that are dysfunctional.*

Perfect knowledge begs many practical questions. In particular there is the problem of perception: perception is the means by which administrative systems of States are related. State behaviour, in responding to the environment, is not determined by what might be deemed by philosophers to be the nature of Man, the State or the inter-State system; it is conditioned by the perception the State has of its environment. Communication, information, prejudice, and ability to store, interpret and employ information are, consequently, factors that condition State relationships. Given the systemic framework of conditions between States, and given that the translation of conflict into dysfunctional conflict is the inability of authorities to anticipate responses and reactions and to prevent the escalation of conflict: 29. *Particular dysfunctional conflicts occur as the result of false perception, false expectations and irrelevant responses.*

That conflict situations inevitably occur as the result of

differences of interests, and that conflict avoidance is possible by cybernetic processes once costs are assessed, would seem to be incompatible propositions. The apparent incompatibility of these propositions is eliminated when they are related to another: there is an incompatibility only if the pursuit of differences of interest at a given point of time is set against the avoidance of conflict by decision-making at that given point of time. If, however, dysfunctional conflict over scarce resources and conflict avoidance by cybernetic means are both regarded as continuing processes involving many decisions and cost appraisals over a long period of time, there is no incompatibility. Restated, the proposition that, given adequate information and foresight, dysfunctional conflict is avoidable, even in conditions of difference of interest, is clearly not valid at the point at which conflict is about to become dysfunctional. The origins and possible avoidance of conflicts are not in final acts, but in decisions taken or not taken day by day over long periods of time, such as power policies that provoke reaction, and such as failures to make adjustments to change that in due course lead to structural breakdowns evidenced in commercial crises and wars. The future consequences of decisions cannot readily be estimated. On the costing side, it is not possible to assess the long-term effects of decisions, especially in terms of other goals that are destroyed in achieving a particular one. That the processes of conflict cannot as yet be perceived at the time, and that costs cannot as yet be assessed at the time, does not mean that conflict avoidance is impossible. It means that at any point of time there is insufficient knowledge, and that insufficient attention is given to the build-up of the final costs involved. There were differences of interest in the thirties between the British Commonwealth nations and others that no less sought the markets of colonial areas: the immediate gains sought were some alleviation of unemployment, but the final costs were a war and the early loss of areas as exclusive trading areas after independence. On a wider scale, decisions taken now by greater Powers that lead to greater inequalities of income between 'North' and 'South' are taken within a framework of differences of interest in the short term, and with little regard to the ultimate costs of dysfunctional conflict. 30. *Decision-making processes controlling conflict are not those taken at the critical point of dysfunctional conflict, but those that preceded it.* Administrative systems are not in themselves well equipped for long-term decision-making. It is only the existence of theories of systemic needs and related propositions that can make up for this deficiency in decision-making.

The study of conflict and conflict avoidance has to some degree been confused with the study of crisis behaviour. A crisis occurs as the result of failure of decision-making at much earlier stages. The critical stage in conflict avoidance is the response to the first change within the State or the environment to which an adjustment was required. There may be a crisis in Fiji in the years to come: the conflict between Indians and Fijians has existed for many years. Dysfunctional conflict in the future could have been avoided only by decisions taken many years ago. Crisis management is an important study; but it is dealing only with situations that have occurred through failures in decision-making that took place many years previously.

VIII. THE INTERNATIONAL CONTROL OF WORLD SOCIETY

States comprise systems each with different and sometimes conflicting values and goals. The values and goals of each are influenced by administrative authorities that allocate resources. The world society has the same feature of inherent conflict. The allocation of values is in this case by direct interactions without the intervention of authorities. In this respect world society is different in character from States. The question arises whether this difference is merely one of development, or whether there are features of world society that are basically different from States, and would prevent the creation of world authorities, with a legitimized status, having power to determine values within world society, and to provide law and order.

Political organization designed to maintain stability is no less designed to control responses to change. The common fallacy of alliance and collective security organizations is the belief that States can be coerced not to pursue systemic values. Fundamental systemic needs include freedom of internal adjustment and of response to external change, and opportunity to influence the world environment, especially in order to gain reciprocal advantages and to remove disadvantages imposed by power relations. No alliance or collective security organization can deter demands for social change, including the development of new administrative structures, and the promotion of new ideas and values; and no outside control can prevent demands for external change, including the alteration of terms of trade, and the elimination of discriminating practices. Demands can be frustrated; but this only means that they will take some other form, such as internal revolution and the elimination of persons and values associated with foreign coercion, and the nationalization and acquisition of foreign property. 31. *No State can accommodate the dictation of any other State, or even all other States together, in matters affecting its systemic values.*

Alliances and collective security have usually been designed to deter attempts by States to influence the world environment, and to bring about changes induced by ethnic, cultural and other systemic needs. Boundaries that are arbitrarily drawn and imposed upon ethnic groups, partitions such as those in Germany and Korea that are imposed upon unitary societies, and unifications that are imposed upon non-unitary societies (and these may include many of the African type where multi-national States emerged out of colonial administration, and even the common European multi-national States that were the creation of other Powers) cannot be maintained once they become the subject of systemic demands. Germany and Japan faced systemic needs: their systems could not meet demands made upon them within the world environment in which they existed. Internal adjustment required was beyond systemic capability; the environment had to be changed. International organization, whether of an alliance or collective security type, cannot impose its will upon a State in respect of systemic needs. The analogy between civil and international enforcement is a false one. For 'international law' to exist it must be based upon a universal consensus: if so based it has no operative role except to act, like a theory, as a guide to States in the pursuit of their interests, and if not so based it has no existence. 32. *Enforcement procedures can never be a part of international organization.* The only exception is where enforcement is legitimized, and for this to happen the subject of the enforcement would need to be a non-legitimized authority, as are authorities in South Africa and Rhodesia.

Deterrence is a concept that has a clear application to individuals and small groups within a unified State. It is not clear that it is relevant to the behaviour of States. Colonial powers could deter only until nationalist movements were established, then threats and punishments had the effect of promoting behaviour they sought to deter. Vietnamese response to escalating deterrence strategies was a dramatic example. Systems depend upon legitimacy and system integration, and where threats succeed this is due to the policy errors that occur when it is assumed that systems behaviour corresponds to individual and small group behaviour within a system. 33. *Threats and punishments deter when systemic values are involved only to the extent that costs exceed values being defended.*

International collective security is not different in form from devices arranged by great Powers, and the threat of particular Powers. Once the international system of States was controlled by great Powers. In contemporary world society States of greatly different power are tending toward an actual as well as a legal egalitarianism. Values, such as are held in communities that are foreign- or class-dominated, and the destructive capability of modern weapons, are two contemporary influences giving rise to egalitarianism. The one acts upon the powerless and tends to leave them undeterred by threats, and the other acts upon the powerful and tends to restrain their actions. It was these influences that hastened the end of colonialism, and are beginning to give opportunities to small States to exist without defending boundaries, to determine their own affairs, and to achieve alterations in their environment. Foreign intervention even by great Powers is gradually being forced underground. 34. *The bargaining power and force capability that arise out of specialization and inequalities between States decrease in effectiveness as values are universalized, and as capability to destroy increases.*

Once force at the nuclear level appears not to be a utility, and once value systems begin to influence policy, the advantage of size and greatness diminish, and this is particularly true once the organization of industry has jumped State boundaries. This observation draws attention to the political viability of very small States that have been and are likely to be formed under pressures of participation demands. 35. *Great Powers that comprise many federated States play a role in international society of less significance than the combined roles that would be played if each were sovereign.*

There was a time when United Nations peacekeeping was welcomed as a major advance in the international control of conflict: now it is less certain. What has become clear is that peacekeeping can maintain or institutionalize a situation of conflict. Peacekeeping may succeed in not allowing internal conflict to spill over into international strife; but, unless it is accompanied by some means of resolving the conflict, this might prove to be an achievement in the short term only. 36. *Inter-national peacekeeping forces prevent the elimination of the weaker communities, prevent the creation of new States, prevent violence, and institutionalize the conflict at non-violent levels.*

This study has not been concerned particularly with the resolution of conflict, which is the subject of the companion study. But in passing it is relevant to note that, in the development of conflict, choices are progressively limited, and at a certain point dysfunctional acts of violence may have a value within the States concerned: action relieves tension after prolonged uncertainty and crisis. Over-confidence and wishful thinking, invented values and leadership interests, tend to make resolution of conflict by peaceful means politically unacceptable. In this short period it could be said that there is a systemic need for dysfunctional activities. In the absence of appropriate means of resolution of conflict the usual development is for the conflict to become institutionalized, especially in modern conditions of warfare in which the parties have no face-to-face contact. Once conflict is institutionalized at a non-violent level it is difficult to persuade parties to engage in reperception. A measure of escalation of conflict leading to further cost assessment may be required before institutionalized conflicts can be resolved: conflicts that do not escalate may be the most prolonged. Acceptable solutions are not usually perceived prior to negotiation; but that acceptable solutions are possible is a proposition parties entertain once costs and goals, and the possibility of not attaining goals, have been reassessed. In short, 'blood-letting' is usually necessary before parties are prepared to discuss their conflict: at a certain stage the parties reperceive the costs, the value of the goals, and perhaps the impossibility of achieving the original goals, and tacitly agree that they are prepared to find some means of reaching agreement. 37. *Resolution of conflict is possible when all parties agree that the conflict is not functional.*

Systemic needs for independence require the absence of international organization with enforcement capabilities, but not the absence of international organization. On the contrary, systemic needs for participation in decisions of direct concern require international organization in which each unit is an equal, no matter how unequal in power and size, and through which systemic needs of interdependence can be met. Functional organization is one form which meets the systemic requirements both of the international system and its components, and for this reason its expansion can be anticipated. A greatly increased number of independent States integrated by greatly increased functional activities are features of the developing structure of international society. 38. *International functional organization amongst States promotes and does not infringe systemic needs.*

It is possible to conceive of a world society that remains reciprocal, in which change is followed immediately by an adjustment, and that maintains a peaceful condition: such a society could evolve and develop without conflict. Under certain conditions conflict exists, and for this reason must enter into systemic relations and development; but conflict is essential to these relations and to development. 39. *Conflict has an influence on the development of international society.* This is self-evident, but it is necessary to state the proposition in order to falsify the more usual formulation that conflict is integrative and an essential part of an evolutionary process.

IX. THE NATIONAL CONTROL OF WORLD SOCIETY

Thus we are led to the view that inter-State conflict has its source within the States that constitute world society, and that dysfunctional conflict occurs by reason of the inefficient management of internal and external relationships. The inter-State control of State relations is not the solution: what is required is increased wisdom and foresight of State authorities in the pursuit of State interests. Up to the present societies have not insisted that States managers should be trained for their profession. Until two or so decades ago, this was reasonable enough: there was little on which to base a training. This is no longer the case. The study of international relations still lacks cohesion, and still requires more testing of hypotheses; but so do all sciences. The inadequacies of medical science are no excuse for practice by untrained people.

The traditional view was that States required the supervision and control of international institutions. This directed academic attention away from the main sources of conflict—those that are within the decision-making processes of States. Now academic attention is focused upon this area and the study is developing rapidly. Knowledge of the fact that control of world society is within the capability of its State members is what needs now to be incorporated into conventional wisdom, thereby forcing authorities to acknowledge their responsibilities for the consequences of their policies. The proposition that may be the most important of all is that conditions of international peaceful relations will increase as theories are developed, tested and employed to guide perception, response and interaction amongst States.

BIBLIOGRAPHY

WORKS CITED IN THE TEXT

Abercrombie, M. L. J. *The Anatomy of Judgment*. 3rd ed. Hutchinson, 1965.
Albinski, H. S. *Australian Policies and Attitudes toward China*. Princeton, 1965.
Allport, G. W. *The Nature of Prejudice*. Addison-Wesley, 1954.
Banks, A. S., and Textor, R. S. *A Cross-Polity Survey*. M.I.T. Press, 1963.
Banks, M. H. 'Two Meanings of Theory in the Study of International Relations.' *The Year Book of World Affairs*, vol. xx. Stevens, 1966.
Blau, P. M. *Exchange and Power in Social Life*. Wiley, 1964.
Boulding, K. E. 'General Systems Theory: The Skeleton of Science.' *General Systems*, vol. 1, 1956.
Bull, H. 'International Theory: The Case for a Classical Approach.' *World Politics*, vol. xviii, no. 3, April 1966.
Burton, J. W. *Peace Theory: Preconditions of Disarmament*. Knopf, 1962.
Burton, J. W. *International Relations: A General Theory*. Cambridge, 1965.
Burton, J. W. 'The Analysis of Conflict by Casework.' *Year Book of World Affairs*, vol. xxi. Stevens, 1967.
Campbell, D. T. See Levine, D. (ed.).
Cantril, H. *The Pattern of Human Concerns*. Rutgers, 1965.
Carthy, J. D., and Ebling, F. J. (eds.) *Natural History of Aggression*. Academic Press, 1964.
Claude, I. *Swords into Plowshares*. Random House, 1956.
Claude, I. *Power and International Relations*. Random House, 1962.
Cohn, G. *Neo-Neutrality*. Translated from Danish by A. S. Keller and E. Jensen. Colombia University Press, 1939.
Coser, L. *The Functions of Social Conflict*. Routledge and Kegan Paul, 1956.
Dahl, R. A. *Modern Political Analysis*. Prentice-Hall, 1963.
Deutsch, K. W. *The Nerves of Government*. Free Press, 1963.
Deutsch, K. W. Contribution in a CIBA Foundation Symposium, *Conflict in Society*. Churchill, 1966.
Deutsch, K. W. 'The Growth of Nations: Some Recurrent Patterns of Political and Social Integration.' See McLellan, D. S., Olsen, W. C., and Sondermann, F. A.
Easton, D. *A Framework for Political Analysis*. Prentice-Hall, 1965.
Easton, D. *A Systems Analysis of Political Life*. Wiley, 1965.
Eayrs, J. *Right and Wrong in Foreign Policy*. University of Toronto Press, 1965.
Fanon, F. *The Damned*. Présence Africaine, 1963.
Farrell, R. B. (ed.) *Approaches to Comparative and International Politics*. Northwestern, 1966.
Fifield, R. H. *Southeast Asia in United States Policy*. Praeger, 1963.
Fleming, D. F. *The Cold War and its Origins*. Allen and Unwin, 1961.
Friedmann, W. *The Changing Structure of International Law*. Stevens, 1964.
Ginsberg, M. *Sociology*. Oxford, 1963.
Goode, W. J., and Hatt, P. K. *Methods in Social Research*. McGraw-Hill, 1952.
Green, P. *Deadly Logic: The Theory of Nuclear Deterrence*. Ohio State University Press, 1966.

246   Bibliography

Guetzkow, H. Contribution in *The American Perspective*, vol. IV, no. 4, 1950.
Haas, E. B. *Beyond the Nation-State*. Stanford, 1964.
Halpern, M. See Rosenau, J. N.
Handy, R., and Kurtz, P. *A Current Appraisal of Behavioral Sciences*. The Behavioral Research Council, 1964.
Harris, E. E. *Annihilation and Utopia*. Allen and Unwin, 1966.
Hobson, J. A. *Imperialism*. Allen and Unwin, 1948.
Holsti, O. R. *Perceptions of Time, Perceptions of Alternatives, and Patterns of Communication as Factors in Crisis Decision-making*. Stanford, mimeograph. Also in *American Political Science Review*, vol. LIX, 1965.
Horowitz, D. *The Free World Colossus*. MacGibbon and Kee, 1965.
Iyer, R. (ed.) *The Glass Curtain Between Asia and Europe*. Oxford, 1965.
Kerlinger, F. N. *Foundations of Behavioural Research*. Holt, Rinehart and Winston, 1966.
Levine, D. (ed.) *The Nebraska Symposium on Motivation*. Nebraska Press, 1965.
Lipset, S. M. *Political Man*. Doubleday, 1960.
McClelland, C. A. *Theory and the International System*. Macmillan, 1966.
McClelland, C. A. See McNeil, E. B. (ed.).
McLellan, D. S., Olson, W. C., and Sondermann, F. A. *Theory and Practice of International Relations*. Prentice-Hall, 1960.
McNeil, E. B. (ed.) *The Nature of Human Conflict*. Prentice-Hall, 1965.
Mack, R. W., and Snyder, R. C. *Journal of Conflict Resolution*, vol. I, no. 2, 1957.
Miller, J. G. *Behavioral Science*, vol. X, no. 3, July 1965; and vol. X, no. 4, October 1966.
Mintz, J. S. *Mohammed, Marx and Marhaen*. Pall Mall, 1965.
Modelski, G. *A Theory of Foreign Policy*. Pall Mall, 1961.
Modelski, G. See Rosenau, J. N.
Morgenthau, H. J. *Politics Among Nations*. 3rd ed. Knopf, 1960.
Nettl, P. 'The Concept of System in Political Science.' *Political Studies*, vol. XIV, no. 3, October 1966.
Nicholson, M. B., and Reynolds, P. A. 'General Systems, the International System, and the Eastonian Analysis.' *Political Studies*, vol. XV, no. 1. February 1967.
Nicolson, Sir H. *Diplomacy*. 3rd ed. Oxford, 1963.
Parsons, T. *The Structure of Social Action*. Free Press, 1949.
Penrose, L. S., and A. *British Journal of Psychology*, no. 49, 1958.
Rokeach, M. *The Open and Closed Mind*. Basic Books, 1960.
Rosenau, J. N. (ed.) *International Aspects of Civil Strife*. Princeton, 1965.
Russett, B. M. (ed.) *World Handbook of Political and Social Indicators*. 2nd ed. Yale University Press, 1965.
Schwarzenberger, G. *Power Politics*. 1st ed. Cape, 1941.
Schwarzenberger, G. *Power Politics*. 3rd ed. Stevens, 1964.
Schwarzenberger, G. *A Manual of International Law*. 7th ed. Stevens, 1967.
Singer, J. D. *Deterrence, Arms Control and Disarmament*. Columbus, Ohio, State University Press, 1962.
Snyder, R. C., Bruck, H. W., and Sapin, B. *Foreign Policy Decision-making*. Free Press, 1962.
Thyne, G. M. *The Psychology of Learning and Techniques of Teaching*. University of London, 1963.

Ulrich, R., Hutchinson, R., and Azrin, N. 'Pain-elicited Aggression.'
   The Psychological Record, vol. xv, no. 1, January 1965.
Vernon, M. D. *The Psychology of Perception*. Pelican, 1962.
Waltz, K. N. *Man, the State and War*. Columbia, 1959.
Weber, M. *The Methodology of Social Sciences*. Translated by E. A. Shils and
   H. A. Finch. Free Press, 1949.
Weber, M. *An Intellectual Portrait*. Heinemann, 1960.

INDEX